I0896535

COOPERMAN!

COOPERMAN!

THE LIFE OF TOMMY COOPER

IAN CARROLL

FONTHILL

Fonthill Media Language Policy

Fonthill Media publishes in the international English language market. One language edition is published worldwide. As there are minor differences in spelling and presentation, especially with regard to American English and British English, a policy is necessary to define which form of English to use. The Fonthill Policy is to use the form of English native to the author. Ian Carroll was born in Liverpool and educated in Liverpool and London; therefore, British English has been adopted in this publication.

Fonthill Media Limited
Fonthill Media LLC
www.fonthillmedia.com
office@fonthillmedia.com

First published in the United Kingdom and the United States of America 2018

British Library Cataloguing in Publication Data:
A catalogue record for this book is available from the British Library

Copyright © Ian Carroll 2018

ISBN 978-1-78155-685-6

The right of Ian Carroll to be identified as the author of this work has been asserted by him in accordance with the Copyright, Designs and Patents Act 1988.

All rights reserved. No part of this publication may be reproduced, stored in a retrieval system or transmitted in any form or by any means, electronic, mechanical, photocopying, recording or otherwise, without prior permission in writing from Fonthill Media Limited

Typeset in 10pt on 13pt Sabon
Printed and bound in England

Acknowledgements

This book is meant to be a user-friendly and subjective account. It does not aim to be overly academic. I have attempted to acknowledge quotes and sources within the body of the text, though some deserve a very special mention. *Always Leave Them Laughing* by John Fisher remains the definitive biography of Tommy Cooper. The level of detail and personal insights offered by the author cannot be bettered. I doff my cap to him. Jeremy Novick wrote another biography of Tommy, one that is even more subjective than my own. The plethora of British newspapers offer no end of stories covering Tommy's life and career, and the internet is also a rich source of enquiry. I would like to thank John Miles OBE, trustee of the Cooper estate, for help and permission in the production of this work, and to Tommy's daughter, Vicky, who offered up a few precious insights into her father's life. I would also like to thank the comedian Russ Abbot for inspiring the title of this work.

Also, a mention to the Victoria and Albert Museum for allowing me privileged access prior to the archive's opening in 2018. I would also like to thank the audiences, the cast members past and present, and the team behind *The Tommy Cooper Show*. Please check it out at a theatre near you.

Most of all, I would like to thank my family and my darling wife Lesley. I could not do this without your love and support.

Last, but definitely not least, a big thank you to Tommy Cooper himself, for giving me such a laugh along the way as I wrote this book. I hope that I have done him justice. Thanks for reading.

CONTENTS

Acknowledgements		5
Prologue		9
1	The Last Performance	11
2	Who Was Tommy Cooper?	16
3	Where It All Began	20
4	Schooldays and Workdays	25
5	National Service	29
6	Meeting Gwen	33
7	Starting Out	36
8	Making His Mark	40
9	The Early Gigs	44
10	A Rising Star	48
11	The Home Front	52
12	The Seasoned Pro	56
13	A Real Magician?	60
14	The Magic Circle	64
15	More About Miff	68
16	Comedy and Magic	72
17	Contemporaries	76
18	Falling Out with Miff	80
19	Mr Personality	84
20	The Legendary Meanness	88
21	Family Man	92
22	The Television Appearances	96
23	The V&A	100
24	The Joke Files	106
25	More from the Archive	111

26	Going Out Live	116
27	The Gag Writers	120
28	Forever Working	127
29	Branching Out	131
30	Opportunities	135
31	Nightclubbing	139
32	Feeling the Effects	143
33	A Rose Among Thorns	146
34	The Affair	150
35	Tommy Remembered	154
36	Touring	158
37	Playing Cards	162
38	A House Full of Memories	166
39	A History of Magic	171
40	Tommy's Heroes	174
41	Drinking to Excess	178
42	The Final Performance	183
43	The Legacy	187
44	The Magic Lives On	190

Prologue

In 2013, Channel 5 ran a competition on British television to find the fifty greatest stand-up comedians of all time. The list contained many legendary entertainment figures, as well as some new faces who may or may not figure on such lists in years to come.

The comedians could come from any era and from any nationality. There were some stellar names among the cast, including such comedy giants as Richard Pryor, Eddie Murphy, Robin Williams, and our very own Billy Connolly. Despite the level of competition, at number three on the all-time list was a certain Thomas Frederick Cooper. The result was all the more surprising for the fact that Cooper had died almost thirty years beforehand.

In 2004, a full two decades after Tommy Cooper's sudden and tragic death, he was voted Britain's number one all-time favourite comedian in a *Reader's Digest* poll. What was it about the man that caused his light to still burn so brightly for his legions of fans? Why was he not usurped by all that had happened since?

The answer lies in the unique quality of his act and in the abundance of his skills. Was he a comedian, a magician, or a legendary clown? In fact, he was all three, for who else but a clown would be able to get a laugh—and I mean a proper belly laugh—without even opening his mouth. It is as a comedian and a magician that he is best known. His was a brand that could not be replicated. His physical presence and his looks alone were enough to ensure that he stood out from the crowd. He was a giant, and an awkward one at that. With an appearance that was once famously described as 'unfortunate', Tommy Cooper scaled the heights of stage and television for almost four decades, but he had been practising for much longer than that to become the star that he eventually became. No one worked harder to achieve success, and no one deserved it more, for he simply ingrained himself into the consciousness of a nation, into their hearts, and into their lives. Was there ever a man more imitated? Was any dinner party ever complete without someone doing an impersonation of his act (as if it were that easy), or by telling one of his many silly jokes?

The routines themselves would be almost impossible to copy, for hours and hours of practice went into each and every one. Indeed, many professional magicians would probably concede that it is more difficult to get the tricks wrong, especially in the manner that Tommy did, than it was to get them right. A critic writing in the Magic Circle's own monthly magazine summed it up perfectly: 'The skill with which he ruined his act was amazing!'

That is not to say that Tommy Cooper did not take his magic seriously—nothing could be further from the truth. His family aside, magic was the real love of his life. He could entertain himself for hours practising his magic tricks. He sought perfection in the craft, if only to then spend more time undoing all his hard work to make something new and comical out of it.

Many people around the world hold him in the highest regard as their favourite comedian. He simply had funny bones, and a magical act to go with it. What audiences were watching was a finely honed performer, who had worked his way up from the very bottom rung of the show-business ladder. No one was more determined or deserving to ultimately scale the heights of success.

My own involvement with the Tommy Cooper story came about by accident. Before 2010, my only claim to a connection with Cooper was that my favourite joke was one of his. That particular gag came from one of his many series recorded for Thames Television.

Tommy comes on stage in his dress tails and trademark fez hat. In his hands (the size of shovels), he is holding a violin and an oil painting. 'I took these to the auctioneers to get valued. He said, "What you've got there is a Stradivarius and a Rembrandt. Unfortunately, Stradivarius was a terrible painter, and Rembrandt made awful violins!"' He then proceeds to smash both objects to bits.

So apart from that being my favourite joke, and loving Cooper as so many people in the country did, I had no other connection to Tommy. However, as an author, playwright, and theatre producer, I had an eye for a story, and when I witnessed one of my actors doing an amazing Tommy Cooper impersonation during rehearsals for another play in 2010, I knew that this was something special that I wanted to share with an audience. I immediately set about writing the play, which was finally produced in 2013 to showcase the talents of the actor Daniel Taylor. We invited Chris Brunt along, the chairman of the Tommy Cooper Society. He called the play a 'tour de force'. The show now regularly tours across the country as *The Tommy Cooper Show*. In 2017, for his unique portrayal of the comedian, Daniel was voted the 'Best Actor on the British Stage' by the Break A Leg Awards.

For fans of Tommy Cooper, and for those coming to him afresh, the show is a wonderful celebration that captures the magic and humour of a true original and comedy giant. Tommy Cooper left a legacy that has not dimmed in nearly half a century. His genius, and the joy he gave to millions of people, will ensure that he goes on being appreciated for a long, long time to come.

1

The Last Performance

On Sunday, 15 April 1984, London Weekend Television were broadcasting a variety showcase of some of the world's great entertainers, including Donny Osmond and Howard Keel from America, as well as an upcoming British comedy duo, Les Dennis and Dustin Gee. The compère was Jimmy Tarbuck, a Liverpool lad with the task of introducing a showbiz legend. He began by saying 'If you asked 100 comedians to name their favourite comic, they would all say the one and only Tommy Cooper'.

He then stepped aside and, to thunderous applause, Tommy appeared on the stage. He looked okay. He had cut down on his legendary cigar smoking and had even reduced his alcohol intake. His huge frame was still slightly shambling, but he appeared to be getting back to his old self, as he had not been in the best of health for some considerable time.

He had suffered a major heart attack seven years earlier, but he had then quickly regained his place as a perennial headline act and an audience favourite. Now, here he was, performing live at Her Majesty's Theatre in London. To be honest, he was a little nervous about his performance. He had trodden the boards for forty years and had appeared thousands of times on the cabaret circuit but appearing live on television was another matter. Still, he had practised his material over and over, and the seven-minute set he was about to reveal was a good one, featuring several jokes, some old and some new, and a couple of classic routines together with his cod-magic tricks.

The normal dressing rooms at the venue were hidden in the basement, with a long flight of stairs leading to the stage. Due to Tommy's poor physical condition, he had been afforded a makeshift changing area in the wings to avoid the long climb.

Cooper made his way onto the stage after Tarbuck's glowing introduction and then began his routine. Everything went smoothly until close to the end. He had his usual props table nearby, with a pair of false lady's legs holding it up.

He would have felt at home, surrounded by his familiar paraphernalia. He looked assured, his earlier nerves having dissipated with the warmth of his reception and the success of his act on the night. He was performing for hundreds of audience-members in the theatre, with more than 12 million people watching it at home on television.

There was just one more routine to enact, and then one short joke to deliver before the ad break. As Tommy moved into position towards the back of the stage, a female assistant called Sandy Lawrence, a dancer on the show, appeared at his side carrying a large bronze-coloured cloak. It was a familiar gag, and the audience laughed with recognition in anticipation of what was to follow. Tommy placed his arms in the garment and pulled it over his shoulders. When the assistant bent down in front of him to fasten it, Tommy looked out towards the audience, as if to say 'That's nice!' It was probably the closest he came to innuendo in the whole of his career. Sandy Lawrence walked to the front of the stage, collected the microphone and stand, and carried them off with her, smiling at the crowd as she went. Behind her, the expression on Tommy's face suddenly changed.

He mouthed inaudibly, as if he had been struck by a sharp pain. There was nothing dramatic in the gesture, just a look of surprise as he realised that something was not right. Then, he slumped to a seating position, as crumpled as the cloak he was wearing. His legs were sticking out in front of him. The audience laughed. It looked like he had been overcome by the beauty of his blonde assistant and had been physically floored. Then, he slowly fell backwards, as if completing the move or the joke. The audience laughed even louder. The fez on his head came down over his face as he disappeared behind the curtain. Cue more laughter. The microphone he was wearing picked up the noise of him gasping. It sounded like he was snoring. Had he fallen asleep? The audience still found it funny and thought it was all part of the act. A hand appeared from behind the curtain and then quickly withdrew. It was meant to tap Tommy on his shoulder to check that he was okay. The hand belonged to Jimmy Tarbuck. The audience found that hilarious too.

Backstage, no one was laughing. The show's producer realised that something was seriously wrong, a fact confirmed by Tommy's son who was standing nearby and stated that this was definitely not in the routine.

The producer called immediately for an ad break and cued the orchestra to begin playing the music that preceded the commercial break. The show was being broadcast live to the nation, and viewers were left wondering what was going on. Behind the scenes, help was being mustered. Thomas Jr rushed to his father's side and tore off Cooper's bow tie and unfastened his shirt. Tarbuck's manager, Peter Pritchard, became the first of several first aiders to attempt resuscitation. He was joined by one of the show's painters, then a rigger, and eventually the production company's resident nurse.

Meanwhile, the adverts were coming to a close, and the show had to continue. The curtain was pulled forward in front of Tommy's size thirteen feet. Jimmy Tarbuck quickly prepped the next two acts. The first of these were the comedy duo of Les Dennis and Dustin Gee. When Dustin Gee said he did not think there was enough room on stage to perform their act properly, Tarbuck told them, basically, to get on with it. They were in an extraordinary situation—an emergency situation. If they wanted more room, they were not going to get it. Like professionals, the duo went on and performed, which involved the pair impersonating well-known soap stars. As they carried on with their act, behind them, they could hear people pounding on Tommy Cooper's chest backstage.

As well as the kiss of life, Tommy was receiving CPR, but it was all to no avail. Paramedics arrived, placed the comedy giant on a stretcher, and wheeled him to the ambulance. In the back of the vehicle, Cooper was accompanied by his son, Thomas Jr, and by Mary Kay, Tommy's personal assistant, with whom he had been having a long-standing affair. Mary held his hand and gazed with grave concern at the man she had fallen in love with some seventeen years earlier. The ambulance made its way to Westminster Hospital where, upon arrival at 8.40 p.m., Tommy Cooper was pronounced dead. He was sixty-three years of age. Mary Kay said that, in the ambulance on their way to the hospital, the paramedic told her that Tommy was really fighting—fighting for his life. He did not want to die.

His wife Gwen, whom he affectionately called Dove, was watching the programme on the TV at home. She immediately knew that something was terribly wrong. Tommy had a bad back. He would never slump to the floor like that without good reason. Besides, she was well-acquainted with Tommy's act. She had helped him choose the gags and routines and watched him practising for that night's performance. She had timed it for him, and she knew exactly what he was meant to do and when. This was definitely not part of the show. It would not be long before the telephone rang at the family home in Chiswick, West London. It was their son, Thomas Jr, with the devastating news that Tommy Cooper had died.

It was the end of an act that had given joy to millions of people over many years. Even his death had, unwittingly, made people laugh. The routine he was about to perform, before his untimely collapse, was one of his very best. He had enacted it countless times, but his audience never tired of it. It was the magic cloak routine. He would climb into an over-sized garment and, accompanied by some jolly music, he would produce a number of increasingly-ridiculous items from within the cloak, all delivered with a look of astonishment on his face.

First, there would be a bucket, then a plank of wood, followed by a mannequin-leg, and finally a ladder. The audience were in on the gimmick, but no one seemed to mind. At its conclusion, the person handing the props to Tommy (in this instance, it was going to be Jimmy Tarbuck) would appear from the bottom of the cloak, and Tommy would then look disgruntled because they had gone and given the trick away.

At the end of this favourite routine, Tommy planned to deliver his parting gag, which would have been 'Is there a Mr Smith in the house? Could you please remove your Jaguar from the car park. It's already bitten a policeman and we're a bit worried about what it's going to do next!' Then would have come the adverts, and Tommy would have waltzed off stage to huge applause. Instead, when the broadcast resumed after the commercial break, the compère told the audience that Tommy Cooper had been taken ill. It was a tough job for Tarbuck, who had first met Tommy twenty years earlier when they shared a dressing room at the *Royal Variety Performance*. That had been Tarbuck's first appearance at the event, while Tommy was by then a show-business legend. Tarbuck said that he never forgot how kind and helpful Cooper had been to him. Now, the Liverpool comic was experiencing what he later called 'The saddest night of my whole career'.

The death was announced to the nation that evening on the news at 10 p.m. The funeral was held five days later, and Tommy's ashes were scattered in the garden at the family home where he had lived for many years. His daughter Vicky described him as a man whose overriding ambition was to entertain people and make them laugh. Aside from his wife and children, she said, it was the one thing in the world that he loved most.

When he performed his final act, his last words were those he spoke to Sandy Lawrence, the young dancer who was acting as his assistant. As she placed the gown over him, he said, 'Thanks, love'; his last word on earth was 'love'. It is fitting that it should have been so, for love is what millions of people felt for him. There have been some attempts in recent years to portray Cooper as a violent drunk, or as a womaniser. Most people find this unfair, and it is certainly not how he is thought of by his millions of fans. There is a Tommy Cooper Society that has thousands of members, and he is still considered our greatest-ever comedian. He is still impersonated to this day. The fez cap is still intimately associated with him, and his catchphrase 'Just like that' seems destined to last forever.

His death was attributed to coronary occlusion due to atheroma, while his daughter, in more prosaic fashion, puts it down to the booze, the cigars, and the late nights that he kept for many years. He had been suffering from numerous ailments including bronchitis, lumbago, sciatica, indigestion, and circulatory complications. He was not a well man. Still, he appeared to be coming back from the brink at the time of his death. He claimed that he drank to eradicate stage fright. When it was said that Tommy only had to walk out on stage and the audience would start laughing, he would reply 'Yes, but you don't know what it takes to get up on that stage in the first place'.

Tommy had made his first television appearance more than thirty years earlier. That he should make his last appearance live on stage is not entirely inappropriate. Shortly after the funeral, talking about the manner in which he had left us, Thomas Jr said that his father would have settled for that, had he known the manner in which he was going to go. Tommy Cooper's death was treated like the passing of a head of state. There was profound grief across the country, that this man who had given us so much pleasure was gone in the blink of an eye.

The tabloid press were eager to report that Tommy had died on stage. It made for a better headline. London Weekend Television, the company that produced the live show, stressed that he had, in fact, died in the back of the ambulance and had been pronounced dead upon arrival at the hospital.

One of the paramedics who had been called to the theatre said he knew that there was nothing he could do for Tommy as soon as he looked at him. At that point, Cooper was still on the stage, behind the curtain, desperately being treated by his friends and family. He died out of view of his adoring public, but their love for Tommy Cooper will ensure that he will never be forgotten.

2

Who Was Tommy Cooper?

Who was this man whose death made the front page of every newspaper in Britain, and was the lead item in every news bulletin? The widespread coverage was not simply for the public manner of his demise. He was, as he was called in every report, Britain's best-loved entertainer, and he had been for almost four decades. There were other personalities who could possibly claim to be more popular at certain times throughout that period. Morecambe and Wise were a national institution, and the Two Ronnies were national treasures, but they were comedy duos, and no other single personality had held the country so spellbound for such a long time. Benny Hill was a household name, and Les Dawson was adored by the general public, but even those two do not come close to equalling Tommy's towering presence.

How should we define Tommy Cooper? He straddled a fine line between comedy and magic. He had a unique ability, one that no other performer in the land could claim to have—of being able to reduce an audience to hysterics without even opening his mouth. It has been said many times that the audience would be laughing while standing in the queue to enter the theatre. The mere thought of him was enough to set them off.

This was due, in some part, to his huge physical appearance. He was 6 feet 4 inches and weighed more than 15 stone, with size thirteen feet. He was, to all intents and purposes, a clown, in the most flattering form of the word. He was big-jawed. In fact, he was big everything. His wife would say to him before a performance, 'You get out there, big 'ed and knock 'em dead!'

He invariably did. Jimmy Tarbuck says he cannot recall a single bill where Tommy failed to steal the show. He was simply majestic, the king of comedy.

For Tommy Cooper, there was little distinction between his life and his art. He was a perennial joker. He loved nothing more than to search out new magic tricks, either to include in his act or simply to perform to his friends at their regular get-togethers. He would do the same for his kids at the dining table, in the living room, or in the garden at home. He was really just a big kid himself, and his act was littered with the sound of his own laughter. It did not matter to the audience that this was irregular and almost taboo for a comedian to do. Tommy had a bond with his audience that did away with convention. There was a community of hilarity that blurred the distinction between audience and performer. They were all in it together. They had to be, for Tommy's humour was not sophisticated in the truest sense of the word. In fact, it was almost ridiculous.

'My feet are killing me,' he would say. 'Every morning when I wake up in bed, I find them around my neck like this!' and then he would mime being strangled. Then, he would laugh, a huge guffaw that invited you to join him—of course, everyone did.

He was Britain's best-loved comedian, respected by his peers, and his admirers came from every corner of society, from working-class coal-miners to the Queen of England herself. Tommy appeared on stage at no fewer than five *Royal Variety Performances*. The first came in 1953, followed by others in 1964, 1967, 1971, and 1977. Those appearances are now the stuff of legend. He was the Queen's favourite comedian, despite the fact he came very close to the knuckle on many occasions.

He even managed to make the Monarch shout out loud at one royal event for the audacity of a particular gag when, in the middle of his act, from his busy table of props, he seized a large sword and placed it on the ground in front of him. Then, he knelt down on one knee in the direction of the Queen. The audience could not believe what they were seeing. There was Tommy, effectively saying 'Go on. Knight me!'

At first, the crowd were in shock as they struggled to believe that anyone could be so daring. Yet, after they got over their initial astonishment, they were rocking back and forth in their seats, with tears streaming from their eyes.

Her Majesty turned to her companion, the Duke of Edinburgh, to acknowledge the naughtiness of it. Then Tommy continued; he turned to the audience and said 'Well, you never know!' Cue more laughter. Tommy continued. 'She might. She might not, but she might. You don't know, do you?' Eventually, he rose to his feet, as well he should have done, and continued with the show.

Afterwards, he compounded his cheek when being introduced to Her Majesty backstage. It was customary for the stars to line up as the Queen made her way past them, occasionally stopping to chat. It was her way of thanking the performers and was a treat for those that had been given the privilege of appearing on stage at a *Royal Variety Performance*.

When the Queen reached Tommy, probably for fear that she would burst out laughing, she gave him a perfunctory nod and attempted to move swiftly on. Tommy, though, had other ideas. He coughed, as if to attract her attention, and Her Majesty stopped in her tracks.

'Would you mind if I asked you a personal question?' he said.

'As personal as I'll allow,' came the royal reply.

'Is Your Majesty a fan of the football?' he asked.

The Queen looked momentarily flummoxed. 'No,' she eventually replied. 'I can't say that I am'.

'In that case,' said Tommy, 'can I have your tickets for the FA Cup final?'

If he had not been heading for the Tower of London already, that should have been the final straw.

So how had he managed to achieve such a lofty status and maintain it for so long? His broad appeal certainly helped, from Monarch to miner. He also never resorted to smut. His act was clean and wholesome. It was nothing other than funny. He never thought he was smarter, or bigger, or better than the crowd who were watching him. All he craved was attention, and in return he offered top-drawer entertainment that was a sure-fire hit.

His energy levels were amazing. He was constantly in motion. He would move between his props tables, rummaging around among the various tricks and visual gags stored there. He often appeared chaotic, but this was a clearly measured act that had been practised to perfection beforehand. He was said to be the hardest working man in show-business, and not just for the number of performances that he would put in. At its height, he once did fifty-two shows in a week. It was instead more to do with the hours that he spent rehearsing, burning the midnight oil, until he had his act completely honed.

He was also the most imitated man in the country, and not just by his fellow professionals. School children up and down the land would try and do it, their hands out front before uttering his famous catchphrase: 'Just like that'. He was just as funny off-stage as on, according to his family and his many close friends.

In 1954, on one of his first visits to America, Ed Sullivan, the esteemed television show host, described Tommy Cooper as 'The funniest man ever to appear upon this stage'. In 1969, he was voted Britain's Television Personality of the Year, and that is not to mention those five *Royal Variety Performances*.

Despite this, Tommy was never honoured in any official lists. There would be no knighthood after all—not even an OBE, MBE, or CBE. One wonders if even the Queen thought that he had gone too far on occasion. Still, there was nothing innately offensive about his act. It was suitable for children, and whole families would gather around the TV set to watch one of his many television broadcasts.

For all that he was a giant of comedy, his real love was magic. Had he not stumbled upon his career when observing how much laughter he received whenever one of his tricks went wrong, he may have attempted to work as a true exponent of his favoured art. Instead, as he explained to the legendary scriptwriter Barry Cryer, 'There must be a hundred great magicians out there. I'll be the idiot, the one who gets it wrong'. He realised there was a living to be made doing just that. As a family man with mouths to feed, and with more than a passing obsession with money, he stuck with the act that earned the most applause. Besides, a lot of magic tricks require a degree of reverence from an audience that simply did not suit Tommy's style. How could he ask an audience to concentrate in silence when they were cracking up at the mere sight of him?

He soon accepted his lot in life, that he would never be a great magician, and he started playing it for laughs. Fellow magician Paul Daniels once said 'He was forever on the lookout for new tricks, but not to amaze or astound. Instead he would be thinking, how can I mess this up?'

He would never do topical gags. There were no current affairs and no politics included. That may be part of the reason behind his enduring popularity. He never went stale. All he had to offer was silly, harmless humour, and he had it in spades. One time, he was due to give an after-dinner speech at a charitable function for his peers. These were trained veterans, masters of their own crafts, with many of them coming from the same entertainment field as Tommy. They should have been a tough audience. Paul Daniels was there to witness the event, and he later described what had happened in an interview with the *Daily Telegraph* in 2003.

Tommy, at the top table, rose to his (huge) feet when it was time to deliver, and that was it—the room fell about laughing, while Tommy just stood there with a confused expression on his face, wondering what on earth was going on. This continued for five whole minutes. The audience were convulsed, and Tommy was none the wiser. Then, as the laughter gradually subsided as people paused to take a breath, Tommy turned to his wife, Gwen, who was seated beside him and said, 'I haven't said a thing yet,' and that sent the whole room up again.

To ask about his position among the all-time comedy greats, in 2010, the *Daily Telegraph* ran a poll to find the nation's fifty favourite jokes. Thirteen of the top fifty belonged to Tommy Cooper. In 2004, *Reader's Digest* voted him the funniest Briton of all time. When the Victoria and Albert Museum took possession of his archive of material, the curator, Simon Sladen, said simply that Tommy had been one of the best-loved performers of the twentieth century.

Ken Dodd, the veteran comedian, said of Cooper that 'He simply loved laughter and he loved to laugh'.

Jimmy Tarbuck said that 'Tommy was one of those comics who could just walk on stage and be hit with a wall of love'.

Finally, Eric Morecambe declared, 'I've never met anyone who disliked him as a man. If you didn't like him as a comic, then you didn't like comedy'.

All of this was for a simple man who would arrive for a show with his homemade sandwiches, lovingly prepared by Gwen, and a few cans of beer in a plastic bag, no matter the venue or the status of the gig. He was hugely popular, onstage and off, despite some personal flaws that have lately been blown out of all proportion. So where did he come from, this comedy king?

The story begins in Wales in 1921 with the birth of Britain's greatest ever entertainer.

3

Where It All Began

In March 1919, a young man and woman approached a house at 19 Llwyn Onn Street in Caerphilly in the Welsh region of Glamorgan. The young woman was seven-months pregnant at the time, and the couple were desperately in need of a place to live. The landlady, Mrs Maud Shattock, took pity on the pair and offered them a room on the ground floor, facing the road, at the front of the small terraced house. The bathroom and the kitchen were to be shared with the other tenants.

Four days later, the couple, Thomas Samuel and Gertrude Catherine Cooper, went out for the evening to the local cinema. At the time, he was twenty-seven years old and she was twenty-six. It is not known what film they watched, or what emotions it brought out in the pregnant woman. They could have been watching Charlie Chaplin's first full feature *The Kid*, which was released that year. Maybe this reduced her to hysterics. Perhaps it was *The Sheik* starring Rudolph Valentino that possibly caused her to swoon. I would like to think it was a comedy that she was enjoying at the time. Buster Keaton and Harold Lloyd were both prominent in the box office listings that year. Imagine if Tommy heard the laughter in the auditorium and came rushing to the fore, thinking he was on next. It means he would have started life in the same way in which he eventually left it, to the sound of people laughing in a large theatre.

Anyway, just as the movie ended, Gertie's waters broke and she began to go into labour. They struggled home and, a few hours later, Maud Shattock served as midwife at the birth of Thomas Frederick Cooper.

Two months premature, little hope was held out for the infant child. As Tommy Cooper later joked, 'When I was born, the midwife picked me up, turned me upside down, and slapped me on the backside. Already I knew that life was going to be hard!'

In reality, Mrs Shaddock had served in this capacity many times before. She was the unofficial 'go-to' person in the neighbourhood for such situations. This time around, she placed the child at the end of his mother's bed and left him in the hands of fate.

The odds were against a child born so early into the pregnancy, especially in that day and age, where death in childbirth was still a common occurrence. Indeed, Mr Cooper had been married once before and had lost his wife and first-born child in just such tragic circumstances. It appeared that history might repeat itself in some part, but Mrs Cooper had other ideas. With a concoction of condensed milk, sprinkled with a few drops of brandy, she stuck by young Thomas and nursed him to full health.

Gertrude Catherine Wright was a practical lady, no-nonsense, and not used to failure. She was said to have been tall, dark, and mysterious. She had been born in Devon in 1893, the daughter of a farmer, and from a family that was believed to have money. They certainly knew how to use it, and how to keep it when they had it. It was just as well, for the man she had chosen to marry was cut from a different cloth.

Thomas Samuel Cooper came from Caerphilly, which lies in a valley in Wales overlooked by green rolling hills. He was one of seventeen children in his family. His dad worked down the coal mines, and so he followed him there when he was old enough to go out and earn a living. After the tragedy of his first marriage, Thomas Sr served in the First World War, eventually being invalided out after he was gassed on the front lines. The medical condition would remain with him throughout his life, leading to bronchial and respiratory problems that would undermine his efforts to find suitable employment.

Luckily for him, he had backed a winner in Gertrude Wright, now Cooper. She was hard-working and knew how to earn a buck. She was also quite stern, and not given to open signs of affection towards her husband or her son. Rare were the hugs and cuddles that one might expect for a first-born child.

Joy came in other ways, however, as Mr Cooper was a very funny man. He was a people-person, had time for everyone, and was always searching for an audience and an opportunity to tell a funny story. Anything, it would seem, except for getting down to some honest work. It must have driven Mrs Cooper half-mad.

Everything was a joke to him. He liked nothing better than having a good laugh. It was a trait that ran in his family. His brother, Jimmy, was a trickster of the highest order. When Jimmy was made redundant at the mines, he took to the cabaret circuit. His act consisted of jokes and conjuring tricks—sound familiar? He also played accordion, and even appeared as the prankster alongside a straight-man in a comedy duo. He was a moon-faced clown in full theatrical make-up.

He would do one particular piece of magic involving real eggs, which he would attempt to make disappear. All the while, the women of the house would be fretting in case he broke them, due to the rationing in place at that time and the extreme poverty prevalent in the country at the end of the First World War.

Thomas Sr was very much like his brother. At every family gathering, weddings, Christenings, and the like, everyone would be reduced to hysterics at the antics of Jimmy and Thomas. Luckily for the latter, his wife was serious and industrious and kept the family on track. She was a seamstress who would knit and embroider for others, running effectively a cottage industry from their one-room home. In the summer months, she would make ice cream in the kitchen and flog it out of the front window, making it literally an ice-cream parlour. Today, there is a plaque outside the house in Llwyn Onn street commemorating the birthplace of the young Tommy Cooper.

Meanwhile, with Mr Cooper senior's chest problems continuing, it was felt that the damp and dusty air of the mining town was not conducive to his recovery; the family upped sticks and moved to Exeter in Devon when Thomas Jr was three years of age. They moved into a house at 3 Fords Road, from where Tommy attended Comrie House prep school.

There is an old photograph of young Tommy as a boy, sitting astride a tricycle. He is grinning, and his looks reflect those of an early photograph of his parents. He has his father's brow and eyes, and his mother's nose, straight mouth, and large jaw.

When it was time for Tommy to go off to school, he attended Mount Radford School for boys. This was a private school, for which his parents would have to pay. Although times were hard, Mrs Cooper always found a way. She continued with the ice-cream business only, instead of selling it from their home, they bought a van and peddled their wares around the fairgrounds, race meetings, and resort towns along the Devon coast.

Tommy would cycle to school each day, and his mum would disperse his dinner-money throughout the individual pockets of his clothing, a portion in each. That way, should he ever lose any of it, he would still have some left over. This thrift with money would be a trait that would live with Tommy for the rest of his life. He would always be careful with it, and mindful of it, to an almost paranoid extent.

While Mrs Cooper was set in her ways, her husband was having a hard time of it. Apart from helping out with the ice-cream business, he had no real trade of his own. He was effectively no more than an assistant in his wife's business, and the toll on his esteem saw him to turn to gambling. This would later severely affect the young family and would be the reason behind their next house move.

By this time, Tommy was settling into school. He was not the brightest academically, although as he later joked, he was close—about 3 feet away. He would copy the answers from his classmates and he would invariably be caught. He was not even clever enough to cheat and get away with it. In one school photo, he is seen standing on the back row, already one of the tallest among his peers. Another picture shows him with wavy, almost curly hair, sticking out at the sides like a large pair of ears. It could be an early indication of how he would later wear his hair when performing, with wild, crazy tufts jutting out at the sides from beneath his fez.

He was described by classmates as introspective and a bit of a loner. He was not part of any gang. He had, at this stage, no siblings to play with. That would change in the future but, for now, Tommy was largely without playmates both at school and at home. Though he had been born in Wales, it was Devon where he acquired the accent that he would carry for all of his life.

He was said to be reclusive and preferred his own company to that of others. He was, though, already showing his unique sense of humour whenever the opportunity arose. At one point, he escorted his mother to a hardware store where she planned to buy a few household items. While there, Tommy managed to draw a crowd by taking a pew on a lavatory that was being displayed for sale in the window.

His mother eventually turned around to see what all the fuss was about, as a group of people had stopped to chuckle in the street. 'Get off there!' she said, in her best posh accent.

'I can't,' said Tommy. 'I haven't finished yet!'

It is a joke worthy of a much older person. It is probably worthy of a professional, and Tommy was still in short pants at the time. His humour deserved an outlet, and his solitary nature was also in need of a hobby. The solution came at Christmas time in 1929, when Tommy was eight years old. His aunt Lucy, full name Lucy Westcott, who came from Cardiff and was from his mother's side of the family, bought him a magic set. She little realised that this would set the course for her nephew's future.

From there on in, Tommy would spend hours practising the tricks in order to master them. He was truly fascinated with the medium, and it would prove to be no passing fad. The local kids rarely saw him playing out after that. He would be in his room, practising, practising, practising.

When he thought that he was ready to showcase one of his tricks, he would come down to the living room and perform for his parents. When he had finished whatever sleight-of-hand manoeuvre he had chosen, he would ask them if they knew how he had done it. 'Yes,' they would reply. As Tommy himself later said, 'God, they were a tough audience!'

Tommy was so beguiled with his new hobby that he strived to master every last trick, over and over, and all-day long.

Whereas before Tommy had been insular and shy, now he went forth in search of an audience. He had come out of his shell, awoken by this fascinating art form. The cinema held no interest for him. Sports held no interest for him. Magic was his all-consuming passion, and he was intent on sharing it with as many people as he could.

Even in class, he could not contain himself, as each day saw a different prank performed. It did not take long for the teachers to spot who the culprit was, and every episode would finish off with a shout of 'Cooper!' One hopes it was returned with a Tommy Cooper belly laugh.

This one festive gift changed the course of Tommy's life. When later he was asked if he was a good magician pretending to be bad, or a bad magician pretending to be good, Tommy replied that he did not know. Perhaps the best response is the one he gave live on television in 1958, when asked to explain the origins of his act. 'I got my first magic set when I was eight years old from my Aunt Lucy. Auntie if you're watching, I just want to say thank you for the Christmas present, but I still can't do the tricks!'

The question of whether Cooper was a good magician or not is one that is still debated to this day. For sure, though, Tommy fell in love with magic and, soon, audiences fell in love with him.

4

Schooldays and Workdays

Tommy took to magic instantly. It became an obsession. It was one that would take over his life. If he had been introverted and reclusive beforehand, he now became even more so, devoting every minute of his spare time to his new-found passion. Oddly, while he was completely lost in his own little world, he found that he was able to mix more easily with the children playing in the street or in the school yard, for he now had something to talk to them about. Rather, he now had something to show them, which happened to be whatever trick he was practising at the time. For Tommy, his peers were simply an audience, and he would do anything he could to impress them or prank them.

While Tommy would spend hours in his room with his magic set, he was also constantly on the lookout for new novelties that he could put into his 'act'. Whereas the other kids in the neighbourhood bought comic books for the stories, Tommy would scour them for the adverts, always searching for new gags and tricks. He would also supplement his list of props with everyday items from the home, much to the annoyance of his mother. His repertoire was expanding, as was his skill-set, as he repeatedly tried to make coins disappear, rabbits appear, and whatever else he could come up with.

He was captivated by the world of magic, and it was a love that would stay with him for the rest of his life. He was still a long way off from converting to comedy, and the thought would not enter his head for a few years to come. He never seemed to understand how funny he actually was. His looks and mannerisms, his hysterical laugh, and his penchant for humour all seemed to be lost on him. He had no self-awareness of how easy it was for him to raise a laugh. One story has him walking into the local sweet shop, his face darkened by shoe polish, wearing a colourful robe, and clutching a suitcase. He looked for all the world like a peddler from an Arabian bazaar.

'Very cheap. Very cheap,' he would say, imploring the shopkeeper to purchase some of his wares.

He was a natural clown, yet he did not seem to get it. He still had his heart set on becoming a serious magician.

As for his home life, Tommy was no longer an only child, as the family welcomed baby David into the world in 1930. There was a nine-year difference between the two boys, and the new arrival was too young to be a playmate for Tommy, but one can imagine the look of wonder on the younger boy's face as his elder brother, as he surely must have done, beguiled him with his sleight-of-hand magic tricks.

Then came the event that Mrs Cooper later described as being the hardest day of her life. Thomas Sr managed to gamble away everything that the family owned, and they were forced to leave their Exeter home and relocate nearly 200 miles away. Their next abode would be in Home Farm Lane, in the village of Langley, near Fawley, about 7 miles from the south-coast city of Southampton. Mrs Cooper would remember with sadness carrying baby David out of their former home and heading into an uncertain future, with the cause of her embarrassment in tow in the shape of Mr Cooper.

Luckily for Thomas Senior, he soon found work at RAF Calshot. It is not known if the job was the reason the family made the move, or whether it happened once they arrived on the scene.

The Army had a reputation for looking after its own. Presumably, they would have found it hard to turn down a request for help from a veteran who had been invalided out of the war, especially from a man in such chastened circumstances. At least, having secured this employment, Mr Cooper was temporarily off the hook with his wife.

Mrs Cooper herself wasted no time in putting their finances back in order. She started another cottage industry at home, this time with a haberdashery business, returning to her earlier trade in needlecraft. Now, with two incomes, the family could relax a little. In fact, they were soon able to build their own home a short distance away. They purchased a plot of land and constructed a detached bungalow, which they named Devonia in a nod to their roots.

Tommy, too, would soon be able to help with the family finances, as he was fast approaching the age where he could leave school and get a job. There was no suggestion that he was capable of doing anything except manual work. While it was true that Tommy had attended private school, the budding magician was a non-starter academically.

As for his hobby, it would remain just that—a part-time passion rather than a full-time career option. Still, it gave Tommy an enormous amount of fun, and it became his calling card and a route to popularity that his own personality had not thus far produced. People would see him riding a bike down the road while reading a newspaper, the broadsheet opened fully out in front of him, completely obscuring his view. The sight was funny enough, with Tommy's long, gangling legs knocking against the handlebars as he peddled along. While many wondered at the feat, and how he managed to do it without crashing the bike, the trick was made possible by the fact that he had earlier cut two holes out of the paper, just big enough for him to see where he was going.

He was by this point acknowledged as the class clown. He would take empty display bars of chocolate from the local sweetshop and place them in the school playground, where they would be found by some unsuspecting fellow pupil. When the unfortunate kid rushed up to seize it, Tommy, hiding behind a nearby wall, would pull it away with the aid of a clear nylon thread. It gave him a good laugh.

Finally, at the age of fourteen, it was time for Tommy to leave school. He had been a practical joker all the way through, and now it was time to grow up and get down to the serious business of work.

First up, he tried college. He enrolled on a course and only lasted a week. His parents, by now doing well with the haberdashery shop, were able to pay a subsidy for Tommy to join an apprenticeship scheme at a boatyard in Southampton. He proved hopeless, and he was still far too interested in playing the clown.

He would visit the town centre of a weekend, scouring the magic shops for new tricks, before returning to work on a Monday morning with the words 'I've got a good one here to show you'. Then, he would beguile his workmates with his latest gag or gimmick. On more than one occasion, he managed to get half the workforce to down tools and gather around to watch him perform. This did not go down well with the company management. Still, it proved one thing. Tommy could hold an audience, and as he was not much good at anything else, the bosses thought they would put him to use at their annual Christmas party. This would be Tommy's first proper gig, and he was understandably nervous.

That Christmas show has now entered into show-business legend. The party was held in the work's canteen, where Tommy had performed an impromptu set for his colleagues on many occasions during their lunch breaks. This, though, was something else.

For all of the hours that he had spent practising, and as much as he knew how to do each of the tricks, the spirits must have been in a mischievous mood on the evening of the actual performance. No matter how hard Tommy tried, everything he did turned out wrong. Firstly, the trick where the pint of milk was meant to stay inside the upturned bottle did not go according to plan. The milk went everywhere, saturating the stage, and causing the audience to fall about laughing. Then Tommy dropped his wand. Items that should have disappeared from view were left dangling in full sight of everyone. It was a complete disaster and Tommy knew it.

He was distraught. He had worked so hard to get there. It was the pinnacle of everything he had been practising for. If he had ever harboured the dream of doing this professionally, that hope now appeared to be spectacularly dashed.

Tommy left the stage in disgrace and made his way to the make-shift dressing room. He sat, head bowed, in tears. The audience, made up of his colleagues, hardy dockers, and sheet metal workers, had all willed him to do well, and he had failed miserably and monumentally.

Yet, as he sat in the darkened dressing room, unsure how he could ever face his co-workers again, he realised that, fully five minutes after he had left the stage, the audience were still laughing. They had found the show funny, hysterically so. It was then that Tommy had his light bulb moment. 'Wait a minute,' he thought to himself, 'there could be something in this. There must be 100 great magicians in the country. I'll be the one who messes it up!' It was an idea that Tommy would embrace and set him on course for the career and the life that he was to lead. Then, with Europe on the brink of another world war, Cooper was enlisted into the Royal Horse Guards. He was Private Tommy Cooper and his journey had just begun.

In truth, Tommy would have struggled to continue with his apprenticeship had he not volunteered for the Forces. By his own admission, he could not knock a nail in straight. He was a liability, and his larking about would not have been tolerated during the war years when the work was deemed to be of national importance.

So, he put down his tool bag, donned his uniform, and turned up at the family home to surprise his parents with his sudden change of career. They could hardly refuse him the opportunity to serve when countless young men were doing likewise in the cause of their country. Tommy, now fully grown into his 6-foot 4-inch frame, already looked the part. He still had that gormless expression, but he had a boxer's gait, a ready smile, and he was becoming a force to be reckoned with. He was nineteen years of age, and about to leave home for the first time. He embraced his uncertain future with all the wonderment of youth.

5

National Service

The barracks of the Royal Horse Guards were based in Rotten Row in London, close to Hyde Park. Tommy was part of a unit of 100 men. As the name implies, Cooper's was a cavalry unit, and over the years, the young recruit became quite proficient in equine handling. This was despite an inauspicious start.

At an early ceremonial parade, to be carried out in full dress uniform, the men were responsible for saddling their own horses. The older men in the unit knew that their horses were none too keen on the idea, and that they would puff themselves out a little to ensure that the saddles were not pulled too tight.

Once the leathers had been fixed, the animal could breathe out, relaxing a little, and giving themselves some room beneath the straps. Yet Tommy did not know this. The trick was to wait out the horse. Once the animal had exhaled, more experienced hands would give a final tug on the buckle to ensure that the saddle was firmly affixed. So, one glorious morning, the whole company stood, resplendent, beside their charges. The order came, 'Prepare to mount'. Everyone stood to attention. Then, the final instruction. 'Mount!' Everyone, including Tommy, placed one foot in the stirrups and propelled themselves up on their horse. However, Trooper Cooper, whose own saddle slipped directly beneath the horse, was left a crumpled mess on the ground. Once again, he had unwittingly made everyone laugh. It was getting to be a trait.

Tommy took to military life. He enjoyed the camaraderie and the fact that he had an in-house audience for his magic tricks and gags. He would spend his spare time visiting various magic shops in the West End of London, always on the lookout for novelties with which to wow his comrades-in-arms. There were so many different shops to choose from—Tommy must have been like a kid in a candy store. Raised in the provinces, these magic shops held a mythical allure. Now, they were on his doorstep, or certainly within walking distance. Tommy took advantage of the opportunity whenever the chance arose.

It added a bit of colour to his more prosaic working life. His day-to-day duties consisted of a combination of military exercises and mucking out the stables, cleaning his uniform and rifle, riding out the horses, plus occasional sentry duty on the Mall, close to Buckingham Palace. This was done in his normal uniform, not the red tunic and bearskin hat more associated with the role. One can only imagine how he might have looked, and how tall he would have been, had he been attired in the more ceremonial costume.

With his considerable size, it is not surprising that he did a bit of boxing in the Army. A heavyweight, naturally, Tommy held his own for a few bouts, but does not appear to have taken it all too seriously. As he himself said, 'I look after myself. I can go ten rounds, as long as someone else is buying!'

One famous incident from this period came when Tommy was serving as sentry, which required the soldier to stand to attention for several hours. Only, Tommy could not do it. His feet ached, his back hurt, and he was tired. So, he closed his eyes, which was not conducive to effective sentry duty, and it would result in serious consequences if he was caught.

On this particular occasion, Tommy heard footsteps approaching. He could not open his eyes as it was already too late. It was clear to anyone watching that this young recruit had fallen asleep. This could result in a court martial. So, surreptitiously, he half-opened one eye, where he could just make out the shape of his sergeant and another commanding officer. The officers came to a halt in front of the sentry box and were not too impressed. Yet, before they could issue a severe reprimand, Tommy stole their thunder as he opened his eyes and said 'Amen!' It did the trick and got him off the hook. By now, he was acknowledged as a character around the unit, and it would have been entirely in keeping with the universal opinion of him as the company clown. Still, he was walking a very fine line there, and when his unit was called up overseas in 1943, it was probably a good thing before Tommy exhausted the patience of his superiors at the base.

The Second World War had been going on for four years at this stage. Europe had been set ablaze. Tommy was lucky to have been held back for so long, but with the war spreading across the globe, and the fighting at its most intense, Tommy found himself in Egypt's Western Desert, where the allies under General Montgomery were going toe-to-toe with German Field Marshal Rommel's Desert Rats. Tommy's company were tasked with reconnaissance. It was dangerous work, and on one such mission, young Trooper Cooper received a bullet wound to his arm. Luckily for him, it was not too serious. A few inches to the left and the world would have lost a celebrated entertainer. After receiving his wound, Tommy was removed from those dangerous front-line duties and another role was found for him.

Meanwhile, his love of performing had not gone unnoticed, and he was invited to Cairo to audition for a travelling army concert party. Not surprisingly, given how much time he had spent practising his craft, his audition was a successful one. He now joined up with a talented troupe of artistes, whose sole responsibility was to lift the spirits of the soldiers who were in need of some light relief from the horrors of the war.

When the Second World War eventually ended, thousands of men and women continued to be stationed in the Middle East, acting as peacekeepers as the dust began to settle on the conflict. Tommy stayed behind to entertain the troops. He was a favourite with the crowds, and his act went down a storm. Tommy achieved this success with a cheeky routine that saw him mock his military masters by first ripping up the rule-book when it came to his uniform.

He would arrive on stage wearing a scruffy pair of shorts that ran down to his knees. He had on an old pair of boots, with his socks rolled over on top of them. Finally, he had removed the lining from his Army helmet so that it fell about his head and ended up lop-sided. To an army of men used to daily inspections, where every button and buckle had to be polished until they gleamed, this was hilarious. He would then call an officer on to the stage and continue with the ribbing, breathing on their medals and polishing them with his sleeve, as if to show how important they were. The audience loved it.

Tommy was pleased that things were working out for him. Performing was the one thing he wanted to do for the rest of his life. Who knew if he would ever get the opportunity, once hostilities ended and he returned to civvy street. Yet for now, he was doing something he loved, earning the respect and recognition of his comrades, and hearing the sound of laughter on an almost daily basis.

Then, one evening came the incident that led to Tommy acquiring the image that will forever be associated with him. He walked on stage, as usual, but he had forgotten his military pith helmet, as it was called. Tommy stood there momentarily, wondering what he should do, and at that moment a waiter strode by in front of the podium, carrying a tray of drinks. Tommy reached down and snatched the bright red fez from the waiter's head and put it on top of his own. The look was immediately priceless and was an instant hit with the troops. Now, with tufts of his dark, curly hair protruding at the sides, his image was complete—that of a half-demented, half-confused clown.

His act continued to progress from there on in, and his stage persona was almost complete. He was still doing the magic for laughs, getting the majority of the tricks wrong, and also performing comic sketches and rapid-fire one-liner gags. He continued to perform for the men of the Armed Forces, and soon found himself aboard a troop ship heading from Suez to Alexandria.

Tommy joined the resident troupe. He was, by now, something of a seasoned professional. Whether he could continue to work in this field after his military service would have to be seen, but here he was, performing several shows a day, enjoying the show-business life.

It was while at sea that Tommy Cooper reached another significant milestone in his life, for here, he met the woman who would soon become his wife. Her name was Gwendoline Henty, Gwen for short, and she was already a star in her own right in entertainment circles. Their paths were about to cross, and love was about to bloom.

6

Meeting Gwen

Gwendoline Henty was born in Eastbourne in 1920. She was a few months older than the man she would marry. She was an established performer in the concert party. Indeed, she was one of the stand-out acts, and as well as being an accomplished comedienne and musician, she would turn her hand to most things required to entertain the troops. She had the best legs in the line-up and was not averse to putting them on display to the delight of the mostly male audience. She was also seemingly bereft of ego and thought nothing of dressing up as a haggard, old charlady for a particular sketch—anything in fact to get a laugh and play her part. She was equally as comfortable playing herself, singing and impressing at the piano, which was her forte. She was compared to some of the biggest stars of the day; in fact, to some of the biggest stars in the world at that time. It appears that she could hold her own with the best of the acts in the company. She was more than a match for any of them, a celebrity in her own right.

One day, aboard a troop ship heading towards Alexandria, Gwen was nursing a bout of flu. She was lying in a deckchair, wrapped in a towel to keep warm, and trying to soak up the sea air in an attempt to revive her to health. That was when she first caught sight of Tommy Cooper. He was standing on deck, leaning against the railings, and Gwen could not help but notice this giant of a man. She saw how the blue of the ocean matched the blue of his eyes, and thought he had the most fantastic physique of any man she had ever seen. His looks were attractive, in an unusual way. There was something about him, she thought, and she turned to a friend who was lying on the next deckchair and asked who he was. 'That's Tommy Cooper,' came the reply. 'He's in the show'.

Later that day, Tommy appeared on stage, and Gwen snuck up to the porthole in the door to the concert room and watched him perform. She was still suffering the effects of the flu, so she dared not enter the room, but as she gazed inside, she was able to observe the movement and magic of Tommy's act.

She could see that he held the audience spellbound. People were falling about laughing as Tommy messed up trick after trick. Gwen found him hilarious. She said that it was the funniest thing she had ever seen, even if she could not hear a word. She also thought Tommy was very professional, polished even. Gwen told herself that he was going to be a big star one day.

A few weeks later, back on dry land, the two of them were paired together for the first time to perform a routine.

'Where's your dots?' asked Gwen of her new partner.

'My what?' Tommy replied.

'Your dots. You know, the sheet music'. She was a highly-trained musician, while Tommy was just playing it for laughs. When he realised what she was going on about, he quickly regained his composure.

'Oh, just give me a few bars of 'The Sheik of Arabi' and leave the rest to me,' he said.

After the show, on their way back to their digs, Tommy sat beside Gwen on the tour bus. 'Do you mind if I rest my head on your shoulder?' he asked politely.

'I certainly do!' Gwen protested.

Undeterred, just two weeks later, Tommy proposed to Gwen with the words, 'I don't suppose you'd marry me, would you?'

Gwen replied, 'I suppose I will!'

It was not Gwen's first engagement. She had previously accepted a proposal from an airman who sadly perished during the war, however, when later asked what she would have done if she had met Tommy while still engaged, she replied that she would have broken it off. 'I really fell for Tommy,' she explained earnestly.

The couple married in Cyprus in 1947 with a single night's stay in a hotel on the island for their honeymoon. The pair were well-matched. They were both comfortable on stage, surrounded by fellow performers. They could look forward to their life together, searching for success, whenever they were released from the military service and could head back to England where they planned to set up the marital home.

It was a union of equals, and Gwen had no trouble standing up for herself. Years of professional practice had honed her skills, and she was a confident and attractive lady. Also, the two of them were deeply in love. In fact, Tommy coined an affectionate nickname for her, calling her 'Dove'. It was a sobriquet that she treasured and one that would stick with her for the rest of her days.

Meanwhile, Tommy had completed his active service and he was set to return to England, while Gwen still had a few more assignments with the concert party to complete before she could head back to Britain. Devonia became Tommy's abode again and, from there, he wrote often, explaining how much he missed her and how much he looked forward to their reunion. He would end his letters with the words 'I love you, my beautiful wife'.

It was not long before he was joined by Gwen, and soon they headed for the bright lights of the capital city and moved into a house in Lavender Hill in Clapham, South London. It was from there that Tommy made his first forays into show-business as a civilian, and Gwen was right behind him.

As an experienced theatre professional, she was also on hand to offer advice about his act—which jokes and tricks she thought he should include. She was a fan with a practised eye and she helped him with his routines. At one time, Tommy entertained the idea that they should pair up as a double act, but Gwen was quick to tell him that a show-business marriage was hard enough without the two of them trying to work together.

'You stay as you are,' she told him bluntly, 'and then, if things don't work out, you've got no one to fall out with but yourself!' The fact is that she knew how good Tommy could be. She had no doubts that he would eventually reach the top, but breaking into the variety circuit was going to be tough, and the wannabe comedian would need her help and support every step of the way.

Even before Gwen had joined him in London, Tommy had been lining up auditions. When these did not go according to plan, he began to doubt himself. After all, he was married now. Was it right for a grown man to keep chasing his dreams when he had a wife and responsibilities?

Gwen would not hear any of Tommy's misgivings. She urged him to keep going. She believed in him at a time when he himself did not. Suitably bolstered, Tommy would go out there and give it his best shot, traipsing whatever boards he could gain access to, and showing his face at every available audition.

He managed to get himself in front of an agent called Tommie Draper and applied unsuccessfully for a shot at the Windmill Theatre. Then, he thought his act would be a good fit for the BBC, which was then beginning to showcase talents such as his. He took it upon himself to write a letter to the organisation in June 1947, stating that his act consisted of cod-magic and comedy, with the offered advice that he thought it would be quite suitable for the medium of television.

Just three days later, Cooper received an invitation to audition. The result has since gone down in comedy folklore. The BBC's appraisal is matched only perhaps by the man from Decca Records who turned down The Beatles, saying he thought that guitar bands were finished.

Tommy, suffering from a lack of confidence at this point as he struggled to break into show-business, failed to make any sort of positive impression. The summary of his experience, delivered by some suit at the corporation (probably the Head of Light Entertainment) described him as having 'A nonchalant approach, with poor diction and an unpleasant manner'. He then completed his report with the words, 'And an extremely unfortunate appearance!'

Luckily, Tommy did not know this and he soldiered on, all the while dreaming of a future in the entertainment industry.

7

Starting Out

Gwen took Tommy's de-mob money, when he was officially released from the Army, and bought him a camel-hair coat with it. Back then, as she later said, you could not be taken seriously in show-business without one, and she was not going to see her husband being left behind because he did not have the right attire. She was determined that Tommy was going to make it to the top, but it used to break her heart to see him rise at some ridiculous hour of the morning in order to grab a pitch at the market, where he would use his stage-patter to try and flog whatever wares he had picked up from the wholesalers that day in an attempt to earn a modest income.

The couple were so desperate for cash that their weekly treat was a walk into the West End, where they would have a half pint of bitter each. One time, they each had two halves and had to walk home, a distance of several miles. They were not the only ones in this predicament. Money was scarce and food rationing was still in place as the country tried to get back on its feet after six years of war.

Tommy was still trying to get gigs for himself and, more importantly, he longed to secure the services of an agent who might procure him some paid work. While he still harboured the hope that Gwen might pair up with him professionally, she was adamant that the idea was a non-starter. Besides, Tommy was not really suited to working as a duo. He had tried it before, most notably with Frank Lyons, a skilled comedian who had been teamed up with Tommy for several sketches during their military days. In Lyons's opinion, Cooper was not the sort of man who could work with anyone else. He said that Cooper only had a rapport with himself.

Another colleague from those early performance days described Tommy as self-obsessed, or at least obsessed with his own act. In fact, it was so all-encompassing that people found him hard to get to know off stage. The show was his personality.

Meanwhile, in the basement flat in South London where they were living, Tommy and Gwen were still plotting the comedian's career path, and in November 1947, Tommy secured the audition that was to change his fortunes forever.

It was at the Windermere Club in London's Regent Street that Tommy first encountered the agent George 'Miff' Ferrie. Cooper was called to the stage, with his confidence all-but shattered at this point. The previous six months of setbacks and outright rejection had put him at such a low ebb that he decided to forget the comedy and the magic and to do some impressions instead.

He did a sketch based on the film *Mutiny on the Bounty* with Tommy changing roles and conversing with himself. It was, with hindsight, probably hilarious but it was yet another audition that was about to fall flat. In any event, Ferrie was not impressed, and he was just about to dismiss Tommy when, in a moment of inspiration, he asked if there was anything else that Cooper could do.

'Well, I do a bit of magic, you see,' the nervous performer replied.

With that, Tommy began to do a few tricks from his well-practised act, and the boys in the band, taking a well-earned break in the orchestra pit, started to laugh. Miff heard their reaction and was impressed. These musicians had seen it all before and they did not succumb to laughter easily. The agent invited Tommy to return in a week or two to perform at the club. After that, it can be said, Tommy Cooper never really looked back.

At the time, television was just beginning to come to dominance. For years, film had been the nation's favourite form of visual entertainment. The movie studios immediately felt threatened by this emerging medium. Television sets were still a rare commodity, a luxury item, but as they became more popular, there was a rush to fill a content vacuum, and variety shows soon came to be a part of the expanding schedule.

Theatres around the country were also undergoing a change in fortunes. They, too, were suffering from the popularity of television and were looking to address the problem by changing their programming.

Entertainment was in a flux. Luckily, Tommy was equally at home in front of a camera or on stage, at the end of a pier, or appearing at a nightclub. It was all work to him, and his act had been tested in front of war-weary troops. He was battle-hardened, and his routine had broad appeal. He was prepared to work hard, and he was ready to embrace success. There was still a long way to go, but he could now consider himself to be a professional, for he now had an agent called Miff Ferrie.

The man Tommy had chosen, or who had chosen him, was fastidious and punctilious. It would be a relationship fraught with friction and occasional hostility over the ensuing decades but, in the beginning, both parties appreciated what they had found in each other. Tommy readily put pen to paper and signed the contract, although its content would cause him considerable consternation afterwards.

The document was signed in November 1948 and covered an initial period of five years, with a rolling clause thereafter that the contract could be extended by Miff as long as his client's earnings had not dropped significantly from the previous year.

The agent's commission was set at 15 per cent. This was to cover the fact that Miff was not acting merely as an agent but was also acting as Tommy's personal manager too. Though 10 per cent was standard for agency work, the higher percentage was more than reasonable for the added responsibility of artist management. It was an issue that would rear its ugly head throughout the long course of their working relationship. The contract was bona fide and endorsed by the council of the Agents Association Limited. It granted Miff sole control to manage Tommy's professional bookings, and was the sort of contract every struggling actor, writer, and performer spends years trying to attract. For the moment, everything was going according to plan, and Tommy happily signed, but down the years, the penny-pinching comedian would come to bemoan the sums that he was contracted to pay. He would have been happier with the lesser amount, but that was not the service that Miff was providing. Sadly, for all concerned, Tommy never seemed to understand it, or appreciate it, and he would forever feel hard done by.

It is difficult to concur with the artist's sentiment in this instance. As Tommy Cooper biographer John Fisher states, 'Miff's commission was a fair enhancement on an agent's typical return if management duties were included as well'.

Yet Tommy was tight-fisted, and it is likely that his contract situation with Miff was good cover for his own unwillingness to put his hand in his pocket. He would use it as an excuse to say that he did not have the money to buy a round when it came to his turn. At first, Tommy was happy to sign the contract, and wrote to Miff and thanked him for all the work that he had brought his way. Thanks to his theatrical agent, Tommy was now a fully fledged professional performer, plying his trade on an almost-nightly basis in the world of show-business.

The one thing he had strived for since he was eight years old was now his to truly hold. Tommy had broken through at the age of twenty-seven. Still, it was not like it was undeserved.

Together with Gwen, they polished his material. She was his script editor and number one fan, on stage and in life. She encouraged him every step of the way and made sure he had all the support he needed to become the success that he did. She was a homemaker, content to remain behind the scenes while Tommy chased the limelight.

They were a happy couple. At home, Tommy would play tricks on her. The laundry basket might hide a fake severed hand, so she would jump with fright when she came to do the washing and discovered the offending article. For example, on the night he first secured Miff's services, Tommy invited the agent home with him, just as he had told Gwen he would do if the audition was successful.

Cooper then led Miff into the hallway and asked him to wait outside the living room door. Alone, Tommy entered to find Gwen looking hopeful. One look at Tommy, his downcast expression, and the fact he had no one with him, caused Gwen to explode. At that point, they felt the whole world was against them. Certainly the world of show-business, because they could not get a break. The door to success was firmly shut against them.

'He's not coming,' said Tommy, down-hearted.

'Calls himself a talent-spotter? He wouldn't know talent if it jumped up and bit him on the arse!'

Gwen then let rip with a four-letter tirade, no shrinking-violet her, while Tommy tried his best to keep a straight face. Finally, he threw open the door and pulled Miff into the room.

'Meet my new agent,' he said.

Miff had heard every word. Gwen blushed and went all demure, before giving Tommy a gentle whack on the arm.

'Isn't he awful?' she said. She had been pranked good-and-proper and would continue to be so for the duration of their long marriage. Luckily, she found Cooper's jokes hilarious, and found Tommy adorable—much like his audience did.

With Gwen at his side and Miff behind him, Tommy Cooper was set for success.

8

Making His Mark

Tommy Cooper wrote to all of the major theatres in London in an attempt to break onto the stage. He auditioned five times at the Windmill, a popular venue in the heart of decadent Soho. The show was a blue revue, and the main attraction was the scantily-clad women who, by virtue of standing motionless on stage, managed to bypass the strict rules on nudity in place at the time. The girls were half-dressed, and among their number was a certain Audrey Hepburn, who would soon become one of the leading female stars of American cinema. She can still be seen in old photos from that era, standing in the chorus line, wearing a half-cut brassiere that is certainly not in keeping with her later iconic image.

The crowd were drawn for the ladies, but the entertainment in the revue would also involve variety acts. Unfortunately, for a comedian, it was a graveyard. The mostly male crowd would read their newspapers while waiting for the girls to return to the stage. It took Tommy five attempts to make any impression but, by then, he had learned to weather such storms of indifference and nothing was going to stand in his way.

With Miff securing him regular work, Tommy began to attract an audience of his own. He had already realised that he could make a living by being the magician who got things wrong. He had spotted a gap in the market, there was not another fool on the circuit like him, and he was determined to exploit his position. He worked continuously and accepted every gig that he could. Slowly, the venues began to get a bit more up-market. From the Windmill, with its certain clientele, he went on to work at the Savoy and Dorchester hotels in the heart of London's West End.

He even began to make the odd television appearance. This despite the fact that the BBC had been so dismissive at Tommy's earlier audition. Just six months after his damning rebuttal, Tommy made his first television appearance on the Leslie Hansen Christmas special in 1947. With indefatigable zeal,

Tommy had made it onto the first rung of the showbiz ladder, and there was no way he was about to step off.

The producers liked him and went out of their way to ask for him. He was becoming a star attraction, and he was also earning critical acclaim. Kenneth Tynan, the most high-profile theatre and television critic of his day, was surprisingly won over by Tommy's daft act. At the time, he wrote of Cooper warmly, in the high tones that critics often use. Writing in the *London Evening Standard*, he described Tommy like this:

> Tommy Cooper is a hulking, preposterous conjurer … He finds himself in a jelly of hysterics at the collapse of his own tricks. He is convulsed by his own incompetence. Holding his sides, laughing, he staggers helplessly from trick to trick. No man was ever less surprised by failure. Cooper has a distinct attitude to life. A stoic self-awareness of the futility of human effort. This is what raises him above the crowd.

High praise indeed, and by now, Tommy's career was certainly in the ascendancy. There were still further heights to be reached, but he was established in the minds of theatre owners and their audiences, and also with television producers, directors, and booking agents. No doubt Miff, the dour Scotsman, was pleased with his decision to invest in the hard-working performer.

By now, Miff had ditched his other acts to concentrate solely on Cooper's career. It was a decision that he would not regret and their relationship would endure for the rest of Tommy's professional life.

Cooper was billed as 'the Mad Magician' and 'the Crazy Comic', and his performances were said to be chaotic. They were not; they were well-honed. He was searching for perfection without ever believing that he was quite good enough.

There was a certain desperation about both his work ethic and the delivery of his act. He was a restless bundle of energy. He never stopped talking or moving. The gags came quick and fast, and they were usually one-liners. If he did not get them with the first one (although he invariably did) there would be another straight after that might fare a little better. He appeared to lack self-confidence, yet he was doing remarkably well. There was not a single performance that was not greeted with laughter, and there was usually at least one person bellowing above the crowd, finding him hysterical, and unable to moderate their appreciation. This became infectious, and Tommy had the ability to create a feeling of goodwill in the audience that other performers could only envy.

At this point, Tommy would usually acknowledge the insane laughter and then turn to the audience as if to say 'what are they on about?' He had the whole crowd on his side.

One early television appearance goes like this: Tommy enters, smiling, and smartly dressed. He has a saw in his hand, and nearby is a large wooden chest. When the applause dies down, Tommy begins.

'You've all seen the trick where the lady gets sawn in half?' The audience nod their heads in agreement. 'Well, I won't bother then,' says Cooper, and with that he throws the saw away.

He then does some business with a handkerchief, drawing it through his hand, and eventually making it disappear, showing the audience that he can actually perform magic successfully if he should wish. All the time, he is talking quickly, gag after gag, constantly moving. It is a double act between Tommy and his props.

He then picks up a tin, waits a moment, and then opens it. A huge snake flies out of it, a jack-in-the-box moment that means nothing yet still gets a laugh. Tommy laughs too, as he does with every other joke that he tells.

He waves a hanky in front of his face, talking nonchalantly as if thinking aloud. 'It's hot, isn't it? It's the heat that does it!' None of this would be quite as funny in anyone else's hands, but Tommy is soaring above the crowds, and everything he says is laced with humour. He is anarchic, and no one in the audience knows what to expect next. It appears that Tommy does not either, but nothing could be farther from the truth.

He is talking again. 'I went sunbathing today, and a boy came over to me and said "I'm going to put something on your back that will make you go brown." I said, "What is it?" He said "Gravy!"' Tommy laughs out loud again.

Then Tommy does 'Egg, bag, bag, egg,' and manages to get it all wrong, while allowing the audience to spot the deception. He does not mind. He is still laughing. Laughing along with the audience at himself. Then he gets his hand stuck in a ceramic mug. He feigns trying to get it out. Losing patience, he grabs a mallet off the busy props table and smashes the mug to pieces to free his hand. He tries to do a trick with a vanishing magic wand. He fails twice, so snaps the wand and throws it away. Then he has a male assistant come on, and Tommy places him in an air-tight box, where he leaves him for a full five minutes. Tommy explains that every magician who has tried this trick has died. He says Houdini has died, all of the others have died, 'and I'm not feeling too good myself!'

He then does the trick with the conjoined metal rings. He is all the while talking, and all the while moving. It is a performance full of energy, and the audience must have been exhausted just watching it. He holds up a cricket bat and says 'Bat-man!' and gets a solid laugh.

Finally, he attempts to release his assistant from the airtight box, only to let a look of dismay cross over his face. It has gone wrong, and Tommy produces a bunch of commemorative flowers, which he throws into the box (now coffin) before wheeling his unfortunate assistant away.

He finishes off with 'Goodnight!' It is a whirlwind routine, indicative of Tommy's style and energy at this point. No wonder he was making such a big impression. He was simply giving audiences a lot for their money. He had created a niche for himself and, having finally got his foot in the door, he was not about to slow down. His work ethic, and his unusual act, not to mention his unique appearance, all meant that Tommy was headed for the top.

Some of his jokes were infantile.

'I went to the doctor's the other day. I said doctor, I think I'm a dog. He said, "Take a seat". I said I can't. I'm not allowed on the furniture'.

Or how about this. Remember, this is probably one of his best loved gags.

'I slept like a log last night. Woke up in the fireplace!'

It is hard to conceive that anyone else could have gotten away with such scant material, yet Tommy had a great rapport with the audience. If he did not get you with one gag, the next would not be far behind and he would probably hook you with that. It did not really matter. Cooper was laughing anyway, so there was always a humorous soundtrack in the room.

He always looked as if he had been dragged from the audience and hurled on to the stage. This added to the sense of camaraderie that the watching crowd felt with him. It was not sophisticated, or at least it was not apparently so. Here was a working-class performer who went straight for the comedy jugular with an onslaught of verbal and physical prowess.

He quickly became a brand, with his trademark fez and his catchphrase, 'Just like that!'

Promoters knew what they were getting, and producers knew that they were watching a unique and original performer. Tommy Cooper was by now a regular on both television and the theatrical circuit, with a growing following and fan base to boot.

9

The Early Gigs

Kenneth Tynan, the esteemed critic, called Tommy Cooper 'Britain's best new clown'. Miff put the comedian on the bill at the Windermere club, and his initial one-week run was extended to three. Any misgivings that the agent might have had now disappeared. Tommy's act proved a hit, and Miff realised that he had something special on his hands.

Miff had been a performer himself, having headed up his own jazz band for a number of years. He knew a good thing when he saw it. From the club where Miff was the entertainments manager, Tommy's act was soon rolled out to other establishments. The Coconut Grove, the Panama, and the Blue Lagoon were regular gigs. The Bagatelle, Churchills, the Embassy club, the Colony, Astor, Quaglino's, and Kempinsky's were all Soho attractions where Tommy played to packed houses and an often-boisterous crowd. Despite these being sometimes less than salubrious settings, Tommy never resorted to the lowest common denominator. His routine was never risqué, his material never blue. He did not need swear words. All he had to do was to maintain his own brand of silliness and he was sure to get a laugh. His set was meticulous, and he was constantly on the lookout for new tricks and gags with which to pepper his act.

He was, as Miff was finding out, a professional showman. His work ethic was legendary, and his reputation was growing. Soon, he would even be booked at the Windmill theatre, which was seen as a serious step up the ladder. It was redemption for the man who had previously failed his auditions there. Now, Miff was inundated with enquiries for his boy. Tommy earned £223 in 1947, a figure that was to treble in 1948.

Tommy wrote to Miff at the end of the year, thanking him for working so diligently on his behalf. He said that he would be grateful if Miff would accept 15 per cent commission and continue to manage his affairs. It was a successful relationship, and Miff was fully occupied finding bookings for a client whose star was in the ascendancy.

With the medium of television growing ever more popular, Miff was keen to get his client on screen more often. Before long, Tommy was offered his own television series. This was a fitting reward for an artist who they had earlier dismissed as 'unfortunate'. Now, they were beating a path to his door, offering him every incentive to secure his services.

It was all experience to Tommy, who just loved to perform, and it was all money to Miff. Both had a voracious appetite for the opportunities that came their way. For all their differences, they were on the same wave-length when it came to working and earning. Both wanted it as much as the other, and every offer that came to them was given due consideration. From provincial clubs and theatres to the most successful of television studios, everyone got a fair hearing.

As such, Tommy continued to play the clubs and the lucrative hotel circuits, such as the Savoy and the Dorchester. Soon, he could afford to move to a new flat in Finchley, North London, with Gwen. From there, it was just a short cab or tube ride into the central attractions.

Cooper was a regular at the magic shops in town. He had a group of pals there and stood out for his heightened sense of enthusiasm for the latest novelties. He was a skilled magician in his own right and delighted in the occasional trick that went right on stage. After all, it was his favourite pastime. It was almost like a case of 'I told you so' whenever he performed a magic trick correctly.

Every time he did so, the audience responded warmly. They looked as surprised as Tommy did that he could actually get something right. They loved it when he bungled things. They loved it when things worked out. Most of all, they just loved him.

Left to his own devices, Tommy prepared his act with precision. He would draw a diagram for himself showing his props layout. Audience drawn to the front, he would show his various props tables and then itemise each trick, so he would have everything in order and to hand.

A typical list reads thus:

Tin and music attached.
Box of tissues.
Duck—card trick.
Yellow blindfold.
Assorted cards.
White hanky.
Black hanky.
Large flowerpot trick.
Red watering can.
Hacksaw.
Brown yoyo.

Ball in cup trick.
Frying pan and flash paper.
Plate.
Egg.
Urn.
Tap on a rope.
Three solid rings.
Red bucket.
Red hanky.
Piece of string.
Scissors.
Cane.

He had a handwritten order for each act.

Flat P.
Watches on shirt.
Gun and cards—missed!
Handkerchief.
Bin—help!
Top hat—talking.
Playing cards—mouth organ.
Sponge box—running gag?
Glass milk.
Snake tin.
Goldfish bowl.
Handkerchief in the middle.

In the middle of it all, it is nice to see items as familiar to Cooper fans as the duck and blindfold gag and the gun and cards. Tommy would still be using them decades later, and they would still get a huge laugh.

The list meant little to anyone but himself. Perhaps it reveals Tommy as a bit of a control freak. Perhaps it shows how nervous a performer he actually was, having to plot a distinct path through every set to ensure he never wandered into ... what? Ad-lib land? Heaven forbid. No, Tommy's act was honed. Nothing could be left to chance. As meticulous as any professional magician, Tommy prepared for the show to go right and wrong, wrong and right, according to his own set of instructions. It was a plan that he would follow to perfection.

If he ever found himself in front of a tough audience, or maybe having an off-night of his own invention, he could always reach into that teeming props table and pick up an object for a quick visual gag. It was a fail-safe operation.

Certainly, during the early days, one can understand the performer not wishing to leave anything to chance. Maybe he never lost those early-gig nerves, but it is a trait that appears to have stayed with him throughout his career.

Luckily for him, if he was never quite as confident as he had a right to be, he was not alone in the venture. Miff was playing his part too. In 1950, Tommy's earnings doubled to £1,500 and, in 1951, they doubled again. Cooper was doing something different to every other comedian on the circuit, being known as 'The Madcap Magician'. His appearance also set him apart. His huge frame, his fast-paced movement, and his gormless grin, not to mention his big laugh, all went into the energetic act.

He began to travel outside of the capital. Miff secured him work at a Christmas panto in Morecambe, with Tommy playing one of the Ugly Sisters in *Cinderella*, but such was the demand to see Cooper live that he stepped out of character during the pantomime to do a short set of his own material during the show.

It is hard to think of any other reason to 'break' the story on stage, other than the huge appeal of an act who was, at this point, very much a novelty, and probably the hottest property on the circuit.

He followed this up with weekly bookings in Stockton and Oldham. There was a real buzz about Tommy's act, and one which Miff was happy to exploit. Tommy was sought after by summer holiday camps, nightclubs, theatres, and television shows. The material he was using was adaptable and suitable for any type of venue. The summer camps required family entertainment. Once mastered, this could be re-applied to any occasion. His one-liners had the audience in stitches, while there was genuine affection for his bumbling magic act. There was nobody else quite like him, and soon he had his own show on the BBC. It was 1952, and the Head of Light Entertainment at the corporation gave Miff a contract for a six-part series. The governors had been keen to do a deal as they just could not get enough of Tommy Cooper.

As if all this success in Britain was not enough, Miff was keen to push Tommy in America too. Together, the two men headed for Las Vegas where some bookings had been secured.

Unfortunately, no one appeared to get the joke. They thought that Cooper was an awful magician, and they could not understand his accent, so his gags all fell flat. It did not matter though, as Tommy had two years of bookings back at home.

Miff was kept busy organising everything, and both came to rely on each other. It was one of the most successful partnerships in show-business, even if Tommy would, over time, come to lose sight of all that Miff had done for him.

For now though, both men shared the same goal, which was to see Tommy Cooper conquer all.

10

A Rising Star

From 1951 to 1952, Tommy's earnings doubled again, and rose incrementally in subsequent years. Gwen and Tommy then moved to Maida Vale, an affluent district in the heart of London. From there, Tommy could hang out at the toy and magic shops, always on the lookout for new material, while he would spend every spare minute practising his act. He would perform almost nightly at a club, hotel, or theatre, before heading home to Gwen to tell her how the show had gone.

In the early 1950s, Tommy did the rounds of all the London nightclubs. These were not the most salubrious of venues, and the crowds themselves were often hostile. This was the world of the Krays and the Richardsons, gangsters and hard men who did not laugh easily. One night, the audience decided to see which of them could knock Tommy's fez off his head. Bread rolls were hurled in the direction of the stage as Cooper tried to deliver his routine. Tommy ducked and dived behind the microphone until he had eventually had enough.

'Stop that,' he said to one conspicuous culprit.

'Stop what?' came the reply from the room.

'Stop throwing bread rolls at me,' said Tommy.

'And why should I stop?' challenged the man, clearly enjoying himself.

'Because I haven't got an ad-lib for people throwing bread rolls at me!' Tommy quipped.

The place fell about laughing, and Tommy was all right after that.

The nightclub circuit was not for the faint-hearted, and Tommy had to work hard to get the audience to pay attention to him. As well as the banter in the room, there was the drinking, the smoking, and the distraction of the scantily clad cigarette girls and the glamorous ladies in attendance. To prepare himself for the possibility of a hostile crowd, Tommy wrote down responses to possible heckles that he might receive. He called them his 'Heckler Stoppers', and here's a few of them that he'd keep in his pocket in case they were needed:

'The last time I saw a head like that, a jockey was bending over it'.

'He can't match wits with me. I haven't got any to match with him!'

'You're just lucky that I'm a gentleman, a scholar, and a coward'.

'What's the matter? Did you get up on the wrong side of the floor this morning?'

'I never forget a face, but in your case, I'll make an exception'.

'Anybody's got the right to be ugly, but you abuse the privilege!'

'I live down by the river. Next time you're in the neighbourhood, drop in!'

It is hard to imagine that Tommy would have needed to resort to the harder-hitting of those comments. Usually, he would just shrug his shoulders and pretend he did not know what the offender was going on about. His early material consisted of lots of one-liners and quick-fire jokes that were extremely silly.

'I sleep like a baby. Every night I wake up about 3 o'clock, crying!'

'My wife was crying the other day. I said, "What are you crying for?" She said. "I'm homesick." I said, "This is your home." She said, "I know, I'm sick of it!"'

'I missed my catnap today. Slept right through it!'

'By the way, how do you like my new suit? Do you think this style will ever come back?'

'Everybody's saying television is here to stay. I don't know about that. The hire-purchase company are taking mine back tomorrow!'

'I was walking home the other night and a bloke stepped out of a doorway and said. "Have you seen a policeman around here?" I said. "No, I haven't." He said, "Stick 'em up!"'

'Now this next trick starts very slowly and gradually peters out'.

'Those adverts on television are silly, aren't they? I saw one the other day. It said, "Take this powder for a headache." I mean, who wants a headache!'

'One night I was doing my act, and the audience got up and started dancing. And the music wasn't even playing!' Tommy would look out at the audience as if to say, 'How did that happen?' creating a bond with the crowd. It was almost as if he was sitting among them and watching the act himself.

As well as his incredible movement, and his physical presence and looks, he was also a dazzling wordsmith. He relished some of his material, and all of it was delivered with impeccable comic timing. This is what audiences found so appealing, and no other professional comedian came even close to his ability to deliver a line with maximum comedy effect.

'My tailor said I'm putting on weight. Why don't I wear a corset? I said, "A corset? Will that help?" He said, "A corset will!"'

'It's easy to grin when your ship comes in and life is a happy lot. But the man worthwhile is the man who can smile when his shirt creeps up in a knot!'

Tommy had the ability to make things up on the spot. As he attempted a conjuring trick, he would utter a string of nonsense as he called upon the spirits of the magic world. It would not be much more than 'Wooha, wooha, wooha,' or any variation thereof, but in Tommy's hands, it somehow worked. He would then fix the audience with a challenging stare, as if to say 'What are you laughing at? This is serious stuff. Magic at work here'.

It was all ridiculous nonsense. Of course, he also had plenty of jokes to tell too.

'I went to the zoo the other day and the zoo-keeper started chasing me because I was feeding the monkeys. I was feeding them to the lions!'

'There's a new kind of Russian Roulette. You get six cobras in a room and you play a flute. One of them is deaf!'

'Two psychiatrists passed each other on the street and the first one said "Hello", and the other one said, "I wonder what he meant by that?"'

The material was not sophisticated, although that would change down the years as his one-liners became more elaborate stories. For now, it was joke, trick, trick, joke—the act shape-shifting from comedy to magic and back again in a constant flux. It was much like Tommy's performance itself, which was one of continual motion.

Helped by Miff, Tommy secured seventeen months of work alongside Benny Hill at the London Hippodrome. He made his first appearances outside of Britain on the European continent, and then performed on the BBC show *It's Magic* in 1952. In July of that year, he made his first appearance at the prestigious London Palladium, which was the hottest spot a performer could attain. From there, he was chosen to appear on the Moss Empire theatre tour, the highest grade of the circuit for an artiste.

This was the time of the great variety promoters like Lew Grade, Val Parnell, and Bernard Delfont—men who knew instinctively what would work on stage and were able to put packages together to fill the provincial theatres, such as magic and comedy, music and acrobatics—anything that would constitute an evening's entertainment. Tommy's act certainly fit the bill.

In 1953, Tommy played in the Peep Show Revue tour, and in 1954 headed back to Las Vegas and then on to New York, where he was offered a season at the Radio City Hall. Tommy declined as he was due back in England where he had continuous work lined up.

Upon his return, he played the part of the king in *Humpty Dumpty* at the Dudley Hippodrome. Then it was the Garrick theatre in Stockport and then the Prince of Wales in London, again with Benny Hill. Tommy was happy in his role of support act. He never wanted the pressure of being the headliner. He preferred to just do his bit on the side and leave his ego out of it—get a laugh and move on.

At the Coventry theatre, he appeared in the show *Paris by Night* that ran from April 1955 to September 1956. Later in the year, he played the king in *Puss in Boots*, a Christmas panto at the Manchester Hippodrome.

He kept his screen appearances to a minimum. He would occasionally do a guest spot to keep his name out there, but he did not relish too much exposure on television as it used up too much material. It was 1957 before he accepted his own full-length series, initially titled *Life with Cooper*, doing twelve shows for the ATV network. It was later renamed *Cooperama* and proved to be a big hit. The television company were keen to do more, but Tommy and Miff resisted and decided to concentrate on the theatre circuit instead.

The following year, he did the summer season at the North Pier pavilion in Blackpool, and then came *Robinson Crusoe* alongside the veteran entertainer Arthur Askey, who was one of Tommy's heroes.

'Look at him. Always moving,' Cooper would say whenever he watched Askey perform. Now, the two would be working together. One wonders how much Tommy learned from this music hall legend, who was the star and host of many a Royal Command Performance.

In 1958, Tommy accepted another television series for ATV, this time called *Cooper's Capers*. Then he went back to his theatre work. His panto that year was *Puss in Boots* in Bournemouth. Then he played the Hippodrome in Brighton. He did his next Christmas at Manchester Opera House, the spring season at the Coventry theatre, then summer at the Princess theatre in Torquay with Morecambe and Wise.

Tommy was working with the best in the business, and he was more than a match for any of them, even if he never considered himself quite worthy. He always thought that they were better than him, despite the reverence in which these other acts held him. They considered him a phenomenon, a giant of comedy, well on the way to becoming a show-business legend himself.

Autumn season found Tommy back in Manchester, followed by panto at the Alhambra in Bradford. His diary was full, and his earnings continued to rise steadily. By the mid-fifties, they had passed the £10,000 a year mark. This was just as well, as there had been developments at home. In 1953 came the birth of Tommy and Gwen's first child, Victoria. She would be followed three years later by the arrival of Thomas Jr.

With a wife and family, an agent, and a successful career, Tommy appeared to have it all. He could consider himself a seasoned-performer, and he was popular with his peers and with audiences up and down the land.

Now at the top, Tommy was introduced to a wealth of writers whose work would support him throughout his career. Their material became some of Tommy Cooper's best-known work.

If anyone thought that Tommy had peaked, they could not have been more wrong. His first ten years as a professional act lay the foundations for all that was to follow. There was still a long way for him to go to become the nation's best-loved entertainer, but there was no way to stop him from doing just that.

11

The Home Front

In the 1950s, Britain was still coming to terms with the horrific events of the Second World War. As the country tried to get back on its feet, rationing of daily-goods persisted, and the first half of the decade was a struggle for everyone. Tommy had managed to work through his own struggles and was constantly performing. No matter where he was playing on a Saturday night, he would always make it home to spend Sunday with the wife and kids.

He was a loving father to Vicky and Thomas Jr, and a loving husband to Gwen. That said, they did have their rows. One time, when they were first performing for the troops in Egypt, they were rehearsing the part of a couple having an argument. They were practising backstage in the dressing room, and they were so convincing that a stagehand wanted to call the police. That was acting; now the fighting was real. Cups and crockery would be thrown, especially by Gwen, while Tommy would do his best to calm her down and take the tension out of the situation.

Usually, if not caused by their drinking, which both of them did to excess, it would be due to Tommy's tardiness. He had his excuses as it could not have been easy to make it back to London from Torquay or Blackpool on the roads and railways of the 1950s. Yet, Tommy's awkward clumsiness meant he would often miss his train and he would have to stumble home with an apology on his lips.

He sometimes appeared with a present for Dove. Once, he gave her a musical clock. Gwen was not amused. He was late, so what was he doing giving her a timepiece when it was clearly him who needed one. He started with his excuses, but this time, his wife did not want to hear it. Gwen launched the clock at him, Tommy ducked out of the way, and the clock hit the wall and fell to the floor where it smashed into pieces. As the couple stood facing each other in a stand-off, the clock began to play the opening bars of the song 'Home! Sweet Home!' with the immortal words 'Wherever you may wander, there's no place like home'. The pair of them fell about laughing, which was often the way that their arguments ended. They did not dwell and, for the most part, the couple had a very long and happy marriage.

'I've been very privileged,' Gwen would say. 'It was a wonderful, extraordinary union. We liked to scream at each other from time to time but it was never meant nastily'. As Tommy himself put it, 'if you can't have a row now and again, one of you is unnecessary!'

The kids also remember their father being great fun at home. He would do the 'snake shooting out of a tin' trick for them, or the children would go to get washed in the bathroom, ready for school, and the soap would turn their hands and faces black. Even the dog would look warily at any juicy bone he was given as too many times before, they had turned out to be rubber. Life was never dull in the Cooper household.

The family finally found their dream home in Chiswick, West London, which today bears a commemorative blue plaque to the legendary entertainer. They also bought a holiday cottage on the south coast. It was a lovely little hide-away where they could take the kids for the weekend. It was yards from where Gwen had grown up in Eastbourne. Indeed, the shop at the end of the road was where, as a young girl, she had bought treats on her way to and from school.

Tommy's earnings had been £10,000 a year by the mid-fifties. By the end of the decade, they had doubled again.

The 1960s were the era of rock and roll. From the late 1950s onwards, the music just kept coming, first from America, in the form of Elvis Presley, and then with home-grown acts such as the Beatles and the Rolling Stones. While Tommy's background was in variety entertainment, enterprising promoters managed to include popular music acts alongside established theatrical performers.

One such travelling show saw Tommy on the bill with a high-flying Merseybeat band of the day. Billy Hatton, was the lead guitarist with the Fourmost, and he has fond memories of touring the country with Tommy. The man was as funny off-stage as on, Hatton recalled, and worked hard to ensure a congenial atmosphere whenever their punishing schedule started to get the better of them.

When the tour dates brought them close to the Cooper family home, or whenever she had the time to come and join up with them, Gwen would make a cake for Tommy to share with all of the boys in the band. She liked to mother them, and Tommy was particularly fond of her raspberry sponge cakes. For the young pop stars, often on tour for a considerable length of time, it was a reminder of home that they looked forward to and appreciated.

I knew Billy Hatton personally. Sadly, he died during the writing of this book before I could ask for further anecdotes. He was a wonderful man who is sorely missed by his family and many friends.

Meanwhile, back in the 1960s, Tommy himself was still on the hunt for new tricks and visual gags. Then, on the tour bus or in his hotel room he would 'practise, practise, practise'. He would do his act for Gwen and she would time him and make suggestions, ensuring that his act remained as good as it could be.

'We always laughed,' she said. 'I think I was his best friend. He'd always say to me, "Never a day goes by without you making me laugh."' This was despite the fact that she was often the butt of the joke.

'I cleaned out the attic with the wife the other day. Damp, filthy, full of cobwebs, but she's good with the kids!'

'My wife and I used to go to race meetings and I was told to cut off a lock of her hair for good luck. Eventually, we had £100,000 in the bank, and not a hair on her head'.

He told lots of gags about Gwen, and many more about women in general.

'This woman went on holiday, leaving her husband behind. Before she left, she told him to take special care of her pet Siamese cat. As soon as she arrived, she phoned home to ask after the cat. Her husband said. "It's just died!" The woman burst into tears and then had a right go at her husband. Finally, when her anger abated, she said, "You could have broken it to me gently. When I asked how she was, you could have said she was out playing on the roof. When I phoned tomorrow, you could have said she's fallen and broken her leg. The next day when I phoned, you could have broken the news to me then." She took a pause, having made her point, and then asked, "Anyway, how's my mother?" The man said, "She's playing on the roof!"'

Gwen might have been Tommy's best friend, but she was not the only one, for Tommy had many close mates, usually drawn from his own entertainment circle. These were writers, actors, fellow magicians, and other performers. One of his closest pals was Eric Sykes, a British writer, comedian, and actor. He was respected by his peers long before he became a household name. His sense of humour is summed up by the title of his own autobiography: *If I Don't Write It, Nobody Else Will.*

In it, he tells many stories about working and drinking with Tommy Cooper. He tells them with a genuine affection. In fact, he was a great champion of Tommy's talent.

Eric first met Tommy in 1948. Sykes was already established as one of the finest of the post-war gag writers. The roll call of talent he worked with at the time included established stars such as Frankie Howerd and Max Bygraves. Tommy and Eric used to rendezvous at a pub called the Clachan at the back of the London Palladium. As with many such pubs up and down the country, being positioned close to the stage door meant that it drew a show-business crowd. People could swap theatrical anecdotes, hear about forthcoming opportunities, and maybe find a sympathetic shoulder to cry on if needed.

The two men became firm friends for life. It is possible that Eric, as scriptwriter, was responsible for one of the funniest lines ever written in British comedy. Frankie Howerd was the star of a hit television show called *Up Pompeii!*. He played the part of Lurcio, a beleaguered servant in the corridors of power in the senate of the Roman Empire. In one episode, his character was dealing with an ever-increasing set of calamities, all of which he was being unduly blamed for. He walked on stage, beset by woes and troubles on all sides. 'Oh, infamy, infamy,' he cried, before adding, 'They've all got it in for me!' It entered into common-parlance, cemented in the minds of a generation of viewers during a golden age of comedy.

Eric and Tommy bonded instantly. At this point, Sykes had not even witnessed Cooper's act. Instead, he recognised a struggling artist—and a man with a passion to succeed. After a pint or two, they would stop at a sandwich shop and grab a bite to eat. Then, the two men would head to the Bag O'Nails where Tommy was due to perform on the late evening show. Eric would leave him at the entrance and head home, and Tommy would head inside and do a late-night performance, often not getting on stage until 1 a.m.

It would be many years before the two men would work together. For now, they were mates, moving in the same circles, sort of. Eric was enjoying some success, while Tommy was merely dreaming of the same.

Eric Sykes said later that Tommy and he were like brothers. They had taken an initial shine to each other, and then they did not see each other for a few years while Tommy went off to tour the provinces. By the time he came back, he was the finished article—a headline act.

Now, he was the real Tommy Cooper.

12

The Seasoned Pro

Tommy made his first appearance at a *Royal Variety Performance* in 1953. At that juncture, he was an unknown quantity, a novelty act. He was just starting to gain recognition. He had risen up to the ranks of the top theatrical circuits and had honed his show to perfection. By the time he came to make his debut in front of Her Majesty, Queen Elizabeth II, he was more than capable of holding his own on that stage among seasoned professionals, even if the stakes were much higher than they had ever been before.

Eleven years later, Tommy made another appearance at the same auspicious occasion. By now, he was an established star, and was very much looked-up to by the rising talents of the day, such as young comedian Jimmy Tarbuck, who forever appreciated the support that Tommy gave him when his nerves were very much to the fore.

Tommy was a nervous performer himself. He confessed to terrible stage fright. He would later use this as an excuse for his excessive drinking; you would never have known he was suffering by witnessing his act, but it is all apparently true. Known as the man who could get a laugh without opening his mouth, people said that all he had to do to have an audience in hysterics was to walk on stage. Yet, as the comedy giant bemoaned to his friend Eric Sykes, 'If only people knew what it takes for me to go out there on that stage in the first place'.

Luckily, his material was becoming more sophisticated. The one-liners were still very much part of the show, but more of a storytelling approach began to work its way in to his act. It was still a combination of gag, trick, gag, trick, but the gags were getting longer. The pay-off was always worth it, and the little asides that Tommy would do midway through, or indeed all the way through, were as enjoyable to the audience as the punchlines themselves. People simply adored him, and just wanted to look at and hear him. He could quite easily have not bothered with the material; he would still have been funnier than half of those who called themselves comedians.

After Tommy had enjoyed a decade and a half of success, he was willing to try out the more elaborate stuff. This created the condition in which he could perform what became one of his best-loved sketches. Written by Val Andrews and Freddie Saddler, it is effectively a spoken ditty, which saw Tommy, usually towards the end of his routine, produce a box of hats from beneath his props table. He would drag the box into the open and look mournfully at the audience as if to say, 'This is going to be tough', and it was.

Then, Tommy would begin.

'It was New Year's Eve in Joe's bar, and a happy mob was there. The tables and chairs were crowded, and lots of music filled the air. In the midst of all this gaiety, the door flung open wide. A worn and tattered Tramp walked in…' With that, Tommy donned a battered hat. '"Happy New Year, folks," he cried'.

Tommy allowed a moment for the audience to laugh at the silly head gear, made ten times sillier and funnier by the expression on that big comical face. He then continued.

'Up jumped a banker, who happened to be there'. At this point, Tommy swapped hats and put on a bowler hat. '"Throw him out", he shouted, "he contaminates the air." "Those are harsh words", said a sailor, standing at the back'. Cue another hat change. '"So what", said the banker'. He changed the hat back. The sailor takes pity on the tramp and offers to buy him a pint. The tramp says he does not drink beer anymore but is willing to share a bottle of rum with him. Then comes a cowboy, and then a fireman, and then a soldier, while the story continues apace.

Tommy then regaled his audience with the addition of a Frenchman, a schoolboy, a pilot, and then an old woman, which gets the biggest laugh of all. Finally, when the place descends into a free-for-all and you can hear the knuckles crunch, a policeman comes in and nicks the whole damn bunch.

In Tommy's hands, it was pure comedy genius. While the act changed slightly with every rendition, and sometimes the hats appeared in a different running order, the story essentially remained the same.

One time, Tommy was running through the routine backstage before a show and, despite having done it hundreds of times before, he became momentarily flummoxed as he tried to remember the running order.

Watching him was Barry Cryer.

'Keep that in,' he said to Tommy.

'Keep what in?' Tommy replied.

'The forgetting part,' said the writer. 'It looks hilarious. The story is complicated as it is. It will look like you really have forgotten it, but the genius is that you haven't. Your face will be a picture'.

Tommy replied, 'But what if they think I really have forgotten it?'

'But you won't have'.

'I know, but how will they know that?'

'They won't, but it will be funny'.

'But what if they ...'

'Just trust me, Tommy. It's funny'.

So, Tommy put it into the act, where it stayed forever more. 'Where was I up to?' and then starting the story all over again. 'It was New Year's Eve' etc., when he was about five minutes in. It raised a genius routine up yet another notch, earning it a place in the nation's hearts.

The 1964 *Royal Variety Performance* was a pivotal point in Tommy's career. He had a solid body of work behind him and, with his continuous touring and several television series of his own under his belt, he was now a household name. As such, he was given the huge responsibility of opening the show. He knew he was scheduled to perform, but he was thrown a curveball by the show's producer, Val Parnell, a week before they were due to go on air when he informed Tommy that he would be going on first.

Tommy panicked and tried to protest. He had his act all prepared, but opening was a different matter. The material he had chosen would play differently in that section of the show. It could be a graveyard slot for an audience starting cold. What was he going to do?

To be fair, the producer had probably been lining up acts for months beforehand, and only when he had everyone confirmed, and there were no last-minute cancellations, could he begin to think about the programming and how he might structure the evening to achieve the best results. Yet it still came as a shock to Tommy.

Producer Parnell explained that he needed some comedy at the start of the show to relax the audience. That way, they would better enjoy the remainder and would have the patience to sit through the acts that they did not know or found harder to get. Also, he could not thrust his other comedian on first as he was a young man making his first *Royal Variety Performance* appearance.

Tommy had to agree. It would not be fair to Jimmy Tarbuck to heap that responsibility on him on his debut. Arthur Askey, Tommy's hero, had hosted the big event several times. On one occasion, after a slow start to the show, the energy in the room sagged, and it was left to the compère himself to hoist the show out of the doldrums. When the next act arrived on the stage, a circus performer of sorts, he asked for a volunteer to help with a dangerous trick involving a horse whip, in which he would strike a cigarette from the volunteer's lips. Askey himself stepped up. Then, with the words 'Now this is where the show starts to get good', the host was as good as his word. The evening lit up (excuse the cigarette pun) from that point on, and Arthur Askey had saved the day.

What was Tommy Cooper going to do in similar circumstances? This was the graveyard spot, when the audience had barely taken their coats off and had just settled into their seats. Tommy turned to his friends for advice, and they put their heads together to try and conjure up a solution. Eventually, Billy Mayo, a variety artist and a veteran of the music halls, came up with an idea.

Mayo told Tommy to walk on stage with a paraffin heater and say 'The producer just told me to go out there and warm them up!' It was a joke that Billy remembered seeing in an old black and white film about the entertainment industry.

It sounded simple, too simple, but Tommy was eventually convinced to give it a try. So, with the rest of his act fully prepared, the *Royal Variety Performance* began. The host was Bruce Forsyth, an old pro himself, a pal of Tommy's and, coincidentally, managed by Miff Ferrie at one time.

Bruce said his opening bit, welcomed Her Majesty and Prince Phillip, and the show began with its usual bevy of chorus girls dancing across the stage. When they departed, Tommy appeared. He was dressed in dapper coat-tails, wearing a more elaborate fez to mark the occasion, and in his hand, he held an oversized paraffin lamp, which he was swinging by his side as he walked on.

When he reached the centre of the stage, he turned to the audience and delivered the line to a thunderous welcome. From there on in, he breezed through his act to uproarious laughter and applause. Indeed, it set up the evening for every act that was to follow, creating goodwill out of the darkness that a poor performance could produce.

In fact, it created such a relaxed mood, and such a confidence boost for Tommy, that before the night was out came the incident with the Queen and the Cup Final tickets that has gone down in show-business legend. It is hard to know whether the story is true or not, but it has certainly been told thousands of times and has endured down the years. Many people claim to have been within hearing distance when it happened, including Jimmy Tarbuck. The only problem is knowing whether to describe it as famous or infamous. Either way, it went down in comedy folklore.

13

A Real Magician?

So, how good a magician was Tommy Cooper? We have already covered the line about whether he was a good magician pretending to be bad, or a bad magician trying to be good. That said, Tommy himself was not averse to repeating material, as we have already seen.

In one performance of my play *The Tommy Cooper Show*, Danny Taylor, the actor playing Tommy, preceded a joke with one of Cooper's regular sayings. 'I can't help laughing. I know what's coming next'.

Someone in the audience shouted out, 'So do we!' It did not matter. The material got a laugh every time.

Cooper's first love was magic; of that there is no doubt. When he started out, he dreamt of being a magician. He practised every available hour to try and master the art. For sure, if he could have made it as a professional, that is what he would have chosen to do, as it would have been his dream come true. Instead, he discovered that he had a gift for comedy, and he was astute enough to realise that he could make a career in show-business out of it. It ticked a lot of boxes, and he loved to make people laugh.

Yet comedy was not what he had set his heart on, if the truth be told. When asked what his hobbies were, Tommy would reply 'Magic'. When asked what his interests were, Tommy would say 'Magic'. When his friends were asked what Tommy's interests were, they would reply 'Magic'. When his family were asked what Tommy's interests were, they also said 'Magic'.

Later on, we can probably add drinking to that list (if one item can ever be called a list!), but it was clear where his passion lay, ever since he first fell in love with the world of magic at the age of eight when his Aunt Lucy got him that magic set. From there on in, and to the end of his life, he practised every spare hour of every day. First, it was upstairs in the bedroom of his childhood home. Then it was in the work's canteen during his lunch breaks. Then, he practised in the barracks when he was with the Royal Horse Guards, and later in his Army tent while stationed in Egypt during and after the Second World War.

When he became a professional entertainer, he would practise in his dressing room backstage, or in his hotel room while on a variety tour, or while doing a season at a theatre a long way from home. There he would be, flicking a coin through his fingers, palming it, practising sleight of hand. He did the same with card tricks—practise, practise, practise. It seemed that he did this mostly for his own amusement; he was that desperate to improve his skills. In fact, without practice, the trick was no trick at all, and this was true of most magic. Luckily, Tommy was so in awe of the craft that he could think of no other way that he would rather spend his free time.

It was the same at hme. Even on Sundays, his only guaranteed day at home with Gwen and the kids. He could not help himself; it was a compulsion. At least he tried to involve Vicky and Thomas Jr, making play of it and asking them if they knew how he did it. Hopefully, they were less harsh on him than his own parents had been all those years before. You might call his actions obsessive, but there was a certain childlike enthusiasm going on there too.

When he was a child, when he first received that precious Christmas gift, Tommy sent off for every trick that he could find to supplement the set that he had been given. His comic books were mere avenues to another world beyond their animated pages. In fact, the only reason he bothered to buy them was for the advertisements.

Growing up, if there was any sort of toy or gift shop nearby, he would venture there on the lookout for items that might go in to his developing routine. When he eventually moved to London, magic shops such as Davenports, Ken Brookes' Magic Place, and the Unique Magic Shop near Carnaby Street were favourite haunts, as were department stores such as Hamleys off Oxford Street, which had its own magic section.

Coincidentally, this is where Danny Taylor, the actor for whom I wrote *The Tommy Cooper Show*, learned his trade as a toy demonstrator.

Once a month, Tommy would venture over to a magician's convention hosted by an entrepreneur called Harry Stanley. While there, Tommy would often be called to the stage to perform for those present. Afterwards, Tommy and his friends would retire to a nearby cafe to practise with whatever items they had procured that day, and there would be competition among the aspiring amateurs and professional magicians to see who could master the latest contraption.

Sometimes, Tommy's extraordinary physique proved beneficial to his magical act. His large hands were good for the art of concealment, while his gormless look was a distraction in its own right.

He exulted in performing a trick correctly on occasion, just to keep the audience on its toes, and usually when it was least expected. He lulled them into a false sense of security, but there was no 'I told you so' about it. He had far too much humility and kinship with the crowd to do anything like that. He was, at all times, adorable.

Even when he managed to get a magic trick right, he still maximised its comic effect, such as with the 'Disappearing egg' trick, which he preceded as always with the 'Egg, bag, bag, egg' speech. The audience would have been disappointed if he had not delivered those lines. So, Tommy says 'The egg will disappear from this bag. Now, if you see anything suspicious [cue giggles of expectation from the auditorium], don't say anything!' Tommy then feigns to place the egg in the bag, while very obviously shoving something into his armpit and clasping his arm to his side to hold it in place. The audience laughs. He had been quick, but not so quick that they had not spotted something afoot. He then turns the bag inside out and, surprise, surprise, there is no egg inside.

'It's where?' asks Tommy, sensing disbelief in the room. 'Under my arm?' he says, answering his own question. 'What, this one?' he lifts up the arm that is not under suspicion and is obviously not holding the egg in place. 'Oh, you mean the other one?' he says, before turning his back to the audience and raising the same arm as before. Finally, he turns around to face the audience. 'Oh, you mean this one', and he raises the right one, and to the surprise of everyone present, there is nothing there. He really has made the egg disappear!

Obviously, some tricks were played out entirely for comic effect, such as what is probably his best-loved gag, which is 'Spoon, jar, jar, spoon'. At every performance of *The Tommy Cooper Show*, it never fails to get its own unique cheer as the crowd settle themselves in for a treat.

Tommy walks to the curtain at the back of the stage and is handed a large clear-glass jar. In it is a silver spoon. He forewarns the audience with a rendition of 'Spoon, jar, jar spoon. Spoon, jar, jar, spoon. Spoon, spoon, jar, jar, spoon', or words to that effect. It is never the same two performances running.

Then he gives it a 'Dat, darrarat, darrarat, da, dat. Stop!' The spoon, which has been dancing up and down inside the jar in time with Tommy's encouraging words, now comes a sudden halt. Tommy looks at the audience as if to say 'That was good, wasn't it? That was magic, that was'.

He repeats the words, and the spoon does the same crazy dance along with the tune. Tommy shouts 'Stop!' once more, and the spoon ceases to move on his command. Then Tommy tries it again. 'Dat, darrarat, darrarat, da, dat', but this time the spoon does not move.

'Well, pull it then,' Tommy says to a hidden stagehand, and the spoon flies out of the jar at the end of an (almost) invisible thread, and Tommy and the crowd fall about laughing.

Even when preparing to do a trick that might go right, this too would be milked for comic effect. Tommy had his own version of gibberish, in place of the usual 'Abracadabra', which would bring the house down on its own.

Many a practised eye will tell you that his dexterity and concentration when performing a trick, such as producing a large number of bottles from a single container, are accomplishments worthy of a master. He was peerless in some regards, which must have frustrated him on occasion. His fame as a comedian stifled his endeavours when it came to performing magic.

He could delight friends with his skills. He would even astound them with some of the things that he was able to do. To them, he could be great, but the perception still remained among the general viewing audience that he was a bad magician trying to be good, and that he would never quite succeed. He was forever to be remembered as the jester, underdog, and clown.

As a young man, Tommy had dreamt that one day he might be admitted to the Magic Circle. His love for the craft was widely known, and he had helped to keep magic in the public eye for many a year. That the top entertainer in the country was a magician gave a huge boost to the discipline. It was only right then that his wish was finally granted when he was eventually awarded Membership of the Inner Circle of the Magic Circle—he was also given the elusive 'Gold Star' status.

Tommy was both humbled and overjoyed and wrote to its secretary to thank him. 'As a young magician, I dreamt of this,' he said, 'but never thought that I would possess this great honour'.

It was validation, if any were needed, that he could consider himself a magician in the eyes of his peers. He had come a long way from that failed performance at the shipyard Christmas party, when all hope of a future doing something he loved appeared lost. With his elite membership granted to the Magic Circle, Tommy finally achieved a life-long ambition.

The truth is that as a magician he was good, but as a comedian he was simply the best.

14

The Magic Circle

The Magic Circle began in London in 1905 as an exclusive club for practising magicians, both amateur and professional. There, at an inaugural meeting convened at Pinoli's restaurant, twenty-three men undertook never to reveal their conjuring secrets to the general public. The motto of the organisation is *indoulis privata loqui*, which means 'Death to traitors!'

Only joking! It roughly translates as 'Not apt to disclose secrets', or words to that effect. The organisation certainly took its motto seriously; their first ever president, David Devant, was expelled after just four years for revealing in a magazine interview the truth behind some of their tricks.

Devant was the finest magician of his day, and he is still considered one of the best magicians of the twentieth century. He is pictured in an old publicity poster performing in front of a packed audience, sporting a dress coat, top hat, and cane. His catchphrase was 'All done by kindness'. Despite the inauspicious end to his presidency, the Magic Circle still award an annual honour in his name.

The club's first ever meeting was chaired by Belgian magician Servais Le Roy. Together with his wife, he was the creator of a famous magic trick, which he named 'the Asrah levitation'. After his assistant lay horizontal on a flat surface, he would cover her with a cloth and then astound audiences as she rose, at his bidding, several feet in the air. The trick was completed by the magician sweeping his hand below the elevated body to show that there was nothing between the person and the table, with no supporting mechanisms whatever. It continues to be performed to this day. Current magician Dynamo has an interesting take on this; he manages to float off the ground from a standing position.

From the restaurant in Wardour Street, the second meeting of the Magic Circle convened at the Green Man pub in Soho. Later on, they took a room above St George's Hall in the city. There, after dealing with any business, the members convened to a performance space where they were treated to a display of all things magical by David Devant and John Nevil Maskelyne. The latter, as well as being a budding magician, was the man behind the introduction of the 'pay-to-use' lavatory, and it is to him that we owe the saying 'I'm going to spend a penny'.

In 1906, the Magic Circle introduced its own magazine, *The Magic Circular*, which was both edited and published by Maskelyne himself. It is now the world's longest running magic magazine and is produced twelve times a year. Today, the organisation boasts 1,500 members, of which three-quarters are male. The decision to allow women to join came in 1994, when 75 per cent of members voted in favour of female membership. The Magic Circle has recently opened up new headquarters in the heart of London, and the venue is available for hire for private parties and corporate events. In 2008, it was voted the British Hospitality Industry's number one venue in the country for corporate hire. It is a specialist club that has created a unique aura for itself, partly due to its subject matter, and also in part due to its many famous members. As well as Prince Charles, whose entry came via the performance of an egg and cup trick, the alumni of this organisation include actor and director Orson Welles, writer Rudyard Kipling, and Prince Charles's own uncle, Lord Mountbatten.

Orson Welles, in particular, had a lifelong love of magic. Indeed, it was said to be his first love, ahead of even film, whether directing or acting. Whenever he was in London, he made a point of visiting the Magic Circle, attending meetings and staying on to watch the show afterwards. It may well have been that he saw Tommy performing there. In the early 1950s, when Tommy was still making his way in the business, he had been invited to entertain the membership. At the time, there were rumours that he had not paid his Magic Circle subscription. Tommy came on stage, met the audience with a stare, and said 'I know you're all talking about me, but you can stop now. It makes no difference'. He then turned around to reveal a rubber knife sticking out of his back.

The Magic Circle events were great get-togethers. Like-minded people would talk passionately about this, their favourite hobby. The stories, like the attendees, came from far and wide. Some were professional performers, others enthusiastic amateurs. All shared a love for magic and its secrets.

Welles had a head start on Tommy. He had received his first magic set at the age of three. Then, aged ten, he was fortunate enough to witness Harry Houdini, the all-time great magician and escapologist, performing in person. The following year, young Orson ran away from home. He was found when a curious policeman was drawn to a crowd on a street corner. There, the runaway boy was doing magic tricks, pulling in punters, with his cap on the ground beside him in an attempt to earn a wage.

All through his life, the 'Boy Wonder' of Hollywood continued with his fascination for magic. In many films, he played the part of a conjurer and man of mystery. He was also talented enough to secure a three-week residency at the Riviera Casino in Las Vegas with his magic act. His wife, the actress Rita Hayworth, acted as his stage assistant while he performed such tricks as catching a bullet in his teeth. He also did Houdini's 'Needle Trick', and in another, he borrowed a note of currency from a member of the audience and asked them to mark it, before the note magically reappeared inside a piece of fruit. As well as his glamorous wife's presence, he also managed to saw another famous actress, Marlene Dietrich, in half, though not literally.

For Orson, his appreciation of the world of magic was a love affair that lasted right up to his death. The very night before he died, he made a television appearance with chat show host Merv Griffin and performed a card trick. As well as his many roles on film where he played a conjurer, it is also possible to detect his sleight of hand and art of suggestion in possibly his most famous, or infamous, outing, when he directed *The War of the Worlds* as a radio play in the 1930s. There, he managed to beguile a whole nation into thinking that America had been invaded by Martians, introducing live news bulletins from the spacecraft landing sites. It was one of the most spectacular radio broadcasts of all time, and only a master of hypnotism, magic, and illusion could have pulled it off. Yet, in attendance at the Magic Circle's regular gatherings, he would be as happy as a little kid in thrall to the mighty men of magic who represented the Circle's upper echelon.

One can only imagine the talent in such a room. Welles himself was no ordinary man; he was an actor, director, writer, and magician. There is a clip on the internet where he comes on stage, in a black turtle-neck sweater, wearing a medallion that looks very much like the Magic Circle's own symbol. He is dressed like Svengali. Firstly, he takes a wooden pail from an assistant, shows it to the audience to make clear that it is empty, before placing it on the floor. Then, he covers the top of the bucket with a silver tray, using it as a lid. When he lifts the lid, there is now a large goose, live and squawking, in the bucket. Orson picks up the goose and hypnotises it. Its squawking peters out to a whimper and then to nothing. It is simply stunning, in every sense of the word.

I would like to have seen Welles's audition for entry to the Magic Circle. Usually, these auditions take place in front of an audience and a panel of three judges who score the artiste out of twenty. Upon receipt of a suitably high score, the magician is invited to join the prestigious outfit. From the 1,500 members, only 300 can achieve the higher status of the Inner Circle. This was the honour that Tommy Cooper received. Previously, he had joked 'I'm a member of the Secret Six. It's so secret, I don't even know who the other five are!' Membership meant a lot to him. He was truly humbled, and even more so for the fact that he had not expected it.

Membership can be attained by submission of a thesis on an aspect of magic, or through performance. Admission to the inner circle was reserved for a select few. One route to the award was the promotion of magic itself. Tommy had been a huge asset in this regard. If one classed him as a magician, he was possibly the most famous practitioner in the world.

When it came to the Magic Circle's centenary in 2005, John Fisher, an earlier biographer of Tommy Cooper, was asked to select several pieces of magic to showcase the art form. He had no hesitation in including Tommy performing the famous hats sketch. Was it magic? In Tommy's hands, everything was.

Today, the Magic Circle boasts members in thirty-eight different countries. It also has a branch for young magicians to secure the lifeblood of this esteemed institution. No doubt, this latest offering was inspired by the success of *Harry Potter*—how many budding wizards must there be, up and down the country, thanks to J. K. Rowling's extraordinary creation? I think she deserves an honorary membership herself.

For Tommy, it was a privilege that he fully appreciated. As he wrote to the Magic Circle's secretary, John Salisse, 'As a young magician I dreamed of this, but never thought I would possess this great honour'.

The word that most members use to describe their relationship with magic is 'obsessed'. It holds a fascinating allure for practitioners. It is an art that can never be truly mastered. Even practice might never make perfect, and Tommy Cooper was certainly its most effective promoter.

Paul Daniels said that Tommy's greatest trick was creating the illusion of chaos. He added that Tommy Cooper was very good for magic, saying 'A lot of people would get bookings just because of him'.

Another comedian and a fellow Welshman, Rob Brydon, stated that Tommy kept magic in the public eye when it could quite easily have fallen out of fashion. 'Even now,' he said, 'if you asked people to name a famous magician, Tommy's would be the first name to come to mind'.

Perhaps unwittingly, Tommy Cooper was one of magic's greatest exponents. For that, and for everything else, his admission to the coveted society was no more than the comedian deserved.

15

More About Miff

As well as Gwen, and the esteem of his fellow professionals, Tommy had something equally as important to his career: an agent and personal manager, Miff Ferrie. When I asked myself what he did exactly to enhance the comedian's career, I was reminded of the movie *Rocky*, starring Sylvester Stallone. There is a fantastic scene in it which I think sums it up perfectly.

Rocky Bilbao is washed up at the age of thirty. He is not just past his prime, he never had one. Now, at the boxing gym where he trains, he has not even got a locker. It has been taken from him by the gym owner, Mickey, and given to some youngster with potential who may turn out to be a prospect. Then, the unthinkable happens, and Rocky is picked at random for a shot at the heavyweight world title.

The boxing world is stunned, and Rocky begins to train alone for this impossible mission. Then, one night, seventy-six-year-old trainer Mickey climbs the stairs to Rocky's run-down apartment. The part of Mickey is played by Burgess Meredith, who is surely one of the greatest actors of all time. Mickey knocks, and Rocky reluctantly lets him in. They make small talk. 'What are those?' asks Mickey, pointing to a fish tank. Rocky says that they are baby turtles. Rocky, despite his brutishness, clearly has a soft side. Mickey counters by saying that they make great soup! Clearly, he does not do small talk.

'What happened to you was pure luck,' the old man explains. 'And like the Bible says, you don't get a second chance. What you need is a manager'. Rocky is unimpressed. Mickey carries on.

'I been in this racket fifty years,' the veteran explains. 'One time, I knocked Guinea Russell clean out of the ring. Jack Dempsey was fighting the same night. Guess who got the headlines?'

'Dempsey?' asks Rocky, on the verge of boredom.

'That's right. And do you know why?'

'Because he was the champion'.

'No. Because he had a manager!'

The scene is beautifully crafted and acted, and is perhaps rendered even more potent by the fact it contains a truth.

Tommy knew that he needed management. Indeed, for a time, it was his Holy Grail as he traipsed across the stage, audition after audition, trying to impress. It was the old Catch-22 situation—how do you get an agent if you have not got any bookings? How do you get any bookings if you have not got an agent?

Miff was born George Ferrie in Edinburgh in March 1911. He grew up to be a jazz trombonist and earned the nickname 'Miff' in honour of another legendary jazz man. He ended up with his own seven-piece orchestra, but never quite made the dizzy heights. He ended up as the bookings manager at the Windmill club. There, he snapped up the best of the talent that he came across and earned a percentage on the side of his day job when those acts went off to appear at other venues.

That said, despite a brief dalliance managing the affairs of Bruce Forsyth, Tommy soon became the sole performer in his care, a situation that suited both parties. Tommy's reputation was rising fast, the bookings were rolling in and, at 15 per cent, Miff was making a good living from his commission.

Miff was acting as both agent (i.e. booking gigs) and personal manager (i.e. heavily involved in the negotiations, travel arrangements, booking accommodation, and career guidance). Taking 15 per cent is not unreasonable or unusual for that level of support.

Gwen herself claimed to have been livid when she heard what Tommy had agreed to, but I think we must view this as hindsight. It is hard to conceive that Tommy signed his contract without first showing it to and discussing it with his wife. She was nobody's fool, as all who knew her would be quick to testify.

Some of Tommy's friends, his drinking buddies, and closest pals saw Tommy's complaints about Miff's percentage as an excuse to cover up his own meanness with money. It does not appear that Tommy had ever complained about his considerable workload—work that Miff had procured for him, it has to be said. It seems that Tommy just could not get his head around the fact that there was someone working feverishly behind the scenes to keep his star in the ascendancy and to make sure that, each year, his earnings went up. Either he was ungrateful or just unappreciative, but Tommy never quite accepted that Miff's contribution was a key factor in his success.

It is just as well that Miff was adequately rewarded for his efforts because what he sometimes had to put up with from Tommy was slander, bordering on abuse. For anything less than their agreed percentage, Miff and Tommy would surely have gone their separate ways. Tommy cannot have been an easy act to manage. He was disorganised, clumsy, and forgetful—in other words, a pain in the backside at times. Without Miff's guiding hand, there is every possibility that Tommy's career would have come to a standstill or gone off the rails completely. How many performers, now since forgotten, were possessed of sublime talent, but failed to reach the heights that they deserved? This could be due to their own laziness (a problem that Tommy never had), or because they did not receive the proper guidance or support, usually best provided by an effective agent or manager.

Can you imagine Tommy trying to procure his own gigs and then turning up on time, or organising his own travel and accommodation? It just would not have happened. He would not have got much farther than the front doorstep. So, Tommy put up with Miff and Miff put up with Tommy.

Despite their differences, if viewed from a purely professional angle, it was one of the most successful partnerships in show-business. That is not to say that Miff was an angel, or even everyone's cup of tea. The most common word used to describe him appears to be 'dour'. One reads it everywhere in the chronicles of Tommy Cooper—Miff Ferrie, dour Scotsman. For sure, he did make some mistakes in how he handled Tommy's career. Some of his decisions seem ludicrous on second glance but, when faced with an abundance of offers, it must have been difficult for Miff to chart the right course at every available opportunity. For all the times when he said yes instead of no, and no instead of yes, the agent and manager guided Tommy to the top of his profession and kept him there for nearly forty years.

Yet there were a few times when his choices could be exacerbating. Eric Sykes, who rarely had a bad word to say about anyone, clearly felt frustrated at Miff's actions on occasion. This was most notable when Eric tried to book Tommy again after the success of their silent film classic together, *The Plank*.

Eric, quoted in Jeremy Novick's biography of Cooper, *Just Like That*, described Miff like this:

> He wasn't very good. He was really not a very nice man. And he didn't have a very good reputation. He could also be quite snide with some of his remarks. Tommy wanted to do more work with me, but Miff stood between us. When Tommy would put something to him, Miff would say 'Oh, you're feeding him again are you?' There was no need to say that. At the time, I was doing a series of one-hour television specials for Thames TV. Tommy enjoyed being in them and wanted to do more, but Miff kept asking the television company for more and more money, so in the end it never happened. Which was a shame. The television company would tell me it was because Tommy was not available, but I found out much later on that it was all down to Miff.

This was not exactly a glowing reference from a much-loved star of British comedy, a man who was one of Tommy Cooper's closest friends. Still, we cannot deny that Miff had been there at the outset and would remain so right up until the very end. That their relationship would be infused with animosity on occasion cannot be denied, but Miff put up with Tommy even when his behaviour became irascible. How many other agents would have done the same? Without that consistency, would Tommy's career have suffered in some way? Would he have faltered? Perhaps even failed?

You never know, for all Tommy's undoubted talent and his comedy connection with an audience, he could have become just another drunk in a bar, head bowed over his pint, slurring to anyone who would listen that he could have made it to the big time, if only he had worked with a manager.

16

Comedy and Magic

Paul Daniels once called Tommy Cooper 'An ordinary magician'. Daniels broke into television in the 1970s after years on the cabaret circuit where he came across Tommy many times. One night, Tommy watched Daniels in action.

In the routine, Daniels had a frog puppet gag that featured heavily. It was a highlight of the show, and Tommy was transfixed. Forever on the lookout for new material, Tommy was desperate to have it. He had always been this way. That was what all those trips to the various magic shops were about. His appetite for the latest novelty trick was voracious. Something original would always catch his eye.

The event was recorded in John Fisher's Cooper biography, *Always Leave Them Laughing*. Tommy pestered Paul Daniels, and Daniels quite rightly resisted. He had an hour of cabaret that he could transport from venue to venue. This was his livelihood, his sole source of income. The frog routine represented a full eight minutes of his act. Yet Tommy was not going to give in, and he kept on at the young magician throughout the course of the evening.

Eventually, when the club had emptied, Tommy dragged Daniels from the dressing room and led him to the auditorium. There, Tommy asked him to take a seat and then got up on the stage and did an impromptu set, apparently made up on the spot.

Daniels later said that he felt honoured and privileged to have witnessed a bit of Cooper magic that no one else had ever seen before and never would. Tommy finished his routine by saying, 'Now give me the fucking frog!'

Daniels could hardly refuse.

Paul Daniels had played the nightclubs for a number of years until he eventually got his break. Asked how he managed to make the transition from stage to the small screen, he had this to say: 'I did my time on the cabaret circuit, but I felt my act was really suited to television, so I was always on the lookout. At the time, there were shows such as *The Comedians*, which were highly popular, number one in the ratings in fact'. These were the guys who regularly shared billings with Daniels in the clubs, and still the magician could not get noticed by the powers that be.

Finally, out of sheer frustration, he asked a fellow performer how he could get on television.

'Oh, it's easy,' came the reply. 'You just give that fellow over there £500'.

The man he was referring to was a booker for the television stations. One payment from Paul was all it took, and there he was on television. He made an immediate impact on the viewing public, and the rest is history. He did well enough for Mrs Merton, played by Caroline Aherne, to once ask Paul's wife, Debbie McGee, during a television interview, 'So what was it that first attracted you to the millionaire Paul Daniels?'

In Debbie's defence, as she later explained, Daniels was not a millionaire when she fell for him. As far as her beloved husband was concerned, Paul was not really criticising Tommy when he called him 'ordinary'. It was just that Paul was a great magician, a great showman as well and, in truth, he was as much in awe of Tommy Cooper as everyone else in the industry. Daniels once recalled Tommy's appearance at the Grand Order of Water Rats.

Tommy explained the derivation of the name of their charitable institution. 'Rats,' he said, 'was "star" spelt backwards'. Indeed, there was a room full of stars listening to him that night. He then explained that 'Air Raid' was diarrhoea spelt backwards, before he concluded by saying, 'And my agent, Miff Ferrie, is just as big a bastard spelt forwards or backwards!' He just could not let it go.

Another comedian to have worked with Tommy Cooper is Russ Abbot. One of his characters inspired the title of this book. Russ is, according to his agent Mike Phillips, a lovely, lovely man. He would have his own day in the limelight.

Russ stepped out of a musical troupe called 'The Black Abbots' and eventually got his own television series. Abbot had learned the ropes on the cabaret circuit. He enjoyed nothing better than sharing a bill with Tommy so that he could soak up his act and learn from the master. One can imagine how exciting that must have been—not just watching one of your heroes perform, but sharing a dressing room, listening to their banter backstage, and watching them prepare.

It must have been a comedy masterclass. Tommy did not so much as take Russ under his wing; he did something much better. He treated him as an equal. He became a friend. It helped convince the young comedian that he had finally arrived.

Russ Abbot liked nothing more than having the ear of the great man. Tommy was a veteran of several *Royal Variety Performances* and a comedian who had been at the top of his game for a great many years. Abbot's favourite joke of all was where Tommy, resplendent in a set of tails, pristine white shirt, and wearing a bow-tie, sat down on a stool and played an organ at the start of his routine. Then, when the music came to a halt, Tommy stood up and walked forward, straight through the organ, which split in two, with each side swinging behind him like a pair of saloon-bar doors.

Russ told Tommy Cooper many times just how much he loved that particular gag. Later, when Abbot was given his own television series, *The Russ Abbot Show*, he came up with the character of 'Cooperman', complete with underpants over his long-legged leotard. It was Tommy Cooper as a superhero. It was an inspired creation and born out of love for Russ Abbot's own comedy hero.

It also speaks about Tommy's standing in the industry at that time. By now, he was an icon, a legend, and he was simply soaring above his contemporaries. He was the epitome of comedy.

All the while, his act purported to be that of a magician trying to amaze and failing miserably. That was the context in which his comedy could ultimately thrive.

After Tommy's death, Russ went to visit Gwen at the family's home in Chiswick to pay his respects and give his condolences. After a cup of tea and a conversation, Gwen asked Russ to follow her out to the shed at the end of the garden. There, she opened the doors to reveal the instrument at the heart of the gag that had tickled him so much.

'He wanted you to have it,' said Gwen. 'He knew how much you liked it'.

Russ revered Tommy so much, affording him superhero status, and it seems that Tommy had found an apprentice in Russ Abbot. Tommy was much looked-up to, and obviously much-loved in the industry. He did not ever appear to have been jealous of other performers. He had a single-minded focus that perhaps allowed him to filter out all challengers to his throne—either that, or he was simply enjoying the ride, or he was just too busy to notice.

Apart from Morecambe and Wise and the Two Ronnies (Barker and Corbett), no one else had that same rapport with an audience. In Tommy's case, that was true for both live and televised appearances. As brilliant as those other two pairs of comedians were, can you imagine Eric and Ernie, or Ronnie and Ronnie, getting up on stage at a nightclub in Blackpool or Liverpool on a Saturday night to perform in front of a room full of beer-swilling blokes and their wives? It just would not have happened.

Yet it was all meat and drink to Tommy. In fact, it was all bread and butter. It was food on the table, and he was not above such prosaic outings. He embraced them with relish.

'Where next, Miff?' Tommy would ask.

'Coventry next Saturday,' would come the reply.

'That's fine,' Tommy would say.

Tommy was astute enough to know that he had to mix things up a bit to avoid becoming stale. It did not matter that the gags were recycled on a regular basis as the audiences expected them.

'Doctor, I've broken my arm in several places. Well, don't go to them places!'

'I backed a horse at twenty to one. Came in at twenty past four!'

These were perennial favourites that audiences wanted to hear. Just moving the running order of the tricks and jokes around gave the impression of a new show every night. Add to that the unpredictability of a live audience, where a waiter might drop a tray of drinks, or a drunken member of the audience might try a heckle, and you create that frisson of unexpectedness that adds to the evening's excitement.

Then there was Tommy's delivery, which was sublime. The 'Just like that. Not like that. Like that', would be different each time. No matter how much he had practised beforehand, he was always in the moment. When he told a story, with that perplexed look on his face, he was always captivating. The journey through the tale was always peppered with his magic way with words.

Here's one with which he kept a Thames Television audience spellbound.

> A lion wakes up in the jungle and he's thinking 'Today's the day I'm going to show them all who's the king'. And he spots a monkey in a tree and he says, 'Hey you, Who's the king of the jungle?'
>
> The monkey says, 'you are'.
>
> The lion say's 'That's right'. So, he moves along, still feeling all proud of himself and he comes across a hyena. 'Hey you, laughing boy', he shouts. 'Who's the king of the jungle?'
>
> 'You are,' the hyena replies.
>
> 'That's right,' the lion says to himself and he moves off again. Nearby, there's a gorilla talking to an elephant.
>
> 'Here he comes, look,' said the gorilla, 'doing all that "who's the king", thing again. I'm off,' and the gorilla disappears up a tree.
>
> So, the lion approaches the elephant and says, 'Hey you, big ears. Who's the king of the jungle?' Well, the elephant picks the lion up with his trunk and bashes him from tree to tree, bashing him about like that. Not like that, like that. And then he finally dumps him in a heap on the ground. Eventually, the lion comes around and says to the elephant.
>
> 'Okay, there's no use getting upset just because you don't know the answer!'

Of course, Cooper laughed at that one too, as if hearing it for the very first time. As Paul Daniels once said, 'If Tommy had kept doing just the magic, the world would have missed a great clown'. Luckily for us, we got the best of both worlds—comedy and magic, delivered by the master of it all.

17

Contemporaries

Tommy Cooper's career spanned the best part of four decades, which was no small feat when you consider that your survival is based on your talent and popularity, and every day of every month, hundreds of newcomers are lining up to take your place. Tommy's career emerged from the music hall age and made the transfer into the era of television. It also encompassed the rise of the nightclub cabaret scene, as well as taking in endless variety seasons at theatres all over the country. He was versatile, with an act suitable to every environment, you might say.

Cooper rose to prominence on the back of such legends of the stage as Tommy Trinder, Arthur Askey, and the 'Cheeky Chappy' himself, Max Miller. Others to have made the grade were Max Wall and Flanagan and Allen. Their day was almost done when Tommy came to the fore, but he revered his forebears and forever held a candle to their contribution. No man, it is said, ever exists in a vacuum. Tommy certainly appreciated that he was standing on the shoulders of variety giants.

Of all his contemporaries, and they were a great and varied bunch, the most similar in terms of comic contribution, and the career that he would enjoy, has to be Benny Hill. There would even be parallels in how both men would come to be judged by history. Hindsight, as we know, is a wonderful thing. In the twenty-first century, a politically correct culture has reared its head to the point where people are frightened to say what they think. We are even analysing the things and the people who made us laugh down the years. Many people feel embarrassed that Benny Hill was ever given prime-time airing to flaunt his particular brand of schoolboy humour. This view is blatantly flawed, for no success is ever undeserved, especially when it endures over time. This, however, gives successive generations the opportunity to alter their opinion.

In fact, Benny Hill's life gives us the perfect mirror in which to view the career and the age that Tommy himself experienced. Alfie Hill (later Benny) was born in Hythe near Southampton in 1924. It was at Hythe Docks where Tommy would one day have his light bulb moment when performing at the boatyard Christmas party. To think that, at the very moment that Tommy was messing up his first professional performance, there was a thirteen-year-old boy living in the same neighbourhood who would follow in Tommy's footsteps.

Benny's father had run away to join the circus at the age of sixteen. He did everything from walking the high wire to mucking out the elephants' enclosure. This teenage adventure was curtailed by the First World War, and he took up the life of a salesman when he rejoined civvy street. Then, he met and married a young woman called Helen Cave, who worked at one of the firms he used to visit.

Benny said of his father 'He had a larger than life personality. He used to walk up the stairs on his hands! He'd never wait till you had finished speaking if he had something to say'. It is strange that this obviously outgoing person should have sired so shy a son, for that is how Benny Hill came across to many people. That said, by the time he reached grammar school, he had started to exhibit a bit of showmanship. He played in goal for the school football team, and whenever the ball came towards his goal, he would wait until the very last second before swooping on it. This made the result look more spectacular than it actually was, and ensured an appreciative response from the teachers, parents, and his fellow pupils watching on the touchline.

A regular family event would be a trip to the music hall. This was still variety's golden age, and there is no doubt that the acts that Benny would have witnessed would have been the cream of talent of the day. Every Wednesday, the Hill family would take in a show. Young Alfie was especially entranced by the comics. Whether he realised it or not, he was soaking up everything he could, and the germ of an idea was beginning to take hold. He himself recalled in a biography written by John Smith:

> I'd watch the comic take all the applause, and it seemed like the most glamorous job in the world. Everyone loved him, and with him were all the saucy girls. At the end of the song or dance routine the girls would put their arms around him and kiss him. Well, I used to think to myself, this man leads the life of Reilly. That's going to be the life for me.

The living room became his arena. With a blanket slung over his shoulder, a nod to the ostentatious outfits worn by Max Miller, he would launch into a routine about 'the Wife' in front of his mum and dad when he was only fourteen. His parents, who had more than a touch of show-business about themselves, encouraged their young son, even helping him to dress up before he would perform for them as they sat on the settee. They would fashion hats, suits, and all manner of wardrobe for the budding young comedian.

At the tender age of sixteen, Benny set forth for the bright lights of London. He had but a few provincial shows in his home town under his belt, yet he was determined to enter the world of show-business. Once he reached the capital, he approached a theatrical agent and asked for a spot as a comedian on the bill at the Chelsea Palace. The veteran booker offered some sage words. 'Start at the bottom and you'll eventually get your chance'. So, Benny joined the company, moving sets, doing whatever was required, and even joining in the chorus until he was finally given his opportunity on the stage.

He was standing in the wings one night when he heard the resident comic calling out for his stooge. 'Where is he?' the man was calling. 'He should be out here,' he said in a voice of desperation. Benny realised that something had gone amiss with the act. The actor playing the stooge had gone missing, probably still in the pub or asleep in his dressing room. So, Benny stepped into the spotlight and improvised for all he was worth. After that, he never looked back.

Yet, as with many a talented performer and sportsman of that age, his plans for a career in show-business were thwarted when Britain entered the Second World War. No warrior, Benny, as he now called himself, was recruited to the Royal and Electrical Mechanical Engineers as a driver. For the next five years, this would be his lot, although he did eventually manage to transfer to the Army's entertainment division where he quickly made his mark.

A natural on stage, he would compère the shows. He always wrote his own material and would continue to do so to the end of his career. He managed to impress a sergeant who was responsible for organising the shows for the troops. The man would eventually become Benny Hill's agent once the war was over.

Following the cessation of hostilities, Benny found himself in London once more, dreaming big but living small. He was part of a coterie of ex-servicemen from the entertainment corps. They were a talented bunch. All of them eventually became household names for a certain generation. Their showbiz careers had been curtailed or sidelined by the war, but they were now free to pursue their goals when released from national service.

The aspiring bunch would often rendezvous at a venue called the Captain's Cabin, which was situated in Regent Street. They would follow this by going for a cheap bite to eat at the Old English Eating House, which served a filling meal for a couple of shillings. Enjoying the camaraderie with Benny were Max Bygraves, Norman Wisdom, Bob Monkhouse, and Tommy Cooper. They would share jokes and information on opportunities in the business, and about agents or bookers who might be looking for acts.

Slowly, the work began to come in. From *Henry Hall's Guest Night*, *Variety Band Box*, *Beginners Please*, and *Midday Music Hall* on radio, Benny drummed up the courage to approach the BBC itself. He literally walked in off the street, up to reception, and asked if he could speak to the Head of Light Entertainment.

In a nod to another era, he was invited in to be greeted by the esteemed gentleman himself. Benny impressed and managed to sell himself, and he was soon a regular face on television. Still an emerging medium, Benny's on-screen persona served as a driving force for how best to entertain people in their own homes. He was a pioneer in how to do comedy on the small screen. While he had succeeded in theatres across the land, he was really best suited to television.

He would maintain his unique standing in this environment for the next thirty years, becoming a global star. He continued to work the stage, but television was his preferred port of call. When he came to do the Paris by Night season with Tommy Cooper in the mid-1950s, Benny took top billing. For Tommy, this was the perfect scenario. There was no pressure, other than the usual pressure to perform. People came to see the headline act. If the support act was good, then great. If the support act bombed, then it was not the end of the world. All of the expectation rested with the main act.

Maybe Tommy Cooper considered himself a niche artiste, or maybe he never quite believed his own hype, but he was happy enough to play second fiddle to the likes of Benny Hill.

For a time, Hill was the most successful and the highest earning entertainment star in the world. He was a ubiquitous presence on British television in the 1970s and 1980s and was a hailed as a genius. The fact that Tommy Cooper held his own in such company is testament to the talent of the great man. Tommy may have been billed as the support act, but he was always a star attraction. Even amongst such illustrious contemporaries, Cooper always stood out as unique.

18

Falling Out with Miff

Jimmy Tarbuck once said that Tommy Cooper had great timing on stage, but no sense of time in real life. Tommy used to drive the stage hands crazy with his nonchalant approach. Twenty minutes before he was due to go on, they would give him notice. 'That's fine,' Tommy would say. The same would happen with ten minutes to go, and then again at five. Finally, the frustrated assistant would say 'You're on!'

Tommy would act all flustered and say, 'Why on earth didn't you tell me?'

He even managed to put his own tardiness into the act. The compère would announce him, the audience would applaud, and then nothing would happen. The applause would die down as the gathered crowd wondered what was going on. Then, off, a voice would come over the public-address system. 'Where am I? What's going on? Why is everything dark? I've gone blind! Oh, no I haven't. I'm locked in the wardrobe'. There was then the sound of a door rattling. 'What's this? My God, a bear. I'm being attacked by a bear! Oh no, it's not. That's my coat. Let me find the key'.

Tommy rattled the door some more. 'That's better,' and then he would make his entrance on to the stage. The routine took a full five minutes, during which time the audience were in fits of laughter and Tommy had not even come on yet.

There was more than a hint of truth in Tommy's lackadaisical approach. He was completely absent-minded. It used to drive both Miff and Gwen up the wall. At least Gwen had the comfort of knowing that she ran the house. She could organise the kids, the weekly shopping, or pay the bills, and there was no need to involve Tommy in any of it. She could work around him. For Miff, it was a different matter. Fastidious by nature, he kept a diary in which he noted every letter and phone conversation between the agent and his client. It does not make for happy reading.

Firstly, there was the undercurrent of suspicion with which Tommy viewed his contract with Miff. Having previously agreed to the 15 per cent commission,

Tommy began looking for ways to get out of it. He approached Equity, the performance union, and had them look over the agreement. They reported that everything was above board. Then he showed the same agreement to his accountant to see if he could help, but he reported that a deal was a deal. Finally, Tommy approached a solicitor. Cooper called Miff ahead of his meeting and talked about it in a roundabout way. He said that his solicitor wanted to know why Miff was taking the amount that he was. Miff replied that it was as per the contract. Tommy was hinting 'But why? Why so high?' Miff asked Tommy if he was unhappy with the arrangement. Tommy said 'No, he was perfectly happy, but his solicitor wanted to know why it was set at the rate that it was'.

Miff nipped this in the bud by calling Tommy's solicitor directly. He explained that the 15 per cent was standard for the inclusion of personal management along with the day-to-day agent work. Besides, the contract was *bona fide* and had been vetted by both the union and Tommy's accountant. The solicitor had nowhere to go. Later on, Tommy told Miff what was really bothering him. He did regard the commission as too high. Could Miff forward a copy of the contract to his solicitors for their perusal? Not only was the agent happy to oblige, for he knew the validity of his case, but he also provided letters of correspondence where Tommy himself stated that he was in agreement with the percentage for Miff to act as both agent and personal manager. The case was closed, or should have been, but not quite.

Sensing an opportunity, the solicitors honed in on the issue of the contract extension. If there was no way around the 15 per cent margin, for that was writ in stone, then the terms of the contract renewal might offer some hope of reward. Unless Miff was prepared to settle for 10 per cent commission going forward, then the contract would not be extended by the artist when it was next due to be renewed. Miff might well have argued that the contract was a rolling one and was valid as long as Miff increased Tommy's earnings year on year. Their contract would be more than ten years old before any such dip in revenue could be found. At the time, Miff was complying with both the spirit and the letter of the contract. He knew he was on safe ground, so he chose to ignore the solicitor's letter. As he rightly suspected that it would, the issue eventually went away, with Tommy continuing to earn good money, and Miff continuing to procure ever more work for his client.

There was no mistaking the fact that Miff worked hard for that extra commission, over and above an agent's usual fee. His diaries again tell the story. One man had a carefree attitude to his responsibilities, while the other was doing all that he could to hold everything in place. Tommy was wandering around causing chaos, and the responsible adult in the partnership was running around clearing up all the mess.

To make his point, Miff wrote to Tommy to tell him that their association had seen the comedian's income rise from an initial £10 to more than £2,000 a week.

To explain what Miff was doing to earn his percentage, another look through his diaries reveals a lot. When Miff would book Tommy's accommodation, the comedian would traipse past the hotel until he found something more to his liking. Then, there were the endless complaints from hotel managers saying that Tommy had left without paying his bill. Miff would then have to attend to it. On more than one occasion, Tommy had been threatened with legal action for non-payment until Miff came to the rescue and sorted it out.

There were the wrong turns taken by Tommy as he travelled the country. He would arrive at the right venue on the wrong day, or the wrong venue on the right day. If a show was pulled due to strike action, a common occurrence in Britain in the early 1970s, Tommy would show up anyway, despite the fact that Miff would have written to him in the first instance and then phoned him to confirm. It did not matter. Tommy was oblivious, forgetful, and disorganised.

'Where do I sign the contract?' Tommy would ask.

'Where it says artist,' Miff would reply.

It was not hard, but it was too much for Tommy. His mind was elsewhere, constantly thinking about his act, the cogs always turning, but not thinking about real life.

The relationship between the two men was on a downward trajectory. If they were wedded to each other through the terms of the contract, with the 15 per cent commission a constant bugbear for Tommy, it appears that they did no more than tolerate each other for a very long time. It was, no doubt, a marriage of convenience, and there would be many rows and disagreements along the way. Tommy would call Miff 'Little Caesar', and tell him to stop snooping in his affairs. However, it was Miff's job to stick close and untangle the situations that Tommy had a habit of getting himself into. This was all before Tommy's drinking got to be a problem.

In the end, Miff wrote to Tommy and told him that he could buy himself out of the arrangement. Knowing Tommy's reluctance to ever part with his cash, he must have been confident that this was a threat that his client would never take up.

John Fisher states that Miff Ferrie was indispensable to Tommy. Likewise, as his sole client, Cooper was indispensable to Miff. Gwen told Miff that he had always been a 'Worry-guts'. Is it any wonder when trying to manage the career of a man-child? He would be on hand to offer excuses and apologies whenever Tommy erred. There were occasions when it all got too much for Miff, as Tommy could be quite nasty towards him.

Despite the fact that the artiste held the upper hand, Miff could stand up for himself. When Tommy declared that he was now too big for Miff to handle and threatened to tear up their agreement, Miff responded by saying, 'Your insults and groundless accusations I find intolerable. My achievement in building you to your present status is being disregarded if not downright forgotten. I should suggest therefore that you execute your threat to tear up our contract without delay!'

Miff was about to take a holiday at the time of this exchange. Tommy's response was to tell the agent that he would be hearing from his solicitors. He finished by saying that he hoped that Miff had a very unhappy holiday!

It seems that Tommy never quite gave Miff the respect that his services deserved. While there have been a few (including Eric Sykes) who have not exactly rushed to praise the little Scotsman, and he struggles within these pages to ever escape the epithet 'dour', he was the first in the business to spot the talent of Tommy Cooper, and he secured him constant work for a period of almost forty years.

To the money-orientated Cooper, Miff's level of commission was an open wound, and one which Gwen was driven to manipulate whenever in the mood. She would wind Tommy up something rotten. She would ask questions like 'Why are you paying him if you're not happy?' and other such stuff until Tommy would be forced to pick up the phone and weakly raise his protest with a bemused and beleaguered Miff.

As Miff often replied, usually on the point of exasperation, 'Don't forget who has always been by your side'. He would say it more than once. Tommy appears to have taken this on board only fleetingly, because before too long the vicious cycle would start again. Miff was a useful scapegoat and a necessary evil. Unfortunately, all too often to Tommy's mind, he was just evil or unnecessary. Miff endured, and Tommy's career endured, but there never was much love between them.

19

Mr Personality

Tommy had been quite a shy child until he discovered magic. It opened up his world. Now, he was forever in search of an audience. With more than one trick up his sleeve, he shed shyness and became more outgoing and, as a result, more popular.

While one school friend described him as a bit of a loner, and an Army colleague said that 'He never had a pal or anything like that', Tommy became more gregarious as he got older. Fame itself does not appear to have changed him, but he is sure to have attracted hangers on, such is the lure of celebrity.

Cooper had a down-to-earth personality. To a watching audience, he was one of them, only a lot more talented. They spoke the same language, lived on the same streets, and fame was almost a by-product rather than the destination that it seems to be today. Tommy did live in the real world, except to him, it was one steeped in endless opportunities for laughter. It was this way of looking at life that he sought to share with his millions of fans.

While Cooper had no capacity for self-analysis, his many friends and colleagues had their own views about this giant in their midst. He seems to me to have been a bit like Peter Pan, the kid who never quite grew up. Certainly, while he attracted all the trappings of a grown-up—the house, the career, the wife and kids—he never lost his sense of wonder at everything that he saw around him.

Eric Sykes says that the two men became like brothers. No doubt, the struggle to break into the big time bonded that particular group of ex-servicemen who used to meet in the bars off the Charing Cross Road in London—Benny Hill, Max Bygraves, Bob Monkhouse, and Norman Wisdom among them.

His long-time television producer Dennis Kirkland said 'Magic was his interest. Comedy was his interest. To some people, that made him a bit of an oddity. He always looked like a man who lived in his own universe. He was, at heart, his own man'.

Gwen said of him, 'He wasn't a shy man, as some people thought. He always got on tremendously well with people because they all loved him. But he was a bit of a loner, and he'd go off into his own little world, thinking about tricks and props and things. Rather than go out with the boys, he loved to come home and disappear into his study to work on some new trick. He just lived and died for his act'.

Always on the lookout for new gadgets, Tommy would tour the magic shops of London. There, he was engaging company, not holding back as he grappled with the latest contraption, bombarding the shop owner with questions as to how the novelty trick worked. If he had any shyness in him, his enthusiasm won over on these occasions.

Benny Hill describes working with Tommy on the Paris by Night revue. While Benny really was shy and reserved when he was not performing and was content to rest up backstage before a show, taking nothing harder than a cup of tea to relax himself, Tommy would stroll up at the last minute with a group of friends in tow. He would then keep them entertained right up until the moment that he was due to go on.

It seems that Cooper was exactly the same off stage as he was when he was on. He was always performing, and forever in search of an audience or someone that he could beguile with his tricks.

Barry Cryer said that Cooper 'Had that faraway look in his eyes, like he wasn't really there. Staring into the distance with nothing to say'. In fact, 'loner' was the first word to come to his mind when Cryer was asked to sum up Tommy Cooper.

> In real life, he looked so singular and strange. He always seemed alone. Even in the middle of a crowd. He would sit and sulk a bit if he sensed the attention that he felt justified to himself was not forthcoming. This usually meant he had a trick that he wanted to show you, while everyone else was deep in conversation about politics or sport or whatever. Then, once he got his opportunity and had enchanted you with a piece of magic or convulsed you with that gag, everything would be alright with the world again.

Whether with an entourage or alone, it seems that he existed in a kind of bubble, and that he communicated with the rest of mankind through the art of performance. As well as his friends in the Magic Circle and the various magic shops and conventions that he would attend, there was also his many showbiz pals, from Eric and Ernie, Spike Milligan, and of course his best buddy Eric Sykes.

By now, he was also accompanied by his son, Thomas Jr, who became his dresser and stagehand. As insular as he appears to have been, he was constantly surrounded by friends and loved ones.

Then there were the young performers who looked up to Tommy—people like Russ Abbot, Paul Daniels, and Jimmy Tarbuck. It appears that Tommy, despite his legendary meanness with money, was really quite generous with his time. As Barry Cryer testifies, Tommy had no animosity or jealousy towards other performers, even those who were at the top of the tree and who could be said to be Cooper's competition for theatrical bookings and the nation's affections.

It is quite endearing to witness someone's passion for something they love. Richard Briers, the British actor, once saw Tommy performing for a group of children. During the show, he blew a series of bubbles, and then managed to catch one in the palm of his hand. Using magician's sleight, Cooper had produced a glass ball that he appeared to pluck from the stream of bubbles. The look of sheer delight on Tommy's face was both wondrous and beautiful to behold. That wide-eyed stare, replete with childlike amazement, was Tommy in his element.

Despite his sheer-mindedness, and his almost monk-like devotion to his craft, Tommy could not help but make friends along the way. The fact that they were, for the most part, just a travelling audience for the comedian and magician is beside the point. Tommy was a popular man, and he was much loved for his ready supply of gags, his innocence, and what he brought to life.

There has recently been a re-evaluation of the life of Tommy Cooper. No one disputes how great he was as a comedian but there has been, of late, both on stage and on screen, an attempt to discredit him as a person, and most notably as a husband. Surely the only person who should be allowed to judge Tommy on this issue is Gwen herself, and her thoughts on the subject are clear.

As she told the *Daily Mail* a decade after her husband's death, the heartbroken wife and mother of two said:

> Sundays are the worst. I was so used to going to collect him from an airport or a train station. Not to have him with me on those days is real murder. He'd always ring beforehand and tell me what he wanted to eat. And he'd ring me every night at seven before he went on stage. Now, when the phone goes at that time, I always expect it to be him.

It is true that she and Tommy often rowed—a fact she was only too happy to disclose in the many newspaper interviews that she gave. Indeed, she almost seems to revel in their recollection—yet it was, by and large, a happy and successful marriage. Tommy thought the world of Dove, and to her, Tommy was her world. I think the current crop of revisionist storytellers would do well to bear this in mind as they attempt to re-write history to the detriment of a comedy legend.

As comedian Jason Manford said, when asked to describe what was unique about Tommy Cooper, 'He had great timing and an incredible rapport with an audience. An incredible rapport. And what they felt for Tommy was love. Real love'.

Jimmy Tarbuck told WalesOnline in April 2014, 'Tommy would walk out and just be hit by a wall of love. It's all about likeability, and by heck, he had that in diamonds'.

On stage, as in life, Tommy Cooper was a much-loved man.

20

The Legendary Meanness

There is one aspect of Tommy's character where he is due some criticism, and that is his legendary meanness. This stinginess was not just confined to skipping the odd round at the bar, but spilled over into every area of his social and professional life. Gag writers would be ripped off, material would not be paid for, and there seems to have been an almost pathological reluctance to part with his money or, on occasion, to give credit where any was due.

It was traditional at the end of a theatre run to give the overworked and underpaid stage hands a tip. In Tommy's version, he would proffer three envelopes and ask them to choose one, which they would do. The envelope would invariably be empty, which is hardly surprising when all three of them were bereft of cash. 'Better luck next time,' he would say. Tommy had no intention of parting with his well-earned money.

At the bar, it was said that he would use every trick in the book to avoid paying for his drinks, and if he was not going to pay for his own, he certainly was not going to pay for anyone else's. Back in the days when he was just another struggling artist, searching for a break, he would regularly meet up with fellow performers who were going through the same experience. At the tea shop where they would congregate, Tommy would shout upon entry to the premises, 'You lot get the teas, I'll get the chairs,' as if that somehow evened things out.

In the pub, Tommy would hang back, pretending to look for his cigars, or he would profess to be desperate for the loo—anything to avoid being first in the queue. He had more than one scheme to ensure he avoided paying. As he became more famous, he was recognised wherever he went. So, he would make for the bar, and someone would do a double-take, and say, 'It's Tommy Cooper'.

Tommy would say, 'That's right. What are you having?'

The bloke would usually reply, 'Allow me'.

Tommy would say, 'Oh, go on then'.

It never failed. In fact, to make sure that he got what he wanted, it was said that Tommy Cooper practically hypnotised his poor victims into buying his ale. By the end of the night, if he had played this trick on everyone, he would have a table full of drinks in front of him.

Tom O'Connor, a friend and fellow performer of Cooper's, recalls how Tommy would pat himself down whenever they landed in a bar. His expression would then change and Cooper would claim apologetically to have left his wallet back at the hotel, or at the theatre, or anywhere in fact where it could not be reached.

O'Connor also explained that Cooper had an expensive cigarette holder that only ever contained one cigarette. By all accounts, this almost sounds like a novelty from a magic shop with which to play tricks on unsuspecting members of the public, except these were his friends and drinking buddies.

Tommy Cooper would quickly pull out the silver case and offer you a cigarette. Obviously, if there was only one there, you could not both partake. So, the person on the other end of the offer would naturally state 'no, have one of mine,' and Tommy would accept; it worked every time. Tommy would have his own packet of cigarettes secreted about his person, but just as he managed to prise drinks out of others, he would do the same with the smokes. For anyone else, this reputation would bring you a wide berth. Only character can compensate; people have to want you there anyway.

Probably the most famous story regarding Tommy's miserly condition is the trick he performed on every cab driver who ever had him in the back of their vehicle. It is customary, almost compulsory, to give a tip when taking a cab in Britain. Tommy would finish each journey with the words 'Have a drink on me'. He would then place a tea bag into the driver's hand.

Gwen appears to have been oblivious to this side of Tommy's character. After all, she has said that she had been spoiled rotten by her husband. She can be forgiven for having suspected nothing. While she took care of the family finances, she always made sure that Tommy had money in his pocket so that he could buy a round down the pub with his mates. She was just looking after him. Tommy, though, had a streak of meanness with regard to his money. He just could not bring himself to spend it. In time, people got used to it, and made a joke of it, but there were times when his friends and his peers were genuinely hurt by his behaviour.

Billy Mayo had given Tommy the idea of emerging on stage at the Royal Variety Performance with a paraffin heater to 'warm them up'. On top of that, Billy had trudged across London to purchase with his own money the item that Tommy so desperately needed.

Much later, Billy and Tommy and a group of friends were enjoying a drink in a bar. Billy was by now an elderly man, and he was not too good on his feet. He asked Tommy if he could be dropped off by Tommy's driver as it was on their way home. Tommy declared that he 'Was not a fucking taxi service!' It was a less than gracious moment from the comedian, who left a similar taste of bitterness with other friends on many different occasions. The fact that Billy had previously done Cooper a big favour was all too easily forgotten.

If Tommy found it hard to express his gratitude, getting money out of him was even more difficult. Some of his showbiz pals, including those tasked with supplying his material, tried every trick in the book to get around Tommy's financial defences. One man, Bill Hall, claimed to have a fail-safe approach. When they had a price agreed for a bit of business or prop, Tommy would always claim, come the time to pay, that he was being overcharged. 'About that money,' he would begin, about to launch into some sob story. Having heard it all before, and being well-prepared, Hall would interject, 'That's right. I quoted you the wrong price. It should have been £4, not £3'.

To this, Tommy would reply, 'No. A price is a price,' and he would quickly cough up the £3. It was the only thing that seemed to work to get him to part with his cash.

Tommy was one of the highest-paid entertainers in Britain, earning many times more than the average wage. He could afford a beautiful house in West London, a cottage by the sea, several overseas holidays a year, and a private education for his children, yet the one thing he could not seem to do was to put his hand in his pocket when it was his turn to buy a round, or to pay for the jokes that the gag writers offered him.

Some of the writers on his staff were forced to take up the issue with Miff directly or, in some instances, with the television companies themselves whenever a routine aired without acknowledgement or payment for the author of the piece. One time, he 'borrowed' a sketch from a writer, saying he wanted it for a party. Obviously, for a small private affair, the writer would be hard pressed to charge for it, so he gave it to Tommy for free. What he did not know, and what Cooper failed to mention, was that the party was the BBC Christmas party to be aired on screen for millions of people.

A fellow magician and a regular attendee at one of the magic shop gatherings was Bobby Bernard. He described Tommy as a 'ruthless opportunist,' adding that the comedian would never pay for anything. As well as pretending to have left his wallet behind, and the various ways in which he would con a stranger in a bar to buy him a drink, Tommy's legendary thrift is the one thing that is universally held against him. Yet, for the most part, it was a trait that was forgiven, simply for the sheer enjoyment that people got out of him along the way.

One of Tommy's established writers, Val Andrews, summed it up like this. 'He had many good qualities and could be great company, but his obsession about the cost of things spoiled things for himself and other people. I was sorry for anyone who had a business arrangement with him'.

Tommy appears to have ridden roughshod over many of the writers who supplied him with the material he needed for his act. Even Val Andrews, who helped create the famous 'hats' sequence for Tommy, could not be assured of receiving anything like proper treatment. If Tommy could not use something he had been given, he would sell it on to other performers and pocket the money. The remuneration for a short gag would have been but a drop in the ocean of Tommy's wealth, but that psychological flaw is ever present when it comes to cash. If a writer spotted a piece of business on television, they would be better raising the issue with the producers themselves rather than take it up with Tommy. At least that way, there was some chance of receiving due payment for their contribution.

John Fisher, the biographer of Tommy Cooper, said that the comedian had a pathological dread of reaching into his pocket. He recounts how Tommy, whenever he was on tour, liked to while away the hours before a show by visiting the local cinema in whichever town he happened to be in.

Cooper would present himself at the kiosk and ask to see the manager, expecting that his fame alone would guarantee him free admission. It is a wonder that he did not ask for the popcorn and drinks to be thrown in as well. He was usually in the company of the travelling show's director. On one occasion, the manager not being available and the teller at the kiosk unwilling to budge, Tommy turned to his colleague and admitted defeat, saying 'You'll have to pay this time!'

Tommy had more than enough money to go around, but the fact is that he just could not bear to part with it. For sure, he worked hard to earn it, but one cannot help feeling a little sorry for his friends and creative team who had to carry him when it came to splashing the cash. Cooper, for all his attributes, was a legendary spendthrift. Luckily for him, his talent and personality ensured that he was usually forgiven.

For sure though, he truly earned the title of the tightest man in show-business.

21

Family Man

Tommy and Gwen met in 1947 and, after a whirlwind courtship, were married in Larnaca, Cyprus. On their wedding night, the couple slept together for the very first time. In her own charming and no-nonsense way, Gwen described the consummation of their marriage as 'Bloody wonderful!'

They moved to London and rented a succession of apartments until, with fame assured and money in the bank, they bought the house in Chiswick that would be the family home for more than thirty years. It was a place of happiness, and it was where the couple raised their two children, Vicky and Thomas Jr.

Vicky was born in 1953, and Thomas came along three years later in 1956. Vicky described her dad in an interview with *The Sunday Telegraph* in 2003:

> He was a real joker at home, but definitely the boss! What he said went. He was always late and used to wind my mum up before they were due to leave for the airport to catch a plane. While Dove was fretting, Tommy would say 'Right, I'll slowly start packing now!' My poor mother. She was a nervous wreck.
>
> He was very strict around my boyfriends. He took a dislike to one and barred him from the house. It was Christmas time and I thought he would bend and let him come round for a drink but, no, it was not to be. He was very fair though and kept to his word. He had a lousy temper, but he would come down quick.
>
> He used to play a lot of games with my brother and myself when we were little. It would always be on a Sunday, as wherever he was in England, he always tried to get home for the weekend. He was a funny, complex man whose life was dedicated to making people laugh.

To Gwen, he was a constant source of frustration and amusement. He would drive her potty with his pranks and his idiosyncratic ways, sitting at the dining table and practising magic tricks for hours on end. One time, he placed a plastic jumping spider under her make-up bag and roared with laughter when Gwen came across it and screamed in fright. He laughed and laughed and laughed, she said, and you just had to laugh with him. Gwen said she would not swap Tommy for anything, not even for a few hours of peace!

Gwen said, 'I think I was his best friend. We always laughed. He'd always say to me, "Never a day goes by without you making me laugh". He was so generous to me. Spoiled me rotten he did. We liked to have a scream from time to time, but it was never meant nastily. It was a wonderful, extraordinary marriage. I've been very privileged'.

Yet they would row and drink, and drink and row. They were both as bad as each other. Gwen was the first to admit that she gave as good as she got. Thomas Jr recalls how his father hated any trouble with his wife. 'They had some colossal fights and Dad would spend all his time ducking,' young Thomas said. Later on, when the drinking began to get excessive, these rows escalated to physical fights. In 1969, Miff Ferrie received the first of a series of phone calls in which Gwen said she was going to leave Tommy because he had struck her in front of the children. Daughter Vicky recalls seeing bruises on her mum after one such altercation.

John Fisher records an entry by Miff in the manager's diary: 'She is divorcing Tommy. Can't take it anymore. He drinks all the time. Stays up until five every morning drinking whisky at the dressing room table. Is violent when drunk'. That said, Miff's diary also recalls that Gwen smashed a chair over Tommy. If it was not always a match made in heaven, it was certainly always a match. Later, she told Miff that she would give Tommy another chance if only he would get to bed at a reasonable hour. That seems to have done the trick, for a little while at least.

Why had Tommy started drinking so heavily? His career was still at its peak. If he had plateaued, it was only because he had reached the highest high and simply stayed there. His health had caused him several problems, and that must have been a source of some discomfort and unhappiness, but it should not have led to the serious battle with alcohol that he became involved in.

One possible cause of anxiety was his relationship with Mary Kay, one of the floor managers at a television studio where he was filming a show. She had now joined his entourage, serving as his PA, dresser, and props manager. They would be close for almost two decades, and Tommy no doubt felt torn by the conflict between his domestic and professional arrangements. He drank to avoid facing up to the dilemma, and Gwen bore the brunt of his inherent anger at the situation he had gotten himself into.

Yet those Sundays at home were special and, as well as being a much-loved husband, Tommy took his parental duties to heart. Vicky recalls the times when she would open up about any problems she had. Tommy would sit there and listen intently, for once, all serious. When she had finished, and Tommy had thought about it, he would offer up a few wise words. Vicky added that his advice was invariably right.

The married couple had started their family late on. Both were well into their late thirties when their children came along. They had some trouble conceiving, for which Gwen insisted that they visit the hospital to have some checks carried out. Luckily, there was nothing wrong with either of them and eventually, nature took its course.

Tommy's gruelling workload and his attempts to climb up the show-business ladder also meant that family had to take a back seat to his career ambitions. As a performer herself, Gwen understood the hard work involved, and she supported Tommy every step of the way. Her innate understanding of the art form meant that she was indispensable to his act. She could also be a formidable force backstage. During one outing, there was another performer who used to wear a fez on stage. 'Not tonight,' Gwen informed him and removed the offending article from his dressing room. Nothing and no one could interfere with Tommy's trajectory.

She also helped him with the personal stuff too. She supplied him with sandwiches and a veritable picnic every time he set off for an engagement. She would prepare so much food that the other performers would also derive fringe benefits from her mothering nature, with her special sponge cakes available to all.

When they were young and carefree, Gwen was happy to come along for the ride and catch his act. Later on, with young children at home, she rationed herself to the odd function, usually a rotary club dinner or some special event. It would be a source of some regret for her that she never travelled with Tommy when the kids had grown up but, by then, she was out of the habit, and it was one to which she never returned. Still, she could at least catch him on the telly, knowing that he would soon be back by her side.

Thomas Jr took up the mantle of supporting his father, becoming a sort of road manager, helping set the props table, and there to provide a helping hand and some company backstage.

The day of Tommy's final performance had been a typical one in the Cooper household. If it was unusual in any respect, it was for the nerves that Tommy was feeling beforehand. Something about this being a live show had set him a-tingling. Gwen knew that the best remedy was to prepare meticulously. Tommy was due on stage for a full seven minutes. Gwen took out a timer that she used in the kitchen—one she used to prepare her exemplary cakes. She had Tommy repeat the act over and over until it was timed to the second. Every gag and every phrase was honed to perfection. The only bit they argued about was how much time to allow for audience laughter in between the jokes—'a lot' would seem to be the right answer.

Finally, Tommy could relax, knowing he could do no more. As ever, Dove prepared his packed lunch. It was a whole loaf's worth of banana sandwiches. She swears these were his favourite.

She decided not to go along with him. Their son would be there to look after him, and she wanted to watch it on the telly to see how he did. For the first five minutes, everything went as she expected it to. She knew every gag off by heart and was pleased to see how well the act was doing. Then it was time for the magic cloak routine, and Tommy slumped to the floor. Gwen knew immediately that something was wrong. She says she knew, just knew. It was his heart. Later that night, her son called with the dreadful news—confirmation of what she already felt. Their love affair, which had lasted nearly forty years, had come to a swift and tragic end.

The following day, the house was besieged by reporters and well-wishers. The phone rang constantly as showbiz pals including Ronnie Barker, Barry Cryer, Michael Parkinson, Eric Morecambe, and Eric Sykes all called to offer their condolences and ask if there was anything Gwen wanted. There was not; the only thing she really wanted was the one thing that she could not have.

Eventually, needing something to take her mind off the pain, Gwen invited one young reporter into her home. Helped by copious amounts of gin and tonic, she asked the man to keep her company while she watched the tape of Tommy's last performance.

When he appeared on screen, Gwen howled and bawled and mumbled incoherently, as if willing the man back to life. Then, when her husband slumped to the floor on the television show, she wept uncontrollably. Finally, when she turned off the recording, she turned around to see the trunk of props from Cooper's final gig, which the television company had returned to her earlier in the day. Atop lay Tommy's uneaten lunch, and the sight of his props chest and the leftover picnic set Gwen off again. 'He never even finished his banana sandwiches,' she sobbed.

There would be more heartache to come, in the form of newspaper revelations, when Mary Kay decided to share her story with the tabloids. For now, Tommy Cooper, family man and funny man, was gone. As Gwen later said, 'I am nothing without Tommy. He was my life. I never wanted a Rolls-Royce or a yacht. All I ever wanted was him'.

The good times were over. Whatever bad times they might have had were also now long gone.

22

The Television Appearances

If the 1950s were all about Tommy's rise to the top, the 1960s saw him out-do his peers until he was unofficially crowned the king of comedy (or officially, if you include 1969's Television Personality of the Year). Despite such contemporaries as Benny Hill, the Two Ronnies, and Morecambe and Wise, Tommy could more than hold his own in the popularity stakes with any of them. Indeed, in terms of the affection the general public held for him, he probably outstripped them all.

In reality, he was not in competition with any of them, for he seemed to hold a unique place in the nation's hearts. It was as if he had been adopted as the country's very own court jester, the favourite performer of every household in the land.

With some acts, the audiences watched expectantly, challenging them to impress. With Tommy, the audience listened, beguiled, knowing they were about to be entertained. The crowds were said to be laughing as they stood in the queue outside whichever theatre he was appearing at. The sheer thought of what they were about to witness was enough to get them going.

It was an extraordinary hold that he had over an audience; it was almost cult-like. It has been said of several great performers down the years that they could read the phonebook out loud and the audience would still sit there transfixed. The reason given is that the audience were simply happy to be in the presence of such a person. It would be something that they would remember forever. How else can you explain some of Tommy's extraordinary openings, other than to say that the audience just wanted to spend time with him?

He opened one show by walking to the front of the stage and began with a seemingly-traditional 'It's lovely to be here'. Then, he took a couple of steps to his left, stopped, and said 'And it's lovely to be here too'. Then, to wring every possible bit of mileage from the gag, he moved another couple of feet away and delivered the line once more. He then laughed as loudly as anyone in the room.

Another time, he stepped onto the stage of a vast auditorium, wandered towards the wings, and delivered several minutes of his routine to the audience

Above: Magic cloak routine.

Below: Then men came and captured the mythical beast...

Above: With Bruce Forsyth and Frankie Howerd.

Below: Tommy with live studio audience.

With 'the boys', Morecambe and Wise.

Above: An early television appearance.

Below: Tommy at his best.

Above: Tommy in demand.

Below: Tommy with saw head.

Left: 'Spoon, jar, jar, spoon!'

Below: Tommy and Thomas Jr on stage.

An early *Royal Variety Performance*.

Above: Cooper's busy props table.

Below: Recording for ABC Television.

Serious for once.

Above: Practising backstage.

Opposite: After dinner speaking.

Above: Trooper Cooper.

Opposite: Tommy and 'Dove'.

Above: Cooper in the kitchen.

Below: Big hands.

Above: Tommy with one of his idols.

Below: Tommy, but not with one of his idols.

Tommy Cooper wears two outfits: split personality.

sitting on that side. Then, after he had reduced that section to hysterics, he wandered over to the opposite side of the stage where he delivered the exact same jokes, this time to another part of the crowd, almost daring the audience to challenge the audacity of doing the same set twice. It did not matter because the auditorium recognised how unique, surreal, and (one wants to say) revolutionary this all was. The laughs for the reprise were even greater than those he got with the material the first time around.

Many people make the transition from stage to screen. If it works, if it has that inherent quality, it should just be a case of packaging it correctly and holding on to the magic. Tommy was perfectly placed to take his act from stage to television. He emerged in the late 1940s as the new medium was coming to the fore and appeared intermittently thereafter. Usually, it was at a time and place of his own choosing, such was his appeal.

He did just enough to earn recognition and retreated whenever he feared over-exposure. It ensured a clamour for his services, and it enabled him to keep control of his career. Miff knew he had a hot property on his hands. The pair were in the driving seat when in came to dealing with television companies. As the 1960s saw a rush to fill the available screen time and cash in on the growing advertising revenue, both Miff and Tommy were cautious in their approach. They did not have to grab, they were not easily seduced, and they always believed that Cooper's popularity would win the day, whatever the avenue they chose to explore. Tommy, at the time, was simply majestic.

It was probably just as well that Tommy was feeling so sharp mentally, because physically, he was feeling his age. By 1971, he was fifty years old. Today, that seems a trifling figure; it barely seems middle-aged. Back then, to what is almost fifty years ago, it was a different thing. Over fifty, you probably qualified as 'distinguished'. For Tommy, his own ailments were induced by a combination of his lumbering frame and his incredible workload. Add to this the fact that he liked a drink, and that he smoked up to forty cigars a day, and what we have is a recipe for poor health.

Tommy had a problem with varicose veins, for which he had to be admitted to hospital for an operation. He blamed the condition on his hours of sentry duty when he had served with the Royal Horse Guards. All that time spent standing to attention had come back to haunt him later in life.

He also suffered from sciatica and circulatory problems. Luckily, his spell in hospital was a success and, after a period of recuperation, Tommy resumed his relentless workload. He was earning £25,000 a year by the mid-1960s, and this was soon to increase significantly when Tommy agreed to do a television run called *Life with Cooper*. After its huge success, he followed it up with another series of the same name.

Tommy Cooper was made for television. It instantly projected him into the homes of millions of people, and there was so much love and appreciation for him that the medium became his natural stomping ground. Yet it ate up a lot of material, and Tommy's was such a quick-fire routine, full of one-liners, that he needed a production line to help him meet the demand. Despite the huge attraction that television had for him, with the ability to turn him into a household name, Tommy restricted the number of his appearances. Fellow comedian Benny Hill had the same idea. He once said, 'I'd rather people said, "I haven't seen him for a while" rather than "Oh, here he is again"'.

Tommy's early television shows followed the format of his live act—gags and magic tricks, all performed in front of an audience. He rationed his appearances throughout the 1950s and '60s until, towards the latter half of that decade, he made several in succession. The shows ran for three seasons and regularly topped the television ratings. Having limited his exposure on screen, this cautious approach was now paying dividends.

Tommy had always varied his act. It moved effortlessly between comedy and magic. His television shows had a similar split personality. There would be a section with him on stage, doing routines that audiences would recognise as authentic Tommy Cooper material. The difficulty came in producing enough material to feed a whole series. The solution came in the form of a series of sketches (written by a team of experienced television writers) that would be interspersed with his usual routine. As innocent as this idea sounds, Tommy's agent appears to have struggled with it. When the producers pitched ideas to Miff, the dour and somewhat humourless man could not get his head around them. He wanted to protect the image of his artist, but even so, it is hard to comprehend what objections he could have raised to sketches that would feature Tommy in a restaurant (Miff said that Tommy would not go to a restaurant as people would recognise him) or a scene in a labour exchange, which Miff objected to because he would never let Tommy be out of work. These sketches sometimes held Tommy back and took him to unfamiliar ground, despite the fact he gave it his best shot. As Tommy himself said, 'I've got acting in my blood. I have. Many years ago, an actor bit me!' Besides, audiences loved seeing him in a new light. In essence, they just liked seeing him, full stop.

The television writers and producers came to regard Miff as a nuisance, and the manager was increasingly side-lined from production meetings where material was being discussed. Tommy himself appeared happy enough with what was being provided, and he jumped into the new format with both feet. He would happily play the part of Hamlet in one sketch, an angry chef in another, or even as a burglar. In one show, he played the part of a prospective son-in-law, trying to make polite conversation with his girlfriend's parents, while sitting awkwardly between them on the sofa, and trying desperately to balance a cup of tea, a slice of cake, and various other objects, even smoking a cigar at the same time.

Despite the popularity of the series, Miff continued to gripe. First of all, he complained to Tommy about the standard of the scripts for the next television series. He tried to get Tommy to endorse a letter to the television company outlining his disappointment. Tommy said that he could not, in all honesty, put his signature to the letter as he thought the scripts were good and that he was sure he could make something of them.

Miff took his opposition up another level. All of these television appearances were actually designed to serve a higher purpose—namely to elevate Tommy's profile with a worldwide audience and, more specifically, with the American market. The agent put this into a letter that he sent to his client in 1970:

> As you know, the object of the last television series was to produce and develop ideas and projects for feature films and television programmes directed towards the promotion and enhancement of the talents of Tommy Cooper throughout the world.

For all of Miff's meddling, and the fact that he clearly riled many of the professionals working in television, his vision for Tommy's advancement seems to have been well-founded. Unfortunately, it would not be Tommy who would eventually make the jump to global stardom and enjoy the subsequent rewards.

Benny Hill was in the right place at the right time when an enterprising television company was looking for a series to sell overseas. Possibly it was his more extensive back catalogue that won the argument. At that juncture, there is no reason to think that Benny was more popular or had more worldwide appeal than Tommy himself. However, Tommy's limited television appearances meant he had left no more than a couple of dozen shows that were ripe for exploitation, whereas Benny had far more to show for his time on TV. It was a mere twist of fate that led Benny to conquer the world and left Tommy to keep the home fires burning.

As we have seen with Tommy's appearances on *The Ed Sullivan Show*, and the host's glowing endorsement of him as 'The funniest man ever to appear on this stage', there is no reason to think that Tommy could not have had the international success that Benny Hill enjoyed if he had been given the same exposure and opportunity.

Yet it was not all doom and gloom and, in 1969, Tommy won the award for Television Personality of the Year when the last in the *Life with Cooper* series ended. There was also another world opening up to Tommy. In the 1970s, working men's clubs across Britain rose enormously in popularity. These were usually decent-sized venues situated in the heart of working-class communities. The beer was cheap, and the masses flocked to them. For performers, it was a gold mine. The money was good, and it allowed Cooper to do his stage act, which was never more suitable than for a live audience.

So, out on tour to the clubs it was. It would be almost four more years before Tommy made another television series.

23

The V&A

Recently, the Victoria and Albert Museum in London took possession of 119 boxes of material relating to Tommy Cooper. It is due to become available to view online in 2018. In October 2017, this author was granted exclusive access to the archive, the first member of the general public to do so.

Now that all of the documents have been carefully archived, they fit nicely into seventy-seven boxes. Some relate to manager Miff Ferrie's personal diaries. Others hold contracts with nightclubs, television companies, and theatres from across the country. With the limited time available to me, as access was still restricted, I headed inevitably for Tommy's personal gag files. These were housed in a dozen boxes, each containing up to fifteen folders.

The archive is held at Blythe House, close to Kensington Olympia Exhibition Centre in West London. It is an imposing and impressive building. There, I presented my credentials, with access granted by prior appointment only, and having passed through all of the security apparatus, I entered the inner sanctuary.

One by one, I opened the boxes and devoured their content. Do you know how hard it was to try and stop a fit of the giggles when you are in the reading room and study centre of a historic museum?

With regard to the material, what surprised me first of all was how much of it came from Tommy's own pen. I have to say that his handwriting is appalling; my own is not much better than spider-scrawl, and Tommy's was just as bad.

I had always assumed that Tommy had a team of gag writers throughout his career, and that there would be evidence of this in the files. I would say, though, that about 80 per cent of the material appeared to be his own. I can now imagine him sitting backstage or in his hotel room dawdling away, coming up with ideas and jotting them down. What tickled me (apart from the material) was what he had chosen to write the jokes down on. There were no notepads (well, just the one, but more of that later) and instead he used the cardboard linings that come inside every new shirt, and there were absolutely loads of them.

You can understand a performer, living out of a suitcase, buying the odd shirt on his travels over the years and then, experiencing a moment of inspiration, grabbing the closest thing to hand to record his thoughts. However, it looked like he had shares in a tailoring business as there were hundreds of them. It did not make any sense. Then again, neither did his handwriting.

There, on the page, or cardboard shirt-backing, lay many of the jokes that the British people have come to love. All of that stuff was there about backing a horse and it coming in so late that it had to tiptoe back to the stable. There were jokes about 'the wife'. 'I took my wife to the football. I asked the man on the gate how much it was for a ticket. He said £100. I asked how much it was for a programme. He said £10. I said give me a programme, she can sit on that!' They were all there in their unedited glory.

It was not just the cardboard shirt-stiffeners that he used, although they appeared to be his favourite. There were gags written on the back of menus and on theatre flyers. Even with jokes that were properly typed out as scripts, he would turn the page over and write his own jokes on the back.

Occasionally, there were pages of material in different (and much better) handwriting. It was touching to think that these belonged to Val Andrews or Barry Cryer, maybe even Eddie Bayliss. One particular routine was fully sketched out with instructions on how to play it. This likely came from Val Andrews, who included the comment that he had used this gag in his act for more years than he cared to remember and that it had never let him down. 'Trust me,' he wrote, 'do it exactly as it is written and it will work for you a treat'. Andrews was a veteran who had performed a magic and comedy act for many years, so it would make sense if it came from him.

Yet most of the jokes appeared to be Tommy's own work. It made me respect the artist even more. There were twelve boxes holding as many as fifteen files, with each file containing maybe fifty sheets of paper, and each sheet containing maybe twenty jokes (because he did love a one-liner), and that was per each side of paper, making for an awful lot of jokes. As Tommy Cooper once said, 'I wasn't the smartest kid in school, but I was close. About three feet away! I was very good at maths. Two and two is four. Four and four is eight. Eight and eight is … and English, I was very good at that too!' Then he would do that laugh.

There must have been 100,000 jokes in there. Some pieces of paper had longer jokes, or whole sketches, or maybe just the one gag, a scribble on a scrap of a page before the idea melted into the ether. They ranged from the sublime to the ridiculous. I went through all twelve boxes, and constantly found myself laughing—a stifled, knuckle in the teeth, fit of the giggles, while I tried to maintain my dignity in such grand surroundings. I was there among several studious researchers, all lucky enough to have been granted access to archives from the worlds of music, theatre, fashion, and the arts. Yet I do not think anyone in the reading room was having as much fun as me.

As well as the gag files, I was treated to a behind-the-scenes look at the remainder of the archive. There are eleven boxes of contract documentation dating back to the 1950s, testament to Tommy's popularity and his propensity for work, and also to Miff's meticulous note-taking. There are letters from Miff to fellow impresarios when Tommy was going off on tour, to television producers, and to club owners.

Unlike Tommy's haphazard approach, grabbing the closest thing to hand, whether it be the back of a postcard or a restaurant menu or even a page of a script on which to write, Miff took a more gentrified approach. He recorded everything in large, bound A4 diaries. On the inside front cover, there would be an annotated summary of the year. Then, on each of the pages within, there would be more in-depth information about the gig. Open up any year and one is met by an avalanche of bookings—Tommy Cooper was busy, year after year.

There are also personal letters between Tommy and his agent. Some of them are very personal indeed, with the two of them arguing, hurling insults, and falling out, then, occasionally, making up. Some are soaked in red wine—a hint of things to come or that were happening at the time. In these, uninhibited by the drink, the anger flows and they are quite sad and moving to read. Tommy goes so far as to insult Miff's wife in one of them, leading to a big falling out between the two men.

Yet as business continued to boom, it appears that both of them were prepared to brush themselves down and get on with their affairs, with Miff taking the bookings, and Tommy continuously on the road. The show, as they say, must go on.

One cannot help but feel drawn into their world, almost like a fly on the wall, imagining Tommy at his writing desk, a glass of Dubonnet in one hand and a pen in the other, hunched over the paper and pouring his frustrations onto the page.

Elsewhere in the files, there are theatre programmes and photographs that, together with restaurant menus from the many hotels where he stayed, serve to give a well-rounded picture of what a performer's life must be like out on tour.

There are newspaper cuttings containing reviews from shows. Miff kept it all, even down to records of phone calls that were made between him and Tommy, or when someone called to try and book the artist. 'You want my Tommy?' Miff would ask.

This would be met with 'Why else do you think I'm calling!' Then, Miff and whoever was on the other end would talk money and dates, usually in that order.

There is also the V&A museum's own collection of cuttings. They are, after all, the research facility for theatre and the performing arts. There are the obituaries from *The Times* and other distinguished newspapers in the aftermath of Tommy's sudden and tragic demise. He is lauded as one of the biggest stars of his generation. Indeed, one of the greatest, possibly the greatest performer of the twentieth century.

The archive is full of rare finds—gems, in fact. There is a postcard to a Mrs Smith of Poulton-le-Fylde, who may have been a friend, or even a guest housekeeper, running a B&B up near Blackpool. It is from the 1950s, in Tommy's own handwriting, and is written like a three-line ditty:

Here's to thee and thine, from me and mine,
And when me and mine, come to thee and thine,
Me and mine, will be happy to see thee and thine!

There were a couple of times when I cracked up laughing as I sifted through the boxes. I skipped over so much in the time available, but occasionally, something would catch my eye and I would go in for a closer look. It was then that I would likely become hooked and, once in, I could not stop until I had reached the punchline. At one point, I was laid low with a fit of giggles by the following joke:

> I used to perform magic on a cruise-liner, and there was this parrot on board, and every time I'd do a trick, the parrot would shout 'Rubbish'. Then, we hit an iceberg, and there was me and this parrot on a raft. After three days, the parrot turned to me and said 'Okay, I give up. What have you done with the ship!'

Remembering where I was, I did my best to contain myself to a hysterical whimper. Then, I found two pieces of cardboard, again from the lining of a newly bought shirt. The first was marked as number one. The second was number two. I started reading and could not stop. It was a sketch, possibly for a television episode, where a barrister was doing his best to present a guilty-as-sin defendant as an innocent victim of outrageous injustice. It was superb—a masterpiece of innuendo, with a total disregard for not just truth but reality.

At the bottom of page two, the story was mid-joke when it suddenly stopped. I wondered where the rest of it was. I laboured on (in love) through the remainder of the files and, later on, I came across page three and then on the reverse, page four of what I immediately realised was the remainder of the sketch I had earlier been so thoroughly enjoying. Should I mess with the prestigious V&A archive, this carefully catalogued memorandum of memorabilia? This sketch was just too good. The pieces belonged together, and I could not resist reuniting both sections. I later confessed my sin to the curator and was relieved to be told that I had done the right thing, but please, for anyone reading this, do not try this at home.

One of the reasons that I had been given privy access was due to the fact that I had earlier been employed as a documenter and conservator on the restoration of the Albert Memorial, working alongside experts from the V&A itself. This, together with the fact that I had a book deadline, got me into the archive early, before its official opening in 2018. I trusted my conservation ethic and was pleased to know that I had done the right thing in restoring the missing pages to their rightful place. I would not have wanted anyone else to get halfway through the sketch, as I had done, only to be left wondering how the story turned out.

The sketch, if filmed, and I hope it was, must have been hilarious. It is hereby reproduced in full.

> Ladies and gentlemen of the jury, for the past twenty minutes I have sat idly by while my worthy opponent Prosecutor for the Crown has stood up here and made a complete ass of himself. The case is very simple. The defendant, Mrs Erwin Crick, murdered her husband, but that is not the important thing. The important thing is she had a reason. You see she loved him. This shows. She did it with six slams of a 45. Ladies and gentlemen of the jury, she should have been given a medal. Another six shots between the eyes. The prosecuting attorney stood up here and called her a liar, a cheat, a blackmailer, and a homicidal maniac. Now, ladies and gentlemen of the jury, none of us is perfect! Look at her sitting there. I want you to pay particular attention to her legs. Notice the well-turned calf, the slim ankles. Now I ask you. Has she got the legs of a homicidal maniac? Of course not. Do you have any idea what this woman has been through since this trial began? Beaten and battered by all sides by questions. She sits on a chair, cowed with fear, hanging like a tense spring. Clerk of the court, will you wake the defendant. Get her up in her seat there. It's been easy for the prosecutor to stand up here and accuse her of all these horrible crimes. It's easy for him. He's got proof! What about me? I've got nothing but trickery and deceit! See what we can do with that. Your Honour. Your Honour. Clerk of the court, will you wake the judge up. Sorry Your Honour, I was talking in your sleep. I object strongly to the unfair, unethical method of the prosecutor trying to influence the foreman of this jury, Mr George Rack, who we all know is a fine upstanding citizen of the community, above and which it has come to my attention that today is his birthday, so the clerk and I have chipped in and bought you this little watch. Eighteen carat gold. Read the inscription on the back. 'To the foreman of the jury that acquitted Mrs Erwin Crick'. Now, I'd like to call to the stand the prosecution's star witness, Mr Ben-Starr. Now, Mr Starr, did you or did you not insinuate on the night in question, January 19th, it was blimey not bloxey

> that was seen at Cathy's place, and also it wasn't until Friday the 14th that you found the pawn ticket in the overcoat, and on the strength of this you have this jury and this court believe that the clerk is in chuffs with the cocker-spaniel, and ladies and gentlemen of this jury, I have in my hand an old copy of a 1953 Taverner's Almanac which states that on that night there was no moon, so how could you have possibly seen anything?

This, and many, many more gems, were contained in the Tommy Cooper archive.

24

The Joke Files

Tommy says he went on holiday and came back to find 2,000 bottles of milk on the doorstep. The next morning, the milkman came around, and Tommy said he had been away. 'Thank goodness,' the milkman replied, 'I thought you'd gone off the stuff!'

This, and much, much more was stashed inside the many boxes and piles of paper in the V&A. There is a routine for a Variety Club luncheon written on the back of a page taken from a magazine, *The Comedian*, Volume 14, Number 5. There is a routine for a double act between Tommy and an unnamed magician, with Jack Benny listed as the compère for the event. Another set-sheet alludes to his second show, with the act listed being completely different to the first set.

Then there is an in-depth routine, one of Val Andrews's, that requires the use of an assistant or member of the audience. It is called the 'eye' card routine. On Tommy's forehead, he is meant to place a playing card, that he has surreptitiously seen prior to placing it there. The assistant places another card on their forehead, on which there is a picture of an eye. Tommy is supposed to read his own card by psychically projecting via the 'eye' card, summoning up all his psychic powers in the process. 'I cannot stress the high entertainment value of this card stunt,' Val writes. 'I have used it for more years than I care to remember, and it has been priceless to me'. What did Tommy do with it? Turned the piece of paper over and wrote on the back of it.

Another card starts with the heading of 'Warm up'. Knowing these jokes off by heart, Tommy has abbreviated his set-list thus: 'Good evening, goodnight gag. Parking gag. Stable gag. Zulu gag. Shakespeare gag. Woolworths gag. Battery hen. Pony trick'. He even opens with a 'Ha!' He knew his stuff.

Another act, for a hotel show, shows how slick he could be: 'Opening, bring on table, rope trick, into spoons and tails, hotel gags, into flying gags, into horse riding gags, into tricks, into hats. Finis!' On the back of this set list, he has written 'The band look upset. I don't know why. Before the show I bought them a drink. So why are they so upset? Looks at band. Oh, you wanted one each!'

From his television appearances, there are also priceless insights in the joke files. There is a letter from Liverpool comedian Tom O'Connor to a man called Dennis. This is presumably Dennis Kirkland, who produced many of Tommy's television shows over the years. The letter is headed 're Tommy Cooper's guest spot'.

It contains a couple of ideas for quick crossovers during the forthcoming show.

> Tom O'Connor on stage. On comes Tommy Cooper dressed as a monk.
> Cooper: Did you know I use to work in a chip shop?
> O'Connor: Really? As a fryer, I suppose.
> Cooper: No, as a chip-monk, you fool!
> Exit Tommy Cooper.

There are dozens more cardboard shirt-backs. One begins with the heading 'Opening patter'. Another reads, 'Opening routine'. Looking through, you come across familiar gags. 'I've always been unlucky, me. When I was a kid, I had a rocking horse. It died!' There are also ones I had never heard before. 'It's only natural to be nervous at the beginning of a show, but please don't be'. There is also a whole folder of the opening patter stuff. Another is marked 'Performance material—tricks'.

His 'Tricks in pocket' is written on the back of a menu from the Old Sugar Loaf hotel in Dunstable, where a three-course meal would have cost seventeen shillings and sixpence in old money. That night's performance featured a range of material, from parachute jokes to wife gags.

Next up is a five-page handwritten sketch, with Tommy playing Sherlock Holmes, someone playing Watson, in a story about a vampire bat; I bet that has been filmed somewhere.

Then it is back to the shorter stuff. 'I went to a Turkish bath. You've never heard such screaming and shouting in your life. How was I to know it was ladies' night!'

There were some more old post cards labelled 'Tricks, props, etc.,' before listing the following items; one long coat, one hat, one fez, one chicken, one battery hen, plates and jug, black suit, grey suit, blue suit, raincoat, overcoat.

Ever resourceful, Tommy has even cut one piece of cardboard into three long strips. He must have been running out of new shirts that day.

Another folder is marked 'Handwritten performance material—Stand up'. Inside, there are routines for everywhere from the Variety Club to Smiths nightclub. One of them opens with the words 'I'm here tonight through the magic of money'. He goes on to say that he makes greetings cards, but 'they are a different kind of greeting card, such as "Happy Wednesday!" No reason for it. Just Happy Wednesday. Or "Congratulations on having your shoes soled," or "Good luck with your haircut"'. Then he moves on to one of those rambling stories that he did so well, always interspersed with his trademark laughs, from short-burst chuckle to manic guffaw, or the inclusion of 'Not like that, like that'.

He stares off into the distance and allows the audience to see what he can see. He begins.

'Elephants are remarkable. They range for miles and miles, over mountains and through jungles to a place where they're going to die, and they die there. The trip, it kills them!' Then, he would laugh at his own joke. Then he would do some magic. 'I call this my pilgrim trick. Every time I do it, I make a little progress'.

Next came a sketch that read like it may have been written for, or performed by, the Goons. It is an exchange between two people.

'What did you do in the war?' one asks the other.

'There was a war?' comes the reply.

It goes on to say that the man had personally shot down eighty-five English flyers, by mistake, and he still has them in case there is another war. Spike Milligan would have been proud.

Speaking of the Goons, there is a great photo in the press cuttings of Tommy and his family on the steps outside a church at Thomas Jr's christening. The fanfare of the day is all too much for the infant and he is bawling his eyes out. Gwen pulls him close to her cheek to soothe him, while Tommy, alongside friends Harry Secombe and Norman Wisdom, all bawl their eyes out too in emulation of the crying child. It is a fabulous picture.

Ad-lib lines complete the 'Stand-up' folder. I then exchanged this box for another, while wondering what I was going to find in this one. I was in a large study room, surrounded by in-depth and weighty tomes such as volume after volume of *The London Stage*, *The Cambridge History of the British Stage*, and *Who's Who in the Theatre*. There were dozens of volumes of *The Theatre Record*, though I knew that I could not afford to get distracted. This was a flying visit, and I had a lot to get through, all of it good. I forewent lunch, asking if there was a place where I could get a drink. I was told there was a café up the street that was quite nice, but time was too precious at the moment and I settled for a trip to the bathroom instead, before returning to the next box and the next gag.

'I phoned the police station this morning and I said "Have any lunatics escaped from the asylum?" The policeman said "No. Why?" I said "Because someone's run off with my wife!"'

He tells us how he was so excited on his first day at school that he cut himself shaving. Then he says that he does not have to do this for a living, he could always lose weight and be a jockey again! This in spite of his size. Then he says he grew up. He had to—what other way could he grow! The gags come thick and fast.

There is stuff belonging to other people. Writer Jimmy Muir presents something that he calls 'Laugh lines'. There is a selection of jokes that were served up like a menu for Tommy to choose from. A couple of good ones, too, like the deep-sea diver who gets the message to come up quick because the ship is sinking, or when the mother-in-law moves in and he says 'Mother, I want you to think of this as your own home' and the next day she sold it. There was also the following: 'Some folks say when they drink coffee, they can't sleep. I'm the reverse. When I sleep, I can't drink coffee!' The gag writer seems to have a penchant for those cardboard shirt-backs too, although his handwriting is much clearer than Tommy's. The question remains: why the ubiquitous use of these pieces of cardboard?

There was more from Jim Muir, including this one, which you can almost hear Tommy saying: 'If your wife enjoys flowers, let her know that you remember by mentioning it occasionally'.

'He got run over by a brewery wagon. It was the first time the drinks were on him'. This could have been a writer's dig at the notoriously tight-fisted Tommy.

Then it is back to Tommy. This must have come from a nightclub routine, probably one that was used to break down a difficult audience, or as an opening line after a less-than-enthusiastic reception. 'I'd like to say something funny, but I don't want to break the spell'.

After sifting through hundreds of single pieces of paper, bits of cardboards, backs of menus, postcards, even the back of old envelopes, I finally came across an A4 notebook with lined paper. It was old and well-worn, called an S. O. book, which had been supplied for the public service. Tommy possibly picked it up in his Army days, and the material within seemed to date from that time.

Already predicting his future performing career, there are heckler-stoppers on one page. Then, over several pages, possibly predicting his future personal life, there is a sketch for Tommy and Gwen that must have been one that they performed for the troops. It is similar in tone to the one where they had a huge row and caused a stagehand, when they were rehearsing, to think it real and almost call the police.

Yet the sketch is quite moving, despite the arguing couple, for in it they refer to a small child, their daughter, who they have named Amber. It must predate Vicky's birth by five years or more, but already the longing and the expectation of family life is there.

Finally, on the second-to-last page of the notebook, there is something of Tommy himself. It is the first personal thing to be found in the gag files, for it appears to be the beginning of a letter from Tommy, possibly to his mother, before he returned to the UK. Perhaps he planned to tear out the page and send it to her.

He writes 'I must say married life is a wonderful partnership and I wouldn't be single again for all of the money in the world. So once again I'll write giving you all the news first hand. Until then, please don't worry. Yours sincerely, Tommy'.

It was a rare glimpse into the real world, in among the thousands of gags that helped form his career.

25

More from the Archive

As well as the professional writers that Tommy worked with, there were some talented amateurs too, such as Eddie Bayliss, a lorry driver from Liverpool who intuitively 'got' Tommy's humour. He sent some speculative sketches to Miff, who immediately spotted their potential. I did not recognise any of Eddie's work among the gag files in the archive, but I did come across another enthusiastic fan who was obviously trying to get his foot on the writing ladder. His name was Bryan Hawkins of Wooding Dean in Sussex.

Bryan had gone to the trouble of sending in what looks like a comic book, with hand-drawn pictures and gags for scenes that Tommy could perform. It is quite a clever idea, easy to get your head around, and Miff must surely have given them some consideration. The ideas, on close inspection, appear to fall short of what would be considered suitable for a television audience of millions. He must, however, have received some encouragement for his efforts, for the sketchbooks keep coming. Along the way, Bryan adds his phone number to the front page, ever hopeful of getting that all-important call.

I did not recognise any of Tommy's jokes in more than a dozen books that Hawkins, the aspiring writer, has sent in, but the fact that they remain in the archive means they may well have played some part. One gag I did recognise came in a slightly varied form. Tommy is to come on stage with an object, describe it as 'priceless' before breaking it apart to show exactly what it was made of. The object in the original sketch had no merit in itself, but Tommy came up with a variant. There is a sketch that Tommy performed on television where the object that he used was more appropriate than the one suggested in the original idea. It was a wand—better suited to a magic act—and Tommy had great fun with it. 'See this wand,' he said. 'It was given to me by the Magic Circle. It is one of a kind, unique, and absolutely priceless'. He then snaps the wand in half. 'I mean, look at that grain!'

As well as the material that came through the post, Miff also took possession of a great deal of fan mail. This would be collated on Tommy's behalf and presented to him when the opportunity arose. I found a large manila envelope with 'For Tommy' written across the front. Never one to waste a good piece of parchment, Tommy had used the back of it to write out more gags. He would probably do this on the tube-ride home after a visit to Miff's office.

I even found a few jokes written on the back of an obituary to a leading light of the Variety Club. This is not in Tommy's handwriting and refers to 'A hat too big for you so it goes right over your ears'. It is followed by a props list, so the author of the piece may have been Thomas Jr, who worked with his dad for many years. The list is very detailed and includes everything, even down to the size of the props table required, which was stated as being 6 to 8 feet long.

Then it was the Crown Court sketch, soon to be reunited with the other parts of the story. Thrilled, I kept reading. Having enjoyed the first half so much, I found gems in the second part too. The barrister defending asks his (guilty) client. 'What were you doing last night?'

'I was in Lovers Lane,' she replies.

'What are you doing tonight?' is his lightning-quick response.

There is a set list for his entire act at the Winter Gardens from Sunday, 4 February 1968, where lunch could be had for twelve shillings and sixpence. Then we are back to the handwritten jokes.

'My wife said she had to go to the beauty shop and have a mud-pack put on her face. And I must say, she looked beautiful. And then the mud fell off!'

Then I found the second item that caused me much embarrassment as I tried to stifle my laughter in the gilded surroundings of the Victoria and Albert Museum. I love Tommy's storytelling, and this was just great. I could almost hear him saying it out loud as I read it.

An actor got a part in a play mid-run when the first actor playing the role fell ill. He was called up at short notice but told 'Don't worry. You've only got one line. It's "Hark, I hear the cannons roar"'. The actor caught a train to the theatre and all the way there, practised his line. Over and over, a thousand times. 'Hark, I hear the cannons roar'. Come the night, the actor was given his cue and he walked out on stage to deliver his one and only line. Then, off, there was a huge, resounding boom, and the actor shouted, 'What the bloody hell was that?' You try keeping that one to yourself in the middle of the reading room at the V&A.

In the next folder in the box, there were thirty-one index cards, each containing about a dozen jokes in alphabetical order. They were meant to run 'A' to 'Z', but only contained jokes from 'A' to 'W'. He had nothing for 'X', 'Y', or 'Z'. They were full of typed one-liners, so again probably came from one of his professional or aspiring writers.

'A' was for audience: 'You lot are looking at me like I invented the Income Tax'.

'B' was for butcher: 'I know my butcher is using dodgy scales. The other day, I didn't buy anything and he charged me six pounds'.

'C' was for children: 'My advice to modern day parents is never to strike your child. They might be armed!'

Another box contained further gag files, also listed 'A' to 'Z'. For 'D', you could take your pick from dancing, deafness, or dieting. We have all heard a few of Tommy's dentist jokes, but I had not heard this one before: 'I always wanted to be a dentist, but my hands were too big. Before I could get to the back teeth, I had to pull all of the front ones out!'

I came across two compendia of jokes, one by Billy Glason and another by Eddie Gay. Billy was a US comic who compiled a twenty-six-part encyclopaedia of gags. Eddie's was a more compact collection of 100 jokes. Both of them had an American lilt, and I found one joke repeated in both. It was the one that Tommy told about the lion and the elephant, and Tommy had placed an asterisk at its side, clearly indicating that this was one that he thought he could use. Which writer he credited, or paid, is unknown—probably none of them.

In the reviews, I came across a piece by the esteemed author J. B. Priestley. He provided a literary summary of an early Cooper performance and dissected the artist's act with some in-depth critique. He said:

> Women do not warm to Tommy's act because it is altogether too daft for them. On stage, where he might be even closer to them, he altogether alarms them. That craggy, convulsed face, the sudden daft grin, those rolling eyes, and above all the insane high giggle that make us feel we might have here a dangerous lunatic. But then we realize that we are watching the performance of a well-known comic.

Cooper had ridden to success in the aftermath of the great era of the music hall and had made a successful transition to television. Stars of the day included Frankie Howerd, and later Benny Hill and Morecambe and Wise. Tommy stood shoulder to shoulder with them all, yet never understood or believed he was their equal. As well as the gag-files, there are many press clippings and interviews that shed light on Tommy's life and career.

He got half of his jokes, he said, by listening to people—a tip that his hero Max Miller had given him. He said he once picked up half a set at a visit to his local barber in Chiswick.

Fellow comedian and a friend of Tommy, Cardiff-born Stan Stennet said, 'In real life, he was very much like he was on stage and television, always trying a gag out and always getting it wrong'. It seems that Tommy looked for the humour in every situation. If he was not on, he was not happy. The first time he met one television producer, he looked nervous. They were in the bar at the studio.

'Roy,' said Tommy, 'I've got to tell you something, Roy. I don't know how to say this Roy, but Roy, I've forgotten your name!'

One interviewer, Peter Black, wrote 'He never tries to analyse why everybody finds him funny'. Tommy said in response, 'The idea of working is to make your life more comfortable, but I get a lot of pleasure out of making people laugh. The longest holiday I've had is about a month. I always like to get back to work. It isn't work, really, doing what you like'.

He talked about that first ever performance at the boatyard Christmas party. 'As soon as the curtains parted, I dried up. I couldn't remember a word. Then the tricks all went wrong'. He would eventually come to see his act as 10 per cent skill and 90 per cent cheek. He had the talent and personality to get away with gags that no one else could. As he once said, at the beginning of a show, 'That was my best joke, from here on in it's nerve!'

Yet he would not be distracted from his goal. In the early days of his career, before he got his break with Miff, his confidence occasionally wavered. Then there would be Gwen to give him a pep talk and pick him up again, and off he would go. He continued to show up for auditions and took whatever bookings he could. He also mixed with other aspiring artists, always on the lookout for openings and opportunities.

Eric Sykes recalled the first time the two of them met. It was in the Clachan pub, behind the famous Liberty department store in central London. The interior was dimly lit and exuded an 'olde-worlde' charm. Eric was talking to the barman. A natural storyteller, he was regaling the man behind the bar with details of the time he was dropped onto the wrong beach at Normandy during the Second World War.

Mid-conversation, Eric became aware of a large presence looming at his side. The pub was not nearly so full as to require someone to be in such close proximity. Eric turned around to see what the gentleman wanted. The big man spoke: 'I'm Tommy Cooper,' he said. 'I know who you are. You do Frankie Howerd's scripts. Can I buy you a drink?'

'I'm okay. No thanks,' Eric replied. Had he known how rare the offer was, Eric might have accepted. That said, Tommy must have been struggling for money at the time, so the offer is twice as surprising. From there, the two men walked to the Bag o' Nails club, where Tommy had a gig, and they parted at the door. It would be years before Eric even caught Tommy's act, but what they shared was a great friendship. By the time they came to do Eric's film together, *The Plank*, Eric was able to describe his old pal thus, as recorded in Jeremy Novick's Cooper biography:

> He is the funniest man in the world. Initially, Peter Sellars was going to play Tommy's part, but Peter went off to Hollywood, so I had to re-cast. When I thought of Tommy, I realised it was an inspirational choice. From that

> moment, I knew the film was going to be a success. And Tommy jumped at the chance to play a part where he didn't have to speak, no words to learn, and only one costume. By now, this wasn't the timid conjurer who had disappeared into the Bag o' Nails all them years before. This was a colossus who sat astride the world of comedy.

This was high praise indeed from someone qualified to know—a colossus indeed, both in life and on stage, and the V&A is now the repository of all the ingredients that went into his act, gags and magic, in their hundreds and thousands.

26

Going Out Live

Apart from that failed performance at the boatyard Christmas party, Tommy said he had never 'died' on stage. The tabloid press made much of the fact that he had died on stage during a live transmission. The broadsheet papers were a little more dignified in their approach. *The Times* newspaper called him 'A first-class conjurer', and friend and actor Ron Moody called him, 'The comedian's comedian'.

The funeral was organised by Davy Kaye, chairman of the Grand Order of Water Rats organisation. He said that, though Tommy was legendarily tight with his money, he was generous with his time. He'd lost count of the number of charity events Tommy had appeared at. He said in *The Times* that 'The response has been absolutely overwhelming. I have never known anything like it. So many people have been in touch. It was all very moving'.

His local paper in Chiswick was similarly full of praise, saying Tommy was a well-known figure in the area, a regular at pubs such as the Barley Mow or the Hole in the Wall, and at restaurants such as the Ganges Tandoori. He was described as a loving family man.

Three months after his passing, there was a service of remembrance held at St Thomas in the Field church in Covent Garden, attended by stars from the worlds of television and variety such as Jimmy Tarbuck, Paul Daniels, Russ Abbot, and Danny La Rue. They came together to pay homage to a giant of comedy who had enlightened their lives and careers.

Six months after his death, Christie's, the famous London auction house, sold eighty lots of Tommy's props and tricks. Among them was a motorised revolving fez with a cockerel weather vane on top, a ventriloquist's dog, and a snake basket. The auction raised £7,500. One lot was bought by Adrian Edmondson, at the time one of the country's finest young comics. Edmondson later professed to be disappointed with his purchase. He had expected to find a world of magic inside the box, but it just looked like a pile of old junk. It probably was, and only in Tommy's hands could it ever amount to magic.

Gwen had decided to hold the sale to free up space at home. Thomas Jr was about to move back in, following the break-up of his marriage. The auction decluttered two whole bedrooms and a garage. Gwen kept hold of a cupboard full of fezzes. She professed not to know why. 'I must be fond of them, I guess,' she said.

Although he had been away on tour almost all of his professional life, Cooper's death left a huge hole in the family home. Further heartache was to come in the revelation that Tommy had another woman in his life. Mary Kay was a stage manager who came into Tommy's circle, first professionally, and then personally. She had filled the void when Dove had stopped going on tour with Tommy. It was not long before her involvement became common knowledge.

Again, the tabloids had a field day. Gwen, still reeling from the loss of the love of her life, now had to contemplate that someone else held a place in Tommy's affections. She processed the information and decided that it was more smoke than fire. It had been, though, an open secret in the entertainment industry. Tommy had needed someone with him. Gwen could not do it; Mary Kay could, and so she did.

Both Vicky and Thomas Jr were aware of Mary's presence and the part she played in Cooper's life. With Thomas Jr joining his dad on tour, it was an impossible secret to keep. By then, Tommy was not in the best of health, so it is easier to envisage this as a relationship about companionship and not necessarily passion. Gwen insisted that her husband and this other woman must have slept together just once. Then, he just could not get rid of her. He was too soft-hearted for his own good.

Vicky Cooper said:

> Dad hated his own company, and he was an insomniac. Mum simply got fed up of the hours he kept and eventually stopped going on tour with him. But he desperately needed someone with him. Someone to look after him. He had ulcers on his legs, and fluid on his lungs, but he was a workaholic and always carried on. Though he cut down on the smoking and switched to non-alcoholic lager in the end, it was too little too late. It was the booze and cigars and the late nights that killed him.

His health had been deteriorating for years. That large frame was a lot to drag around. First of all, he had problems with his legs. One time, he broke his ankle walking along the gangway of a submarine while on holiday with the family in Gibraltar. This only exacerbated the problems that he already had.

There were those varicose veins, the sciatica, and his bronchitis to contend with. After any period of convalescence, he'd soon be back at work. Then, on holiday, this time in Rome in 1977, he had a suspected heart attack.

Ever the performer, Tommy had scheduled a show in the Italian capital for 950 British delegates at an IBM convention. There, he fell ill and was rushed to hospital, before he was eventually released after treatment. Yet he did not slow down. He struggled on, with nightclub performances across the country in the 1970s, where he was billed as a 'Superstar Comedian'.

There were television shows in the 1960s and 1970s, which were hugely popular with the general public, and were critically reviewed in the press. Alan Coren, in *The Times* in 1975, described one such show. He said that Tommy reminded him of King Kong: some strange, outsized, mythical creature, wondering how it got here, and not quite of this world.

Although there was some truth to the opinion that Tommy looked lost in the world in which he found himself, Coren was not so much referring to the everyday world as much as Tommy's predicament in some of the sketches. Coren questioned the very format of the productions. Tommy's act just did not belong on this type of show. The reviewer said he felt sorry for Tommy, and imagined him atop one of those broadcasting masts, clinging to it like the aforementioned creature, trying to tear it down for all the pain it had caused him.

Sometimes, the sketches worked. Sometimes they did not. Alan Coren's review was not very flattering about the format and the success of the shows. He did not blame Tommy for any shortcomings in the production. He merely felt that it was not the best way to use this incredible performer. Fault lay with the television producers themselves, he said, and possibly with the writers, for trying to change a winning formula.

Back to the stage, where Tommy's dresser of nine years' standing was summoned to court and fined £30 for stealing £40 from the performer. It was time for a new helper, which is probably where Mary Kay came in.

Also in Tommy's entourage was his son, Thomas Jr. He had theatrical ambitions of his own and earned his Equity card after studying drama at Chiswick Polytechnic. He had to take his mother's maiden name as the actors' union would not allow two Tommy Coopers, so he called himself Thomas Henty. He did not really mind. He was no comic actor himself. He thought that the villain was the best part to play, and he thought that 'Henty' sounded more menacing than 'Cooper'.

Tommy adored his boy. Vicky recalls one afternoon when the family were all at home. She, a typical teenager, was making fun of her little brother and the new set of clothes he was wearing. When the ribbing reached its peak, Cooper broke in with 'Leave him alone. He's a good 'un'.

Dove recalled her first kiss with Tommy on that tour bus back in Egypt, when Cooper had placed his head on her shoulder. 'It was a lovely kiss,' she said. That was the first time they ever got lovey-dovey, and she thinks that's when Tommy first came up with his nickname for her.

Tommy loved her treacle-puddings—he loved everything she made, in fact, and what Dove really liked to do was bake. It was one thing she really came to miss, cooking for him.

'He adored my home-cooking, did Tommy,' she would tell the *Daily Mail* a decade after his death. He also liked plenty of cheese. She was still minded to recall how much she had loved him from the very first moment she saw him, with his gorgeous blue eyes, and beautiful hair: thick and dark brown. 'I was very much in love with him,' she said, 'and stayed that way for nearly forty years'. She ended by saying that she still missed him terribly.

For Dove, the Mary Kay story came and went. It was yesterday's news, while her love for the man she had married would always remain. They had climbed the showbiz ladder together, Dove supporting and prompting, Tommy trying to reach the top. They had wanted kids, but that did not happen easily. Seven long years they had waited; eventually, it happened, first with daughter Vicky and then with Thomas Jr.

The couple were over the moon. Dove says that Tommy was an excellent father who adored his children and always entertained them. Of herself, she says he used to hug her constantly. She can still feel him doing it. On the night he left for his last performance, he hugged her five times before leaving the house.

He was particularly nervous before the show. He was troubled by the fact that it was going out as a live transmission. Despite his many years on the road, and that he was a seasoned professional, he was more anxious about that night's bill than he had been in years. Gwen noticed it, Thomas Jr noticed it, and Eric Sykes thought it odd that Cooper should have called him on the actual day of the performance to ask him to watch the programme that night. It was out of character.

On top of Tommy's drinking and smoking and his general ill-health, he was stressed about that evening's performance. It was to be his very last. He died exactly as he had lived: making people laugh. Ultimately, that was the thing that he really loved to do; he was simply born to entertain.

27

The Gag Writers

Val Andrews worked with Tommy Cooper for thirty-five years. He was responsible for some of the comedian's most famous jokes and sketches. He was a veteran performer, with a comedy magic act cut from the same cloth as Tommy's. He was born in Brighton, the son of an architect, on 15 February 1926. He was named Val as he was born just a few hours after Valentine's Day. His father introduced him to magic and, like Tommy Cooper, he fell in love with it straight away.

In 1943, Val moved to London and immediately made friends with a group of fellow magicians. He began performing on the stage under the names 'The Great Valentino' and 'Val Vox, the Magical Raconteur'. He was also a talented ventriloquist and music hall artiste, as well as being a prolific writer. In 1952, he published a book called *Commercial Comedy*, and later followed this up with another called *Val's Varieties*.

One night, Val had just finished a performance and was leaving the stage, only to find Tommy Cooper waiting in the wings. Tommy asked him who wrote his material. 'I do,' came the reply.

'Well, I want you to write for me,' said Tommy. It was the start of a relationship that would last several decades. Tommy was always on the lookout for new stuff to do.

Andrews contributed more than 1,000 articles on magic to various magazines, and is also the writer of more than twenty Sherlock Holmes books when the Arthur Conan Doyle franchise was revamped. In 2006, he was presented with the John Nevil Maskelyne prize by the Magic Circle; this was for his outstanding contribution to the field. He even wrote a book about Houdini.

He observed Tommy Cooper closely and said, 'Years of hard work and experience went into honing the perfect comic article'. It was even Val's suggestion that Tommy should remove his fez at the end of every performance to reveal that magnificent mane of hair. It was something that Tommy would do throughout his career, thanks to Val.

Val Andrews's writing partner was Freddie Sadler, a compère and impressionist who plied his trade on the comedy circuit. Sadler attempted to flesh out his meagre earnings by writing material for others, most notably Tommy Cooper. He worked on many of his early television shows and helped create many of Cooper's favourite sketches. Val says 'Hats' is half him and half Sadler. Freddie continued to write for Tommy right up until the end of his career.

People were always trying to talk Tommy into using their material. One time, someone pitched him a new idea. 'There's this trick, see,' the bloke said. 'You take a card, and you crack a few jokes, then you do a bit more with the card, and you tell a few more jokes. You've got the audience cracking up at this point, then you do a bit more with the card, and you crack a few more good 'uns. Then, the card ends up stuck in a rat trap. What do you think?'

A bemused Tommy replied, 'Never mind the bleeding card trick, where's all these fucking gags?'

Another person who wrote for Tommy was Barry Cryer. Born in Leeds, he went to university to study English literature but left after receiving his first-year results. Luckily, he had been spotted performing in a university review and was offered an audition by an agent called Vivian Van Damm at London's Windmill Theatre. He passed with flying colours and started work there that very night.

Barry suffered from eczema and had to be hospitalised several times. He was released from his contract by Van Damm and decided to try his hand at writing instead. He began by doing sketches for The Fortune Theatre, and also wrote nightclub shows for the popular drag act Danny La Rue. From there, he was talent-spotted by David Frost and joined the team at *The Frost Report* alongside such luminaries as John Cleese, Graham Chapman (both of Monty Python), and Marty Feldman. It was an association that lasted for many years and led to Cryer writing for some of the biggest stage and television stars of their day, including The Two Ronnies, Morecambe and Wise, and Les Dawson, as well, of course, as Tommy Cooper. Cryer has even written for American greats Bob Hope and Richard Pryor. He is considered one of the finest television comedy writers of all time. He wrote for Cooper for a great many years. In July 2017, he received an honorary doctorate from Leeds University, so he finally got his degree after all.

Eddie Bayliss was one of Tommy's favourite writers. He contributed many of the most memorable of all Tommy's jokes, including the 'My feet are killing me' and the 'I had a ploughman's lunch the other day' gags. Despite the fact he never gave up his day job, he wrote whole episodes for Tommy's television series such as *It's Tommy Cooper*, which ran between 1969 and 1971. He added further material to *The Tommy Cooper Hour* in 1978 and *Cooper's Half Hour* in 1980. He seemed to share Tommy's worldview, walking that fine line between genius and madness, with a heightened sense of the ridiculous. It is Bayliss that we have to thank for placing the sword on the ground in front of the Queen at the Royal Variety Gala Performance. Even Her Majesty herself laughed at that one. In fact, she literally shouted.

Barry Cryer claims that you cannot copyright a joke—they have all been around forever, and they are either borrowed or adjusted but that they are just there in the ether, waiting to be plucked from the air and then told afresh. It depended on the telling, and who was telling it.

As Barry Cryer said:

> You saw the joke on the page and you saw Tommy telling it. They're not the same thing. Tommy was brilliant. It was a shared joke with the audience: almost like a conspiracy. He would do an awful joke, laugh himself, and the audience would laugh with him. It was almost like he implied to the crowd, 'I know this joke is terrible, and you know this joke is terrible'. That's funny.

Barry Cryer then went on to say that Tommy was highly regarded by his fellow comedians. He broke all the rules and, like all great comedians, he understood that it could end at any minute—maybe this would be the night that audiences would see through his act, would find him out, and his career would end. So, in response, 'knock 'em dead every night. Never let your guard down'. Tommy did this for so many years, his brilliant performances served up on a foundation of gratitude, containing not an ounce of complacency. Yet Cryer then is correct: some of Tommy's jokes were awful.

'I had a dream I was plucking a chicken,' Tommy said. 'I woke up and my wife was bald!' That was probably one of Cooper's own, but I wonder who came up with that spectacular bit of business which is probably one of Tommy's best-known and best-loved sketches.

It is the one where Tommy wheels a large three-sided box onto the stage. He taps all three sides, rapping it with his knuckles, then almost crying with pain at having done so. He delivers the words 'Empty, empty, empty,' to show that there is nothing in the box. To further illustrate this, he climbs inside and pulls a curtain across the front. Then he suddenly throws it open again in one of the best bits of timing in the whole of comedy.

'It's dark in there,' he says, before clutching at his heart as he would often portentously do. He steps out of the box, closes the curtain behind him, and then asks for a drum roll. He pulls in a drum roll from the left of the stage, then a drum roll from the right of the stage, and finally a drum roll from the front of the stage. There's a great big build-up, surely deserving of a suitably momentous pay-off.

When the drums thunder to a crescendo, Tommy pulls back the curtain to reveal nothing. He looks inside, as if someone was there but now they've gone. He looks confused, flummoxed, surprised and disappointed. Then he shrugs as if to say 'never mind' before moving on with the next trick. The failed magician fails again.

Whoever created it must have been an absolute genius. If it was not Tommy Cooper, it was someone with a complete understanding of his comic skills. No one else could have made as much out of the trick as Cooper did. His doleful expression was priceless, the result of yet another disappointment.

Another favourite of mine (and everyone else's) is the trick (or gag) Tommy performed at the 1953 Royal Variety show. This was the first of what would eventually be five appearances at the event. There is a variant of this in the joke files of Billy Glason that Tommy would eventually purchase, so maybe that is the right place to give credit. Anyway, for his inaugural performance in front of Her Majesty the Queen, Tommy did this.

He placed his top hat upside down on his props table and moved about 6 feet away. Then, from a pack of cards, he took one and attempted to throw it into the upturned hat. The card flew through the air and went awry, landing elsewhere on the stage.

'Missed,' Tommy informed us.

He tried again, with the same disappointing result.

'Missed,' Tommy repeated. 'Now, if the next one misses, I shall shoot myself,' he said.

Then he tried again and it missed. Tommy, with the look of a condemned man, walked off stage to meet his fate. There was a loud gunshot. A moment later, Tommy reappeared.

'Missed!' he said and laughed.

Looking through the Cooper archive, I came across a sketch that I know and love. It is one that we have included in *The Tommy Cooper Show*, only this was different—this was more. Imagine finding more of your favourite thing. Fascinated, I read on.

I am referring to the famous story that Tommy told about the girl he once fell in love with. There she sat, on Waterloo Bridge, dangling her feet in the water. She had beautiful golden hair, all down her back, but with none on her head. She had a cute button nose that turned up, then down, and then sideways. They used to go to the beach and play in the sand. She would bury him in the sand, then he would bury her in the sand. One day, he is going to go back and dig her up.

He bought her a stick of rock, and she bit into it, and then she started to cry.

'What's the matter, love?' he asked.

'I've broken a tooth,' she replied through her tears.

'Never mind, love,' he said. 'You've got one left!'

He bought her the best set of false teeth that money could buy, and then she left him. He was broken-hearted, absolutely devastated. A year later, he saw her coming towards him in the street, and she started laughing at him. Then, he added, 'With my own teeth!'

In the archive, in among all of those gems, there were several more to choose from. From whose pen they came I do not know. I credit Barry Cryer, but I cannot be sure.

From that famous Waterloo Bridge sketch, there were these additional items.

> She was a red-head—no hair, just head.
>
> Her brother said to me, 'She smokes in bed'.
>
> I said, 'What's wrong with that'.
>
> He said, 'Face down?'
>
> She rolled her eyes at me, and I rolled them back at her.
>
> It was love at first sight. I wish I'd had a second look.
>
> Next time I saw her she was in her front garden, lying on the grass with a straw in her mouth, siphoning petrol out of the lawnmower.
>
> She was the only girl I know who could eat an apple through a tennis racket.
>
> I said to her, 'I will love you when you are old and wrinkled, worn, bent, and grey, but I won't be with you'. This gets a tick and then a cross from Tommy. He planned to use it and then changed his mind.
>
> We met at the seaside and she gave me a wave. I've still got it at home in a bucket.
>
> She was very fat. You didn't walk with her, you walked among her.
>
> A lorry came along and knocked her down. I said to the driver, "what's the matter with you? Why didn't you go around her?" He said 'I didn't have enough petrol'.
>
> But I was crazy about her. I loved every hair on her lip. She bit an apple and broke two teeth. I said 'don't worry, love. You've got one left'.
>
> Talk about bad manners. She had her own way of eating. Now I don't mind anyone eating with their hands. But soup!

Tommy has placed either a cross or a tick against each, deciding whether or not to include them. The last one got a cross. What survived was a classic sketch. In the archive, there was lots more of it. 'She cocked one eye at me, and I cocked one eye at her, and there we sat, the two of us, cock-eyed!'

In all, I spent two days in the archive, sifting through material. I scanned over a hundred items for later perusal, and I feasted my eyes on the boxes behind the scenes that were still being sorted. As Tommy Cooper said in the preceding sketch, 'Maybe one day I'll go back'. These files contain the work of many gag-writers, Tommy included, who all provided the material that sustained Cooper throughout his career, from humble beginnings to his live television exit.

There are eleven boxes that relate purely to Miff's contractual correspondence with clients, nightclubs, theatres, hotels, and television companies. They all attest to the thoroughness of Ferrie's work. That's what agents and managers do—they free the artist to concentrate on their performance. In Tommy's case, this was especially true because he was so absent-minded. He needed someone to look after him professionally.

The gag files and the correspondence files are roughly the same size and take up the same space in the archive. I guess that is show-business for you—two sides of the same coin.

I was impressed by Tommy's sheer presence in the material. There is a voracious thread running through the collection—of Tommy's manic ability to summon up a constant stream of gags. Following Max Miller's advice, Tommy tried to find the humour in real life situations, just by listening to people. His simple one-liners are drawn from his own experiences. The wife, for example, was a subject that most audience members could relate to, and it was a source of inspiration for Tommy. It also allowed him to portray himself as a put-upon clown.

'My wife does bird impressions. She does. She watches me like a hawk'.

'I don't know what to get my wife for her birthday. A box of chocolates, a fur coat, a diamond ring, or a car. I know, I'll get her a box of chocolates'.

'You know why I call her "dear"? She's got antlers growing out of the side of her head'.

'My wife has a bad memory. She remembers everything!'

'She puts on cream an inch thick. Curlers in her hair. Fishing net over the whole thing. She said to me "Kiss me". I replied, "Take me to your leader!"'

He does a joke about taking his wife everywhere, but she always comes home. Anyone who has seen the film *Goodfellas* will remember the hackneyed stand-up doing the exact same thing. Old jokes seemed fresh and funny when Cooper delivered them, and it was his timing that turned his performance into art.

Spike Milligan, one of Britain's best comedians of the twentieth century, was in awe of Tommy's act. Spike, himself widely acknowledged as a comic genius, would absolutely marvel at Cooper's delivery. Asked to decipher it, Milligan would just shake his head in wonder and compare it to a piece of music by the composer Chopin—high praise indeed.

Tommy would not perform anything on stage until he had practised it to perfection, and if that meant practising it hundreds of times, then so be it. In order to break the rules, you first have to know them. Tommy knew them off by heart. Some said they never knew if Tommy was the stupidest man they had ever met, or the cleverest. He was certainly the best at what he did.

That he worked so hard to achieve what he did is surely his best accolade. If he had worked half as hard, or wasted the talent that he had, he would have been just another mediocre entertainer.

Arthur Askey once said that every show-business generation produced the same thing: 'a lot of crap and a few stand-out performers'.

Tommy belonged in the latter category, but maybe so many more do too. Maybe they just do not have the work ethic that their talent deserves, or they will not make the sacrifices to reach the heights that they could.

For Tommy, it was not work, because he was doing something that he loved—making people laugh.

28

Forever Working

In 1975, Tommy penned his own book entitled, almost inevitably, *Just Like That*. In it, he wrote his life story, sort of. Rather, it reads like one long sketch. It would have been nice to hear his side of events without playing it for laughs, but I do not think he had the capacity for such self-analysis. He probably feared that if he looked too closely, he might lose that innate gift for comedy that he possessed.

It was one of several such ventures that Tommy undertook. Success brings opportunities, as commercially-minded companies seek to jump on the bandwagon and cash in on a brand. Cooper was one of the country's most recognised and popular personalities. He lent his name to several novelty items including board games and other merchandise, including the Tommy Cooper golf game, with a large caricature of himself in the middle of the board.

It was Miff's job to sort through the many offers that came in and, it has to be said, he provided wise counsel in all of the years that they worked together. Tommy's manager certainly had his client's best interests at heart. Despite their differences, Miff had a certain sense for sniffing out what was most appropriate, and he protected Tommy's reputation, and helped ensure his act's prolonged career. He did not just jump at every proposal. He always played the long game.

Between the two men, they plotted a course that would ensure this longevity. The television serials would be staggered. They would do a few TV shows then leave the next few years fallow, this despite the clamour for Tommy's services.

The seventies in Britain were a golden age for television. Families would gather around the set on a Saturday night and watch hour after hour of the biggest stars, either performing their own sketches or presenting a variety of quiz games and contests. Tommy held back, kept his powder dry, and cherry-picked from the selection of offerings.

This did not mean that Tommy was not working. As well as occasional television appearances and performances, Tommy had a busy schedule doing live shows in the nightclubs of Britain. He was much in demand for functions given at the Grand Order of Water Rats, The Variety Club of Great Britain, and at the Magic Circle.

At the latter, he performed one routine that began with the words 'I used to be in partnership with Jasper Maskelyne (son of the Magic Circle founder). We were known as Maskelyne and Feminine!'

It is hard to see how Tommy expected to get away with that, as a less feminine person it is hard to imagine. The joke harks back to a tradition on the stage, where music hall comedians would challenge audiences with innuendo. 'What if I am?' was a Max Miller line. While it was good to keep up with tradition, Tommy's sheer physical stature rendered his own attempt at the joke immaterial.

The only reference I have come across to anything resembling a comment about sexuality was when Tommy was set to appear on a bill supporting Frankie Howerd. As we know, Tommy had no problem appearing down the bill. The promoter explained to Cooper, as if he felt the need to, that Frankie was good at putting bums on seats. 'Safest place for them,' Tommy replied, perhaps a little ungraciously. In truth, Tommy considered Howerd a friend and he greatly admired his talent.

Then, in Cooper's same Magic Circle set, there are better gags: 'When I was young my mother used to pay a woman to take me out in my pram. I've been pushed for money ever since!'

'I saw something funny in the paper today. A father of fourteen has been shot. Mistaken for a rabbit!'

'My wife puts on her face before going to bed. I say "Goodnight, swamp"'.

'Thank you for that thunderous burst of silence'.

There is so much material in the V&A archive that it is no wonder it has been deemed of national importance.

The 1970s brought the inevitable toll resulting from his workload, and also from the passage of time. Tommy was not getting any younger and he was still as busy as he had ever been, but now he had the burden of carrying his huge frame into middle age and beyond. By the time he reached his fifties, he was not in the best of health; also, his drinking had gone from being strictly social to something else entirely. It now became a crutch for whatever demons were eating away at this otherwise simple man.

Tommy came from the war generation. They had been through so much and had developed a stoic view of life. They were practical and realistic. The war robbed many men of their opportunity in life. Promising footballers who might have graced the old First Division instead spent their most athletic years in the service of their country. Luckily, Cooper and his peers in the entertainment world were able to continue with the pursuit of their goals, their best years still ahead of them. Art, unlike sport, did not have a shelf life.

Cooper came from a hard-working family. His mother, especially, instilled this ethic in him. His paternal grandfather had worked down the coal-pit all his life. Tommy, himself, was working class. He never appeared to be too far removed from his audience. Similarly, with his kids, he and Gwen endeavoured to keep their feet on the ground. It was a source of pride to Tommy and Dove that their children could not be called spoilt.

It was also true that Tommy embraced his hectic schedule with relish. Maybe, having found something to do that he well and truly loved, it never seemed like work. It was often said that he was the hardest working man in show-business, and not just for the amount of energy he expended on stage, but for his never-ending workload. It was a title that he justly deserved. For sure, he enjoyed the rewards, but it appears that he never once complained or seemed to mind about the mammoth task that he was set.

As for the drinking, Tommy, who enjoyed playing the working men's clubs, must have been led into temptation. He liked a drink, and gazing out from the stage every night, at tables full of blokes sinking pint after pint, must have given him a hankering he found hard to resist. Possibly, the stress of having two women in his life added to the burden. Mary Kay was now at his side for professional performances, and Tommy obviously allowed her into his affections to some extent. Maybe the thought of betraying his wife, or the shock of leading two different lives, made him turn to the drink in order to blot out the reality of his situation.

It was a case of burning the candle at both ends. Health and age catching up with him, stress and worry coming back at him, and there was Tommy, in the middle, with nowhere to go. Though he played the clubs to avoid over-exposure on television, it sadly meant that he was handily placed to grab the crutch that drink became for him. With so much on his mind, he was not in the best place to understand what was happening and the effect it would have on his well-being.

Yet, after every health scare, every warning that his own body sent out, he just could not wait to get back to work. Rather, he could not wait to get back on stage, or on TV, or in front of an audience. The need to perform ran through to his very core. He had more than earned a rest, and he could certainly have afforded to slow down, but he never would, and he never did.

There was also the ridiculous amount of travel involved. He was all over the country, every week of the year, living out of a suitcase—never mind the additional ones he needed to carry all of his props. Cooper was sleeping in hotels, contacting Miff to see where he was going next, shacking up with Mary Kay all week, and then home to the family on Sundays. This is not to mention the club full of punters he had to entertain each night. That would be enough to wear anyone down and Tommy, at heart, was just a normal bloke.

Testament to this common touch is the fact that a bloke working in a factory all week had every chance of turning up at his local social club on a Saturday night and seeing Tommy Cooper live on stage. It must have seemed surreal, yet it was happening all over the land.

Cooper's success was based on his innate comic ability, and honed in the hours of practice that he put into it. He was blessed with a talent that no one else had, but he also worked harder than the rest of his peers to master his craft. It is no real surprise then that he should have enjoyed such respect and acclaim.

The television shows allowed millions of people to witness Tommy Cooper as a performer. Perhaps *The Plank* gave the best opportunity to see how good he could be on film.

When Tommy said he wanted to work with best pal Eric Sykes when the latter put together a silent film production, Miff did not stand in his way. Shot in 1967, the film featured the two friends on screen. It turned out to be television gold. Made by Associated London Films, and written and directed by Eric himself, the black-and-white short film is fifty-five minutes long. The opening shot shows a huge timber yard, stacked with thousands upon thousands of planks of wood. The credits roll. Tommy is credited first, then the humble Eric Sykes plays second fiddle. Among the supporting cast are Jimmy Tarbuck, Roy Castle (of *Record Breakers* fame), Jim Dale (of *Carry On* film fame), Jimmy Edwards, and Bill Oddie of the Goodies, among many others.

The two stars of the film appear and collect their tools—Tommy a hammer, Eric a work bench. They make their way into a ground-floor room of a house that is being built. Their task is to lay a new wooden floor, but they are one plank short. Off to a timber yard they go, causing chaos along the way.

It has gone down as a great British classic. There were more films in the pipeline, such was *The Plank*'s success, but Miff never endorsed a sequel. For Eric, this was deeply frustrating, even hurtful, and he never truly forgave Miff for denying them the possibility.

The film itself was reprised without Tommy in 1979, such was its enduring appeal. There were no others like it in the entire canon of Cooper's work. He never got the opportunity to make a movie of his own, as others such as Tony Hancock and Morecambe and Wise had done.

Tommy was selective in his television appearances. The film roles never really happened. It was a shame that there was no encore to *The Plank*, but those screen appearances were all the more appreciated for their rare and undoubted quality.

29

Branching Out

In the music hall tradition, most entertainers had more than one trick up their sleeve. Performers were used to turning their hands to anything in order to play their part, doing whatever was required to keep an audience entertained.

Max Miller sang and joked his way through his act, Tommy Trinder did the same—and who knew that Max Wall could sing? Certainly not me, but he was not the only one blessed with a fine voice. Flanagan and Allen had a huge hit with 'Run Rabbit Run', a wartime favourite that seemed to lift the spirits of a beleaguered nation. Even Frankie Howerd and Arthur Askey had a go. One good song could make your fortune, as Stanley Holloway found out with 'Get Me to the Church on Time'.

We could also add Charles Coborn to this list, as the person who sang 'The Man Who Broke the Bank at Monte Carlo'. He made his fortune singing this music hall favourite at every theatre and variety club in the land. In fact, he almost became as rich as the man he was singing about on the strength of that one song.

Of Tommy Cooper's contemporaries, Benny Hill fared best with his song 'Ernie', the man who drove the fastest milk cart in the West. The single was a massive hit, selling in the millions, and reached number one in the pop charts.

Tommy recorded his only proper single in 1961. It was written by Cy Coben and called 'Don't Jump Off the Roof, Dad'. It was released on the obscure Palette label and copies sold for 2 shillings each. It reached number forty in the charts and stayed there for three weeks. Despite its modest success, it became a signature tune for Tommy and, 'The Sheik of Araby' aside, is the song that is most associated with him.

It tells the story of a man who's had a hard day at work, where the boss is driving him mad, only to return home to a house full of shouting kids, and this before he gets bitten by his own dog. He takes himself up to the roof before the kids try to coax him down, not out of any genuine affection, but because they do not want him to ruin the garden that their mum has been busy pruning to perfection. They advise him instead to make his way to the park and jump in the lake. It is delivered with a sort of stoic and resigned response to the situation.

Apart from this, Tommy never really sang. He did a version of 'Me and my Shadow' alongside Arthur Askey, the joke being that they were physical opposites, with Askey slight and Tommy enormous. He also book-ended his classic sketch about the girl he met on Waterloo Bridge, dangling her feet in the water, with a song. He started by singing 'We'll meet again, don't know where, don't know when,' the Vera Lynn song that meant so much to a generation ravaged by war. As Tommy started singing, he then got all emotional and started crying into his handkerchief, before he regaled us with the story of the girl with the button nose. After he brings the tale to its brilliant conclusion, he signs off with a final flurry of 'But I know we'll meet again some sunny day'.

Other than that, Tommy stuck to his stock in trade of comedy and magic. His first forays into the emerging world of television serials came with *It's Magic* in 1953. His appearances were limited to just thirteen minutes of the show's forty-five-minute running length. In between the recurring sections featuring snippets of Tommy's act, viewers were treated to interludes of music, poetry, performance, and almost anything it seems to fill the allotted time. There was also one pure magic trick included with every show to justify the programme's title.

His debut had been on the BBC Christmas party show in 1952. This would be the extent of Tommy's television appearances for a number of years, due to caution against overexposure on Miff's part, and the bureaucracy of the government-run television corporation—at the time Britain's only television station.

The men who headed up the organisation's entertainment and comedy departments at the time were dour-faced businessmen, unsuited to the task of tickling the nation's funny bone. Negotiations for further appearances would drag on through 1954 and into 1955, when the BBC finally got some competition in the form of commercial television. Now the watching public had two channels to choose from, and both of them wanted to work with Tommy Cooper.

The impresarios working at the new television station were better equipped to nurture the comedian's talent, but again negotiations came to nothing while the parties, Miff and the entrepreneurial heads of the new station, looked for the best format to suit the rising star's style.

Ultimately, the clamour was such that it was always going to happen eventually, albeit not to the satisfaction of either side. It seems a compromise was reached, which did not meet anyone's expectations. Despite some misgivings, Tommy's popularity emerged unscathed from *Cooperama*, which premiered in 1957. The best that could be hoped for was that lessons would be learned and that the next series, planned for 1958, would achieve better results.

There were still the occasional one-off appearances (*Sunday Night at the London Palladium* for example) to keep Tommy's stock high, but by now he was established in the hearts and minds of the nation and he was worthy of a greater platform, namely his own show.

He followed the 1957 series with another called *Cooper's Capers* the following year. After that, his diary would be filled with theatrical bookings and limited television appearances. It was probably just as well, as everyone involved tried to figure out how they had failed to harness the full potential of Tommy's act. So potent when doing his material on stage, even on a television show, the two series that had been transmitted in his own name were weak in comparison to what he could deliver under his own steam.

There were offers from both the BBC and what we today know as ITV, but in the time required to put a television series together, heads of department would be replaced or move on, and the ideas would come to nothing.

In 1966, Tommy eventually returned to the nation's living rooms in a television series again called *Cooperama*, a title of Miff's suggestion. Despite a talented team of writers, the show still struggled to capture the magic of Tommy's act, and the comedian was obliged to attempt to make something work, which was never quite the right fit. It is not fair to call a show with ratings in the millions a failure, but if you were a fan of Tommy Cooper looking for a favourite set or routine, you probably would not find it here.

Yet millions of viewers are not to be ignored, and certainly not by the television companies, whose licensing fee and commercial contracts relied on them. Thus, they soldiered on, changed writers or directors on occasion, and made the decision to go again in 1967. This time, the name was changed to *Life with Cooper*. It would follow the same format that had previously underwhelmed, hoping this time it would somehow click.

One tweak to the format was to begin each show with a proper Tommy Cooper performance in front of a live audience. Then, they could move on to the more experimental stuff so that, even if some of it fell on stony ground, at least the show should prove to be an overall success.

Quaint now to watch, the show was recorded in black and white. Britain was still emerging from the dark ages in terms of technology; even the Flintstones had colour television. The show features zany credits, a forerunner of all that was to follow. It began with Tommy appearing on stage to do the sort of routine audiences had come to expect from his live performance. In one show, he tells a joke about an elephant and a kangaroo teaming up to rob a bank. Tommy seemed to delight in the absurd. His jokes were never topical. Did they need to be, when his forte was in silly humour, which he elevated to heights beyond the material's true status?

So the elephant and the kangaroo approach the bank. The elephant goes in first. Tommy says, 'Walks in', then corrects it to 'More of a gallop, really'. He was forever picking over the bones of his own gags, even in mid-sentence. He was a master of mining his every joke, determined to extract its full comic potential. The kangaroo follows the elephant into the bank, using its accomplice's bulk to disguise its presence. The elephant uses its trunk to snatch the money from the teller's till, then proceeds to fill the kangaroo's pouch with the proceeds before they flee the scene. The police arrive and interview everyone present.

'What happened?' they ask.

'We were robbed by an elephant and a kangaroo,' comes the reply.

'Would you recognise them again?' the policeman asks, and the audience laugh, thinking that is the punchline.

'No,' comes the reply. 'They had stockings over their faces!'

Tommy continues. 'I got a new car for the wife last week. Not a bad swap, I thought'.

From gags, he does a bit of magic. Then, as he is about to do his next trick, he introduces it with the words, 'I first did this trick when I was on holiday'.

He then starts to daydream, and we move from the stage performance to Tommy's memory of the holiday, previously captured on celluloid in a pre-recorded segment. This was the format for many of the series in which the comedian appeared. Though there were slight variances to this, subject to the whims of whichever company was producing, it seemed to be a style that would follow him down the years. The quality of the pre-recorded segments were hit and miss, but the shows enjoyed almost unparalleled success. Imagine the heights he might have reached if the material and format had suited him better.

It is easy to see how audiences could not get enough of him at this stage. The show was book-ended with the type of performance that they had come to associate with Cooper. If the quality dipped during the sketches, it was still nice to spend time with the man. In all, there was enough going on in each programme to see how the shows achieved the impressive ratings that they did.

The fact that the show was all about Tommy, audiences would quite happily sit through a half-hour in his company, even if it was not his finest half-hour, and nor would it ever be, as he was dancing to the tune of a production company rather than surviving on his own wit and judgement. Still, it hit the spot—the top-ratings spot at that.

Tommy Cooper had the world at his feet. He was loved on stage and loved by audiences at home. All of his hard work appeared to be paying off.

30

Opportunities

Miff was still not happy with *Life with Cooper*. He thought that some of the material was not good enough, and he was not shy in telling both Tommy and the television company about it. In fact, when the scripts came through for the follow-up series in 1969, Miff turned them down flat. He even went so far as to type out a letter of rejection, which he issued to Tommy to be counter-signed and forwarded to ITV.

It is possible in this action to see something of the true relationship between manager and artiste. Miff felt the need to put words in Tommy's mouth, as if he sees himself as the adult in the room, with the child expected to do as he was told. It is also possible that he thought Tommy neither intelligent or articulate enough to state their case adequately. Either way, it was an unusual way to go about business and smacked of some desperation on Miff's part. As Tommy grew more popular and prominent, and continued to attract the attentions of the powerful media players, perhaps Miff feared losing his hold on the talent, and the letter to be signed was a way of bringing him back in line.

To Tommy's credit, he refused to endorse the letter, and instead penned one of his own to Miff, saying that the scripts, while maybe not perfect, had some very funny parts. He felt that he could still make something of them. Tommy, who had always had an ear for what material would suit, proved himself more adept than Miff gave him credit for. The series topped the ratings chart.

Though the journey to the top of the television rankings had been difficult, at least they had got there in the end. The layers of bureaucracy, the differences of opinion between the heads of department, and the constant job-swapping had not helped matters. Then again, it had ensured a steady rise to the peak of the industry, rather than a swift crash and burn, which Miff had been keen to avoid all along.

As the 1960s drew to a close, Miff received an offer from the entrepreneurial David Frost, who wished to package Tommy in a private venture that would target an international audience, most notably the lucrative American market. The idea was attractive to both artist and manager. They would complete their contracted series for commercial television in 1969, and then look to make another in 1970 for the new enterprise.

In today's world, this is how many films and television series come together—packaged by an astute producer and then sold to one of the many available channels who are always on the lookout for new product. Indeed, this was how many of the earlier theatrical reviews had been orchestrated.

The tradition of variety entertainment was based on creating an eclectic bill that would have broad appeal, with something for everyone. While concentrating on the magic of Tommy Cooper, the show would deliver the star to a whole new audience. For television at that time, Frost's vision was a fresh one, and all parties entered into it with enthusiasm.

Frost had the good business sense to realise that the product he was working with, namely Tommy Cooper, simply had so much more to give. He had just been voted Television Personality of the Year. Why not ship his talent across the globe? It was like delivering the Beatles to America. The market was so much bigger. Tommy was like an untapped oil well or a dormant gold mine. Miff had not taken advantage of the tremendous opportunity that Tommy had presented to him. David Frost was about to rectify that by bringing Cooper in house to work with Frost's own television company.

Then, as the series got close to production, Miff began to have the same doubts—that the format would not show Tommy Cooper in the best light. Maybe it was Miff being over-cautious. Maybe Frost was right in his opinion that there was only so far that a man like Miff could take Tommy. Perhaps Ferrie did not have the vision to guide Cooper to the heights of global stardom. Miff, though, had genuine misgivings, and Cooper would not do anything without the support and approval of his manager, however parochial his outlook might be.

Miff's concern was that the envisaged programmes closely resembled those that had been done previously. The shows would open with Tommy doing a bit of his stage act, and then they would segue into a selection of sketches. Though some of these sketches looked good on the page, and there was undoubtedly some great writing talent on the team, there simply was not enough quality material. Miff thought that the shows would be under-rehearsed, and he did not hold out much hope for the show's success.

The contract was initially for thirteen episodes, with the option for a further series to follow. Despite some highlights, the series offered ever-dwindling returns. The one redeeming factor was the overseas exposure that was clearly expressed in the conditions of the contract. When these foreign sales failed to materialise, Miff felt no compulsion to fulfil the option of another series.

When the producers attempted to put pressure on Miff to allow the second series to be made, he had his own solicitors point out that they were in breach of that particular clause of the original contract, therefore the contract was no longer valid.

It was not simply a hoped-for benefit of producing the series; the overseas exposure was actually the main reason for doing it. It was a fundamental part of the whole process, and the two parties to the contract were now in opposite camps.

Miff could afford to stand his ground. Tommy was very much in demand on the nightclub circuit, and it was there that Miff sent him to keep the cash rolling in. Cooper was earning £7,000 a week, which was as much as he was being offered to do a television spot. While Tommy kept plugging away on stages across the country, the legal stand-off kept simmering away in the background. Miff had a good case. The promised international element of the deal had not been forthcoming. Though David Frost's company kept gently prodding and probing, Miff's answer always remained the same.

'You are in breach. You've failed to deliver on your side of the bargain, therefore myself and my client are under no obligation to renew the contract. Case closed'.

Tommy stayed out of the argument. He was happy enough to be back on tour and embraced the cabaret circuit wholeheartedly. He probably enjoyed the intimacy of the venues. They may have reminded him of some of the places he played on his inexorable rise to the top of his profession.

Always happy in front of an audience, especially one so close, he could actually see the delight register on the faces of the people in front of him. For Tommy, that was all he wanted to do as a performer—delight people. That is what he did with friends and fellow artists back-stage, or with the crew on the set of a television production, or even in a bar with his mates. It was probably what he loved best, that close, personal connection, and now he got to do it every night.

It was an arrangement and an attitude that would keep him from doing another television series until 1975. The initial contract for the series was for four shows, which was later increased to eight. It was called *The Tommy Cooper Hour*. There had been occasional outings on television in the previous five years, but this marked an upturn in exposure, and yet still no such leap in quality.

The show would last an hour and would be filmed before a live theatre audience; at least this was a move in the right direction. The ratings were great, securing top of the rankings every week. Audiences could not get enough of him, even if the show he was packaged in was never quite right.

Tommy was simply ill at ease in this world of television sketches. The Two Ronnies did sketches brilliantly. 'Fork handles/four candles' remains one of the best comedic sketches in British television history. First and foremost, they were both comic actors. Ronnie Barker proved this superbly in the classic series

Porridge. Ronnie Corbett had success in this field too. Eric Morecambe and Ernie Wise were probably closer in style to Tommy, and their success was born out of their amazing chemistry. Tommy, although he had a small supporting cast, had to carry these sketches pretty much alone; it just did not suit him.

Still, the juggernaut rolled on. The next outing was in 1976 with a series of six half-hour episodes in a show called simply *Cooper*. Maybe the producers would have shown more imagination if they had called it 'Simply Cooper'. That is probably what it should have been—Tommy simply doing gags and magic, which is what audiences loved to see him do.

Following these television outings, Tommy restricted himself to occasional guest spots and appearances on behalf of friends Bill Fraser and Eric Sykes on the popular TV show *This is Your Life*.

Despite the fact that Tommy was only supposed to come on and say a few kind words about the guest star, on both occasions he managed to steal the show. At one point, the host actually gave up trying to rein in Tommy's madcap approach and went and sat down with the special guest and their immediate family, leaving Tommy to hold court for a good five minutes of what should have been a tribute show to a much-loved friend. It did not matter. It made for great television, and the all-star casts were left with tears streaming down their faces at an impromptu Cooper performance.

After that, Tommy did several one-off television specials for both the BBC and ITV, but the seventies were overall a decade dominated by the cabaret circuit as far as Tommy was concerned.

Cooper had taken a five-year break from recording a television series between 1970 and 1975, and he had also taken a six-year hiatus in between his *Royal Variety Performance*s in that decade—in 1971 and again in 1977.

Instead, he embraced the emerging nightclub culture. To say that he enjoyed it, well he did so just a bit too much.

31
Nightclubbing

Gone were the days when Gwen and Tommy shared a 10-shilling-a-week flat in Clapham and would walk into the West End on a Sunday afternoon and enjoy half a pint of beer each. Now, it was Dubonnet wine and a healthy dose of spirits, and that was at home. When drunk, they would fight, with Tommy bobbing and weaving, ducking and diving to avoid being struck by the various household items that Gwen would throw at him.

Then there were the clubs. The country was littered with them—smoke-filled testosterone dens, where pint-swilling working men would forget about their lot in life and join friends for a good old 'lads' night out. If they were lucky, they would get to see a decent turn like Tommy Cooper.

Some of these establishments were quite classy places; they had to be to afford the fee that Tommy was earning. From 1970 to 1980, Tommy played literally thousands of club nights. There he would be, this giant of the small screen, the familiar fez and coat-tails, brought to flesh on the stage—his trademark chuckle and exuberant laugh, the famous gait, that effortless motion, sometimes frantic, sometimes elegant, always unique.

He was a delight, and the nightclub owners could not get enough of him, with return bookings year after year. The act was a huge hit, but it slowly began to take its toll. Tommy was not getting any younger. A man's man, he saw no reason to hold back in such a male-dominated environment. He could hold his own with the best of them. Indeed, you could say he outdid them when it came to downing pints. The drink began to get the better of him. From sinking a few to unwind after a show, he now wanted a few before he went on; he said he did it 'to calm the nerves', though these were perhaps the delusions of a man on a slippery slope.

From 1970 to 1975, he was almost constantly touring, and therefore in the path of temptation. Rumours of his excessive drinking began to emerge and somehow found their way back to Miff. Then, there were the complaints.

Tommy would sit at the bar after a show and sometimes stay there till the sun came up the following morning. That the drink was usually free for the acts was not conducive to moderation. Tommy played on the fact that he was such good company. He could usually keep the staff entertained for hours, all the while drinking them out of their profits. It did not help Tommy much either. It not only affected his health, but also his act.

In a week of bookings, audiences and club owners never knew quite what they were going to get. He would come on, do five minutes of his set, and then wander off again to the bar or dressing room, only to be cajoled back on where he would do a few more minutes. In his defence, he would claim that he had done his allotted forty-five-minute set, but that time might include the interlude he had taken during the routine. Other nights, he just would not turn up at all. Although this happened infrequently, it occasionally did happen, and an embarrassed and apologetic Miff was obliged to return some of the fee in compensation.

Cooper was also perennially late. This was not just a problem confined to his cabaret appearances. He had been a source of frustration to television producers and directors for many years. He famously kept one film production waiting all morning, turning up at midday when the call had been for 8 a.m. Tommy turned up in his pyjamas and said, 'Well, I couldn't get out of bed!' No one could be mad at him for long.

When the tardiness started to become a regular event, the people who had booked him, quite naturally, grew frustrated. When he turned up to one club, the owner said angrily, 'You were on half an hour ago'.

'Was I?' Tommy replied. 'How did I do?'

Miff made his feelings known to Cooper. He said there had been some complaints about the comedian's performance of late. Tommy did his best to defend himself.

'You were drinking at the bar till seven in the morning,' said Miff.

'Well, you know I can't sleep,' Tommy replied. As funny (or sad) as that is, it was actually true. He was practically an insomniac. There was even talk of filming his television specials at midnight as that was when he was most awake; years of not going on stage until one in the morning had adjusted his body clock, you might say.

Tom O'Connor has been called the finest stand-up comic ever to come out of Liverpool. For a city known for its humour, that is high praise indeed. The Scouse comedian had trodden a path well-worn by many cabaret entertainers over the years—first, you put in your time on the variety circuit, before television eventually offered you a game-show to host. Legends such as Groucho Marx had been down the same road. In Britain, Bruce Forsyth, Les Dawson, Les Dennis, and many others followed the same career path. Tom O'Connor did it too. Maybe it offered some respite from the coal-face of performing in cabaret night after night at some of the toughest clubs in the country.

Tom O'Connor shared many a bill and many a dressing room with Tommy Cooper. He saw him up close and got to observe both the man and the act. He saw him both socially and professionally. While in awe of the talent of this great performer, he acknowledged many of the myths and characteristics that Tommy was apt to portray.

Miff was an ogre, apparently, and Tommy was his dancing bear, to be struck by a stick if he did not perform. As others have commented, Tommy liked to give this impression to deflect criticism from any defects in his own character. That alone should have justified Miff's extra 5 per cent.

Tom O'Connor was also witness to Tommy's drinking when it was getting out of hand. In fact, according to Tom's testimony, it was already way out of hand. He describes being in a club with Tommy, prior to a scheduled performance, and Tommy going along the bar and asking for a pint of everything on draft and a short measure of every available optic. Unsurprisingly, Tommy failed to appear on stage that night and wandered back to his lodgings. As it became obvious that something was amiss, the club owner phoned Tommy's hotel and asked to be put through to his room. He demanded to know what was happening. Tommy said that he was not coming.

'But I've got 800 people waiting for you, all of whom have paid £20 for a ticket,' the club-owner complained.

'Get me their names and addresses,' Tommy said. 'I'll go and apologise to them in person!'

Luckily, Tommy's position as a giant of comedy meant his many foibles were tolerated. As much as they were unfair, there was a certain acceptance that this was the reality and he would be welcomed anyway. As with his audiences, people were just happy to be in his company.

By the time Tommy returned to television in 1975 for another series, the subject was debated between the producers and Miff. There was some concern about Tommy's 'health', which was how they referred to the problem.

Miff wanted to distance himself from the production, having already expressed dissatisfaction about the quality and suitability of the material they were going to use. However, he did write a letter to Cooper saying that he understood the stress of making a television series, but that he hoped that Tommy would take it easier on himself. He was genuinely worried, and with good reason. Tommy had issues with his legs, with his breathing, and obviously with his drinking. On top of all that, he was not sleeping. Miff was unsure how that was going to work, especially as work was all that Cooper seemed to do. Miff finished his missive by saying that he fully realised that it was sometimes just not humanly possible for all this effort to be maintained.

A holiday might be in order. Tommy was not at all averse to that. He loved to vacation in hot climates; Spain became a favourite. There, he could relax, with a drink in front of him, of course. He was just a regular guy taking a well-earned rest. It was ironic then that it should be while on holiday that he suffered his first major coronary incident. Although he had a work assignment to carry out while there, the trip to Rome in 1977 should have provided some respite from his busy schedule.

Instead, he experienced his first major health scare. One can only wonder why it took so long. With hindsight, the heart attack that he suffered appears almost inevitable, given the drinking, the working, the life that he was leading and the stress he was constantly under. Luckily, Tommy survived intact, before taking up the baton once more.

He was outstanding at the Royal Variety Gala Performance the same year, when the whole country could enjoy the man at his best. The material was original and Tommy was in fine form. It was probably his highlight television appearance throughout a hectic decade that undoubtedly took a toll on his life.

By 1978, his occasional television appearances were starting to creak once more. People were starting to worry about him. He was slurring his words, and the shambolic act, which was actually highly finessed, now became what it purported to be. He could not do the little comic stumble he used to do as he walked across the stage, as people would now think that it was real.

Tommy admonished himself after one television performance, calling it 'rubbish' as the credits were still rolling. The producer later told Miff that the magic was just not what it had been before. Maybe, neither was the comedy giant.

All those years of club appearances had taken their toll. As much as Tommy loved what he was doing, and audiences could relish the opportunity to witness the nation's favourite comic up close, there had to be some payback for all that exposure to such an unhealthy environment.

Cooper embraced the night-clubs with a passion. Sadly, over the course of countless appearances, they appear to have done him much more harm than good.

32

Feeling the Effects

That big lumbering frame was always going to come at a price. It was a lot of weight to carry around, especially when you have done it for such a long time. This was no longer that handsome young guardsman, or the boatyard apprentice, or even the dashing comedian on board the troopships of the Middle East. It was no longer the nervous young man setting foot on the boards at an inauspicious audition, or the adventurous man stepping onto a West End stage for the first time.

This was a man with thirty or more performance years on the clock. This was a man who had foisted himself from venue to venue, resort town to resort town, by plane, train, and automobile for several decades. This was, in effect, a man not given to take care of himself. He was not even able to slow down.

Mary Kay, the 'other woman' (or 'that bloody woman' as Gwen later called her), said 'You don't know the number of times before a show I've said "Please Tommy. Don't drink."' Yet he still would. While Tommy was at the height of his success in 1970, the remainder of the decade would see him deteriorate, not in popularity, but certainly in how he was coping with it. It is amazing that he was able to perform as often as he did, and maintain his ratings, while carrying so much baggage with him.

He had physical problems, but probably emotional ones too as his private life grew more complicated. The affair he embarked upon with the former floor manager, now his unofficial personal assistant, was bound to add to his stress. The double life he began to lead was maybe one of the reasons that he turned to drink. If Tommy had moments where he was less than kind, or less than considerate to the two women in his life, he was never in any way the kind of monster that has recently been claimed. George Bernard Shaw once wrote that 'man makes a beast of himself to hide the pain of being a man'. Tommy, despite recent articles, television dramas, and even theatre plays attempting to portray him as such, was never a beast. That said, Thomas Jr recalled how his father, who never looked for trouble, once knocked a yob unconscious in a pub when the man came in and started giving the landlord a bit of aggravation. Tommy Cooper apparently stood there in silence, minding his own business, until he had had enough. Then he whacked the villain out cold.

Cooper is said to have been mean on occasion. With money, we know that he was monumentally mean, but there are also signs of a short temper that flared up from time to time. Most notably, these all seem to have been in his later years, and one can sense the irrationality of a drunk in these actions. Once, he was at a Variety Club dinner, accompanied at the top table by Gwen. He got up to give his speech and never once acknowledged his wife, who was seated at his side. When she spoke to him after a period of several minutes, he turned to her quite nastily and spat out, 'I thought I told you to wait in the truck'. It was an attempt at humour, but it was meant to belittle her, and it cannot be called funny by anyone's standards. Yet Tommy was not really a nasty man, though there are times when he could have been nicer. He was not a Jekyll and Hyde character, though he once did a routine where he performed a hilarious impression of Robert Louis Stevenson's creation.

'I will now perform Jekyll and Hyde,' he said. He wandered melodramatically to the rear of the stage and disappeared behind the curtain. He then popped his head out, still wearing his fez. 'Nasty, nasty, nasty, nasty, nasty,' he said in a gruff voice before disappearing. He then popped his head out again a few seconds later. 'Nice, nice, nice, nice, nice,' he said, in a lovely voice, all smiles and innocence. It was Tommy at his silly best, and he was always much more of a nice man than a nasty one.

The fact that Gwen continued to pine for her affectionate husband all those years after his death is testament to his inner character. Though Mary Kay recalled several incidents where Tommy lost his temper with her, she still claimed to love the man and said she had spent many happy years, seventeen in total, working with him and being at his side. She wished she could have had him all to herself.

Despite this, Mary said that Tommy once flung her to the floor in a restaurant. Her crime was to have laughed when he made some complaint about the food. Another time, he snatched an expensive watch from her wrist, one that he had bought her, and threw it across the room when she was making a fuss about keeping an appointment.

The cause of this increasingly erratic behaviour was perhaps the struggle to stay on top of his game. The doctors in Rome who treated him after his heart attack were under no illusions—chronic alcoholism was their diagnosis. Tommy tried to brush it off as exhaustion, anything but the truth.

Perhaps that is a symptom of an alcoholic: the ability to lie to oneself. As his mother once wrote to her hard-working son, 'You're like me, Tommy. You haven't time to be ill, but sometimes we have to find time'. Would he listen, despite his need to perform?

It did not seem likely, given all that had gone before. If Tommy was as happy performing a simple magic trick for friends in the pub as he was on the stage in front of thousands of fans, then why the need to put himself through everything that he did? He was not getting any younger. Did he never tire of touring? Did he never heed any doctor's advice? Miff had warned him, his own mother had warned him, Gwen, the kids, and Mary Kay all warned him. Did he listen?

It seems that Tommy was oblivious. Maybe he was just pig-headed. Maybe he just did not want to believe what his friends and family were telling him. If he would not listen to others, maybe he would listen to himself when his own body spoke up.

He had suffered a mild heart tremor in 1965 during a pantomime season, but ever the professional, and against doctors' orders, he decided that the show must go on. Then came the incident in Rome, after which, Tommy could not wait to get back to work. He had a little time off to recuperate and, before the year was out, picked up where he had left off. It seems that Miff simply did as instructed. Tommy said he was well enough, so why not? Miff was not Tommy's doctor, he was his manager. There was still great demand for Tommy's services so Cooper got his wish to carry on.

It was true that Tommy was never happier than in front of an audience. If he wanted to go back to work, then maybe he knew best. For sure, he was feeling the effects of three decades of endeavour, to climb the show-business ladder and to stay at the top for so long. Yet, accompanied by the stress of his lifestyle—living out of a suitcase, leading a double life, the pressure of performing—sooner or later, for once and for all, something was going to give.

Sadly, for Tommy, it would be 'Three strikes and you're out,' but that was still in the future. There was still much mirth to be had with the madcap Tommy Cooper.

33

A Rose Among Thorns

'Struggling Bravely' was the title of the Alan Coren article in *The Times* newspaper in 1975, when he compared Tommy Cooper to King Kong. It is an excellent piece, full of love and respect for the artist. 'One time,' he says, 'the creature roamed wild. Then, men came and caught it, and put it in sketches, and backed it with music, and surrounded it with character actors. It has to perform instead of simply be. It still produces flashes of its old self, then one of its keepers yanks its chain'.

It was not a lament for a lost talent, for the talent was still there. It was just recognition that the man had so much more to give than he was being allowed to do. Those who had seen him at his best yearned for more of the same. They just wanted their Tommy back, the man who had given them so much pleasure over the years.

There were many highlights to fall back on. From the black-and-white picture days for Thames Television, there is a sketch where he performs as if on a ship. The stage is constantly moving, much like the man himself. Tommy makes great use of the running gag as he is propelled from one side of the stage to the other in perpetual motion. He introduces a ventriloquist's dummy into the act. It is Cooper at his manic best as the recalcitrant puppet, as well as the movement of the ship, send the performance into chaos. Tommy ends up completely drenched as the portholes keep opening up behind him, spilling buckets of water onto the stage.

There is a highly polished number with Tommy seated at a grand piano, surrounded by elegantly-dressed ladies, singing 'Autumn Leaves', only to end up with the piano and himself covered in the very thing he is singing about.

There are classic sketches such as 'Spoon, jar, jar, spoon,' which is probably one of the best-known and best-loved in his entire repertoire. Some of these routines were performed year after year, even show after show, but audiences never tired of them; the same can be said of the jokes. Like familiar friends, people were delighted to see and hear them again.

There is one particular fifteen-minute set that is a pure delight, even masterful. It begins with Tommy telling a couple of jokes, including the one about cleaning out the attic with the wife. He then says he went to the seaside and knocked on the door of a boarding house. The landlady opened an upstairs window and said, 'What do you want?' Tommy replied that he wanted to stay here. The landlady replied, 'Well stay there then!'

He then said that while he was there, he decided to go deep-sea-diving. He got all of the gear—the goggles, the flippers, the wet-suit, and the tank of air. He jumped into the sea and he was swimming along—like that, not like that. He was only using one hand. In the other, he was holding the instructions. He was swimming along, at the bottom of the sea, 155 feet down, thinking how quiet it is down there, when he came across a man in a sports jacket and grey flannel trousers. He thought 'that's unusual, for a Thursday'. He scrawled on a piece of paper, 'What are you doing down here?' and shows it to the man. The man takes the pad and pen and scrawls back 'I'm drowning!'

There were a couple of classic sketches were Tommy donned a costume. Two of them in particular stand out. Both feature Tommy in a split costume, half of him playing one character, and the other half playing another. One sees Tommy dressed half as a British officer and the other half in Nazi uniform.

The Nazi begins. 'Well, brigadier, you're probably wondering why I called you to my office'.

'No, I'm not!' the British officer replies. The German officer continues.

'Last night, 370 of your men escaped from this prisoner of war camp. How do you account for that?'

'You left the front door open,' comes the reply.

It ends with Tommy saying the German's lines while in character as the brigadier. It is a wonderful, surreal, and very silly sketch.

There was another routine in a similar vein, with Tommy dressed this time as one-half humble maid and the other half as a sailor.

'Jack. Jack. You've come back,' she says.

The sailor informs her that his name, in fact, is Fred. The maid's home is under threat from an evil landlord, and the sailor says he is going to save her ramshackle home from the developers who are planning to turn it into a multi-storey cowshed. Then she tells Fred that she is so pleased that he is going to take care of her and their little boy, who is two years old.

Fred has been at sea for four years and quickly does the maths. He says the child cannot possibly be his, therefore he is going to leave her.

She pleads with him. 'Can't we start again'.

The sailor relents and says, 'Oh, go on then'.

Tommy then turns back to his female side and says 'Jack. Jack. You've come back!' and they start the sketch all over again.

Tommy could get away with stuff that no other performer would even attempt, such as beckoning with his hand, beseeching the audience to laugh harder and clap louder, hand over his own mouth shouting 'more' in an ill-disguised attempt to encourage the audience. If it was not part of the act, you would have said he had no shame or that these were the last desperate acts of a comedian dying on stage.

One routine saw Tommy come on and stand next to a table, on top of which he had placed a chair. 'Now this trick is very dangerous,' he informed us. 'I could break my neck. I could be killed, so I'd like to request my round of applause now, while I'm still alive to hear it'. Obviously, not having done anything thus far, the audience response was lacklustre. Tommy took it all in and then said, 'Well I'm not breaking my neck for that,' and walked away, laughing.

Another time he said, 'Before I do my next trick, I'd like to say this. "This!"' He was delighted with himself. 'I've always wanted to say that,' he said. Then he said 'that!' He then added as if he had only just noticed, 'That is funnier than this'.

As usual, by the time he had finished with his set, the stage was littered with abandoned props, playing cards, bunches of flowers, a skipping rope, and other items from his crowded props tables.

These television shows were written by an eclectic mix of writers. As well as those previously named, and apologies to those not mentioned, the names of Dick Hills and George Martin, Johnnie Mortimer, and Brian Cooke appear in the credits of the television shows.

Despite the fact that many critics, and even interested parties such as Miff, felt that Tommy was not best used in the television series format, they still produced some wonderful comedy moments.

The tactic of going off to do other things was an astute managerial decision that kept Cooper fresh. Miff would think nothing of devoting a whole year of Tommy's time to cabaret to keep him off the telly. Besides, as Miff explained, there were so many people doing Tommy Cooper impressions that it felt like he had never been away.

It was true. A whole host of professional impressionists included him in their act. It would have been rude not to. It was not like Tommy was hard to do. The fact is, he was simple to impersonate because he was not a complicated man, either personally or professionally. He resonated with an audience because he was so down-to-earth, even though he was a larger than life character in every sense.

Tommy literally, stood out from the crowd. He was revered by his peers, and he was truly unique. He was adored by the general public, and yet surely, he could not carry on at the pace he had set for himself.

There was an attempt by Tommy to rein himself in. He promised to take more holidays. When Gwen was recovering from an illness of her own, they convalesced together in the Channel Islands. Tommy said he would now take one week off for every two that he worked. He had earned the right after being at the top of the entertainment business for three decades.

Financially, he could afford to do so, and this would have suited Miff just fine. He was batting away offers as it was, from the television stations and from nightclubs across the land. He also turned down numerous requests for Tommy to do adverts on television. He did not want to sell out his star and hurt the brand. There was no need as Tommy Cooper was still at the peak of his game.

34

The Affair

Of course, no Cooper biography would be complete without reference to the extra-marital affair that no doubt took place. For me, although it is important, it is not as important as many would make out. It happened, but I do not think it should be allowed to outweigh the contribution that Tommy made to entertainment in the twentieth century.

If you are a fan of Cooper, it matters not. To his family, it matters little. To the 'other woman', it obviously matters because she cared, but it should not be the ultimate memory of a much-loved star. Instead, I believe we should concentrate on the comedy, just as Tommy Cooper did.

A man went on a safari and he was walking through the jungle in Africa when he came across an elephant, limping along. The man went up to the elephant and saw that it had a huge thorn in its foot. So, he pulled the thorn out, just like that, and the elephant gave a roar of approval and then went on its merry way. Years later, the man was back home and the circus was coming to town, so the man took his family down to the street corner to watch all the clowns, jugglers, acrobats, and animals arrive. There, at the head of the parade was an elephant. It took one look at the man and ran up to him and lifted him triumphantly into the air. Then it smashed him to the ground and trampled all over him. It was a different elephant.

Now, Tommy liked elephant jokes. There was the one about the elephant and the lion who thinks that he is the king of the jungle, until shown otherwise. Then there are these:

'How do you make an elephant fly? Well, first you find a zip that is three feet long ...'

'My uncle used to work in the circus. One day he said to me, "Every day I used to carry the elephants to the water." I said, "don't you mean you used to carry the water to the elephants?"'

'"No wonder I was tired!" The uncle replied'.

Undoubtedly, the elephant in the room in Tommy's own story was his mistress, Mary Kay. The couple, if that is what we can call them, met in January 1967 in a church hall that was used for rehearsals by Thames Television. At the time, both were married. Cooper's partner Gwen was at home raising the kids, Vicky and Thomas Jr, then aged thirteen and ten respectively. Mary was married to Norman Fieldhouse, a music composer, and they had three kids of their own—Tony, Peter, and Simon, aged between six and fifteen.

Mary was a former singer who had moved into stage management at the television company. She described that first meeting with Tommy as 'Very nice and unexpected'. She thought he was just gorgeous, charming, and beautiful. She acknowledged that many people found him ugly. His looks were unusual and very much an acquired taste. By now, Tommy was a national treasure, a television institution, and Mary was impressed when she met such an icon for the first time.

Her son, Tony, would later tell the *Daily Express* in an interview in 2011 that his mum was very much in love with Cooper. That she was free to do so adds a further twist to the tale, for Norman Kay, the composer, was conducting an affair of his own.

At that first encounter, one of the directors said to Mary 'I think he fancies you,' after Tommy put an arm around her. The comedian then looked deep into her eyes and asked if she would like to be on holiday at that very moment. Mary melted, and said she definitely would. Thus began their affair.

She began to go on tour with him, becoming his personal assistant, props maker, driver, and companion whenever he was away from home. In her own words, she said that she looked after Tommy because his wife did not wish to help with props, clothes, and cooking. I am sure Gwen would dispute the latter, but there was no malice in Mary's version of events and she said of Dove, 'She was a great lady and I know they had a good relationship, but I'm glad I was able to help with so much'. It seems that Mary became indispensable to him, and the two remained close for seventeen years.

Friends and colleagues of Tommy, such as Barry Cryer, find laughable the idea of the big comedian as some sort of lothario. It was a relationship of convenience. Tommy needed help on the road, and Mary was there to supply it. Obviously, there was more to it than that, but it is easy to see how two people working in such close proximity, especially in the rarefied air of an industry as capricious as show-business, could have allowed the lines to become blurred.

Tony Kay, however, is in no doubt about the impact that Tommy had on Mary. He recalled the following in that *Daily Express* interview:

> He was the love of her life ... I'm sure my mother would have loved to be completely with Tommy, but I don't think he had any intention of leaving Dove. He needed someone to take care of him on the road and took advantage

of her feelings. That's the way I view it. My mum always saw the best in people. She saw him through rose-tinted spectacles and would not admit that he was not perfect.

The pair travelled the country, sharing hotel rooms, and checking in as Mr and Mrs Cooper. One time, Tommy forgot to pay his bill and the invoice was sent to his home address. It was not the first bill that Tommy ever forgot to pay, but this time, the repercussions threatened his marriage. When he returned to Chiswick, Gwen gave him hell, and it took all of Miff's tact and ingenuity to get the hotel to say that they had sent the wrong bill. They suggested that there had been another Mr and Mrs Cooper staying there at the same time, hence the confusion. A close shave, and it was a wonder that there were not many more such incidents, for in the industry, Tommy and Mary's relationship was well-known.

Even their children were aware of it. It seems that Dove was the only one who was not. At the time, Norman Kay was essentially living with another woman, Janice, and he and Mary would take turns looking after their three boys. They were good parents in all other respects, and the kids eventually came to terms with the unusual living arrangements. Norman and Tommy even became friends and would send each other humorous anecdotes.

While Tony Kay acknowledges his mother's great love for Tommy, his assessment of their affair is tinged with a hint of bitterness too. He says that overall, he liked Tommy, but he was not entirely convinced that he was as perfect as Mary believed. 'Tommy would make an effort to keep things humorous, but you wouldn't get any real idea of him behind the scenes'. If Tony raised any objection to how Tommy was treating her, Mary would protest and say 'Oh, but he's lovely'—rose-tinted glasses indeed. She would blame it on the pressure that Tommy was under.

The most disappointing aspect of the affair, Tony believes, is the lack of provision that Tommy made for her after his death. Mary was convinced, probably naively, that Tommy was preparing to divorce Gwen and marry her. He told her that he wanted to be with her until the day that he died.

He said that she would never have to worry about money because he would make sure that she was all right. Whether he ever planned to or not is a subject for debate. The reality is that she did not feature in his will and was left with nothing but her precious memories. I am sure she would have settled for that, but I am equally sure a little provision would have been appreciated too.

In all, Kay described their relationship like this: 'We had a wonderful life, full of fun and love. He was an absolutely beautiful man to be with'.

Many affairs fade and die. In this instance, it seems that Mary loved Tommy right up until the end.

'She never got over it,' Tony Kay has said. 'I think Tommy Cooper may have loved my mum, but I know that she was besotted by him'.

When the affair eventually became public knowledge, the newspapers tried to portray her as 'Mad Mary,' a kind of stalker. She was not; she was very much a part of Cooper's life, but she was not the only one.

At that time in Britain, divorce still carried a heavy social stigma. Having worked so hard to establish the career that he had, there is no way that Tommy Cooper would have risked everything to create a new life with another woman. His marriage, his family, and his relationship with Dove were what counted. Ultimately, Tommy wanted to continue in show-business, so his affair with Mary Kay was always just a practical solution to his endless life on the road.

35

Tommy Remembered

The doorbell would ring, long and loud, announcing the arrival of the man of the house, back from a week's cabaret. He struggled to keep track of his keys and was laden with a suitcase full of clothes and another full of his essential props; it was better for him to stand there and ring and let the family come to his aid, which they would. The door would open, and the children would fling themselves into his arms for a cherished cuddle. He might also be bearing gifts—souvenirs brought from whichever town he had been appearing in. Sundays, most definitely, were 'Father's Day' at the family home.

Vicky remembers a loving father, a joyous, boisterous presence to have around, as she told the *Daily Mail* in 2014 in the aftermath of the television show *Not Like That, Like This* in which Tommy's reputation was trashed. His comedic reputation was very much intact; indeed, it was as esteemed as it had always been. Yet the programme-makers decided that the drama lay elsewhere and chose an overall tone to the piece which sometimes left viewers feeling that they were watching some kind of monster. He was a bumbling clown, who was occasionally unkind, but was he a monster?

Tommy's daughter was keen to set the record straight. Despite the show's claims that she had approved the script, Vicky was left flabbergasted by the whole premise. 'My brother and mother would have been mortified by the result,' she said. 'I think Dad would have been incredibly upset too,' she added. 'What sort of daughter would I be to even consider approving a pack of lies?'

She describes her father as a flawed human being, like the rest of us. She disputes the fact that he was a violent alcoholic, and there is something very touching in her defence of him and in her fury at the television producers and writers who dared to defile his reputation. She has a point, particularly when the man is no longer here to defend himself. 'He wasn't this tortured soul you see in the drama. He had an almost childlike quality to have fun'. She said that she wanted her father to be remembered as a man who above all wanted to entertain people and make them happy.

Of the affair with Mary Kay and its effect on her father, Vicky finds solace in the fact that he did not gloat or even relish the situation he found himself in. 'Looking back, he did change during the affair,' she said. A couple of times, she caught him crying. He appeared morose and would have quiet moments. It is easy to believe that he was feeling guilty, rather than revelling in thoughts of being some sort of gigolo.

Yet those Sundays at home were the best, Vicky told the *Daily Mail* in 2014. The family would all pile into the parent's double bed and watch television in the afternoon, drinking tea, and eating sandwiches. Tommy's huge laugh echoed around the house. They were happy times.

The children found it difficult having such a famous father. They much preferred it when he was just 'Dad'. They thought he put his audience before them and were only too happy to be reminded that this was not the case. He would do practical jokes and practised his gags and magic tricks on them. The children, exactly as Dove had done, would comment on their suitability for his act. Just like before, Tommy would take note of their opinions.

Vicky says Gwen and Tommy were fantastic parents. They made each other complete. He would fuss over Dove if ever she had a high temperature and would even postpone engagements if she was unwell. It was a happy marriage, despite its occasional feisty nature.

'When Dad died, Mum was devastated,' Vicky said. 'She went into a slow decline. It was like she'd lost a part of herself'. This was hardly the reaction of a battered or downtrodden housewife. Vicky does acknowledge the part that Mary Kay played. At first, she said, she did not want to believe that it was anything serious. She also did not want to see her parents' marriage break up. Divorce was still a rare thing in those days. Though never desirable in any age, at the time, it came with added social stigma. She calls Mary 'the woman on the side,' who filled the void once Gwen decided to stay at home. 'There was simply a gap in dad's life on the road'.

It was an arrangement that came to be accepted by all who knew about it, while the secret had to be safely guarded from Gwen. Tony Kay recalls seeing both Vicky and Thomas Jr accompanying his mother to the Kay family home. The children all met each other and did their best to make light of it. They were all aware what was going on. Tony says Vicky and Thomas Jr became friends with his mother and saw her as a stabilising influence. Yet Vicky would not be so forgiving when Mary published a kiss-and-tell book two years after Tommy's demise, entitled *For the Love of Tommy*. It may have been motivated by money, to recompense for what she thought she would get from the estate. It may also have been an attempt to tell the world that she had loved, and had been loved by, a man she so clearly and deeply missed.

Vicky added that she was sick to death of people trying to cash in on her father's fame and name. It may be one reason why she had no show-business aspirations of her own. She wanted to become a beauty therapist, but took shorthand typing as well so that she would have, at her parents' insistence, something to fall back on. It was indicative of the way the children had been brought up. Both Tommy and Gwen were determined that, despite the family's wealth, their kids should not be spoilt.

Thomas Jr showed most inclination to follow his father's career path. He studied drama at the local polytechnic, but then chose to go and do something else. He had long been embarrassed by shouts of 'Just like that' wherever he went, as it was common knowledge in Chiswick that Thomas and Vicky were the offspring of one of the most famous men in Britain. So, young Thomas found a job on a building site, changed his surname to Henty, and relished the anonymity.

Speaking of anonymity, Tony Kay recalls a story where, now a grown man, he and Tommy Cooper were hanging out at the Kay family home in North London. Tommy suggested they go for a pint down the pub, and Tony watched as Tommy began to rummage around in his suitcase for something.

'What are you looking for?' Tony wanted to know.

'My sunglasses,' Tommy replied. It was dark outside, so why the need? Tony wanted to know. 'Well, if I'm wearing dark glasses,' Tommy replied, 'no one will recognise me'. The most famous man in the country, and the most imitated, needed far more than that to go incognito; what he planned to do about the 6-foot 4-inch frame and size thirteen feet, we will never know.

Blissfully unaware of Cooper's affair, and recognising that Tommy needed a helping hand, Gwen thrust Thomas Jr forward into what she thought was a vacant position. One can imagine the awkwardness that greeted his arrival, with Thomas Jr and Mary working out what each of their roles would be. For Gwen, she had peace of mind knowing that Tommy had someone on the road with him who could carry his bags, get him to bed at a reasonable hour, monitor his drinking, and help with all the props, setting the stage and the like. Now Tommy had two helpers, but he did not seem to have minded. He could hardly have objected without revealing the extent of Mary's presence in his life.

For Thomas Jr, it was a labour of love. It enhanced his drama studies and gave him a priceless opportunity to work behind the scenes on television and to soak up some of his father's fame at nightclubs across the country. He also managed to make the odd television appearance himself, playing stooge in several of Tommy's tricks and gags on screen. It may have fulfilled any acting ambitions that the youngest member of the Cooper household held.

It is only fitting then that, come that fateful occasion, live at Her Majesty's theatre, it should be these two fundamental elements of Tommy's life and work, the family and the affair, that should be present with him in the ambulance for that final journey. Mary claims that she and Tommy had made love in his dressing room before the show. 'Ridiculous!' Gwen later exclaimed after she read the widely disputed story. 'My Tommy had a bad back and couldn't possibly have done so'. The idea does seem far-fetched, especially as Tommy was using a makeshift changing area at the side of the stage. Also, where was Thomas Jr? Setting the props table, no doubt.

Whatever the truth is, it was all meat and drink to the tabloid journalists, and later the television drama experts who decided that there was much more to Tommy Cooper than met the eye. There certainly was, but I fear that it is not the kind of thing that the media seems presently concerned with. It is the fact that this much-loved comic was a much-loved man. His children adored him, and Dove, despite their occasional flare-ups, loved him more than anyone else. She loved him with a passion that left her a changed woman when he was gone, for a large part of her died with him on stage that night. That Mary Kay loved him too is not in doubt. Her own children know that better than anyone. If Tommy felt anything more than affection in return, I do not suppose that we will ever really know.

Yet Tommy Cooper as a bad man? Tommy Cooper as a monster? The closest he ever came was wearing a Frankenstein mask in one television sketch, and even that was hilarious.

36

Touring

Why do some people run away to join the circus? Why are some people drawn to a life on the stage? It is a question only a performer can answer. Maybe it is the sound of the applause that keeps them going, night after night, week after week, year after year, but it must get wearing.

Tommy once said, 'I was going to play Leeds, and I was going up by plane, and it got foggy and the plane was diverted to Manchester. I was really cross about it. So I got all my props and cases together and I thought I'll go and have a drink in the bar. True. And I'm standing there, and a young fellow came up to me and said "Hello. What are you doing here?" I said, "What am I doing here? Well, I live in Chiswick, and I got fed up walking around there, so I thought I'd come up here and walk around here, and when I get fed up here, I'll go back to Chiswick and walk around there again!"'

He was clearly in a grumpy mood that night. Occasionally, even for someone who loved his work as much as Cooper did, maybe all the travelling and the endless merry-go-round just got too much for him. Tommy said that he had stayed at every hotel in the country and had the towels to prove it.

Luckily for Cooper, he would often get a summer residency at a resort town, perhaps a pantomime, or a week-long run at a club. He did not have to move residency every day. Still, it did not provide the comforts of home. He missed Gwen's cooking and seeing the kids growing up on a daily basis. In order to stay at the top of his game, he gave up a lot.

Before the children were born, Gwen was happy to accompany Tommy around the country. They would hole up together and live like the newlyweds they once were. Then, Tommy spent many a year touring on his own. As his circumstances improved, he found better accommodation, ate at better restaurants, and enjoyed a better glass of wine with his meal.

In later years, he had Mary Kay for company. They would share a room, twin beds of course in case any questions were ever asked, but he lived his life on the road for the duration of his show-business career. He became adept at using his living situation in his act.

Here is an extract from a Tommy Cooper set that you may not have seen before. It was written, or more correctly, scrawled, on the back of a menu from the Blackpool Winter Gardens from February 1968, where the luncheon cost 12 shillings and sixpence and contained such delights as Clear Princess, Fylde Capon, and tapioca pudding for dessert.

The act runs over two pages. It begins:

> When I was two years old, my parents moved. I found them when I was four. I was born with a silver knife in my mouth. My father was a sword swallower. My father came from a musical background. He used to hit me with a violin! I was six years old when I discovered I was full of music. I had swallowed a mouth organ. I decided to become an inventor. For my first experiment I crossed a mule with a cow and I got milk with a kick in it. Then I crossed a pig with an elephant and got the biggest pork chops in town. Then I crossed a kangaroo with a raccoon and I got a fur coat with pockets. Then I went to a salesmanship school. The first thing they teach you is how to get your foot in the door. The next thing they teach you is how to get it out again! I've had my foot in so many doors there's a groove in it. The years flew by and I was soon a fully-fledged adult, high heels and everything. I got my first job right here in....

From there, his act would have consisted of stock jokes about Blackpool, which could be easily adapted to suit whichever town he was in. Obviously, jokes about Blackpool would be easily transferable to other seaside resorts such as Southend, Torquay, Bournemouth, or Eastbourne.

It did not matter how many times Tommy would do the rounds, the audiences never waned. There was never a time when Tommy Cooper was not the star attraction at whatever club he was due to perform, and he would make a joke of it. 'They say that everyone plays the [insert name of club] twice in their career. Once on the way up, and once on the way down. It's nice to be back!'

As well as local references, which always went down well, he might include the name of the club's patron in the act. 'My voice has been a bit hoarse today. Before I came on, I asked Danny Thomas if he could give me something for my throat'. He produces a cut-throat razor. 'Nice guy!'

'I've played some dives in my time. At one club they stabbed me goodnight'.

'But it's not all bad. One time the audience carried me shoulder high into the street after my performance. I said there's no need to carry me home, boys. They said "home? We're taking you to the river!"'

'I've got to get my glasses fixed. I walked in here tonight and bumped straight into eight people I owe money to'.

At these venues, usually the preserve of a crowd of drunken men, the 'wife' gags were a sure-fire hit. 'I was driving my car and a policeman stopped me. I said, "What have I done?" He said "Nothing, but do you realise your wife fell out the vehicle two miles back." I said, "thank goodness for that. I thought I'd gone stone-deaf!"'

'My wife spends a fortune on cold creams and oils. Puts them all over her body. Last night I went to grab her and she slid out of bed!'

'My wife's a magician. She can turn anything into an argument'.

'I said to my wife, I've been thinking about the quarrel we had last night, and I have to say that everything you said was right. She said, "It's too late. I've changed my mind."'

'She's into DIY, my wife. Any time I ask her to do something, she says "Do it yourself."'

'I met my wife at a dance. I thought she was at home with the kids!'

'My wife's a light eater. As soon as it gets light, she starts eating'.

He might then do a bit about his family.

'My people are in the iron and steel business. My mother irons and my father steals!'

'My brother used to work in the circus. They used to shoot him out of a cannon. Was he hurt? I don't know, they never found him!'

He also did jokes about his children.

'My boy is six-months old and he's memorised the *Encyclopaedia Britannica*. He's a real genius, but he can't talk, so nobody knows about it'.

'I hate making decisions. I have an eleven-year-old daughter I haven't named yet'.

'The trouble with kids today is that they're spoiled. I spent twenty pounds on a space-suit for my little boy, and then he wouldn't go'.

He even made jokes about himself.

'My father said to my mother, "Do you think he gets his intelligence from me?" She said, "He must do. I've still got mine."'

He also had gags for the more salubrious venues that he would play. He said, 'I'll never forget when I was playing the Palladium. I drew a line a mile long, but the manager made me go out and erase it!'

Whatever the venue, Tommy and his audience were a match made in heaven. His material was perfect for the clientele at these working-men's clubs. Whether it be a summer season, a Christmas production, a *Royal Variety Performance*, or one of his many charity functions, Tommy made himself available. Whatever hardships he experienced on the road, whatever disruption the constant touring caused to his daily life, Cooper accepted it as part of the path he had chosen.

For twenty years, Tommy had practised his act to perfection. For a decade after that, he was the most popular entertainer in the land.

What was driving him to keep on touring when he was clearly rich and not in the best of health? He had heard enough laughter to last anyone a lifetime.

Was he still searching for the perfect gig, the most appreciative audience, the funniest gag? Was he simply trying to give back to the fans who had supported him for so many years.

Whatever the reason, there is no doubt that Tommy had a love of performing in his blood. He must have done, to have put himself through so much for so long.

When anyone else might have slowed down, taken it easy, or semi-retired, Tommy just kept going. He was still the hardest working man in show-business, even when he had reached the very top. The touring years took their toll on Tommy, but in that time, he gave joy and laughter to millions. Tommy Cooper gave us everything, until he had nothing more to give.

37

Playing Cards

One staple of Tommy's act was the card trick. It is amazing what can be done with a simple set of playing cards. There are many true magic tricks that can be accomplished, and there are also a thousand gags that can be inspired by their inclusion. Tommy had some of the best:

> Take a card. Now I'll write the name of the card you picked on this piece of paper and I'll put it over here. Now think of your card. Got it? Now double it. Okay? Now add your weight. Now double that. Now add your height. Okay? Now divide the number in half. Right? Okay then, what's your card?' Tommy picks up the piece of paper and reads the result. 'The 217 of clubs!'

Every serious magician had a pack of cards in his repertoire. Every child's magic set would also include a pack. How far you manage to get with it is entirely up to the performer because there are endless varieties and hundreds of different routines, adding up to infinite opportunities to amaze.

Even today's most innovative and current magicians are fine exponents of this ancient art. David Blaine learned his trade with nothing else, and spent years mastering the cards. His ability took him from his front porch to the local diner, and eventually to palaces in the South of France, performing for royalty and to millions of people on television. He devotes a whole chapter to them, which he calls 'The Secrets of Cards', in his book *Mysterious Stranger*. He states that, to most magicians, the cards themselves are marvels.

The great card magician Dai Vernon, probably the most influential card manipulator of the twentieth century, said that a pack of cards should be treated like a living, breathing thing. The whole process of working with cards is almost poetic. He goes on to say that if you are in a room full of magicians and someone even mentions the word 'cards', within seconds, everyone is reaching into their pockets and pulling out their own deck.

David Blaine relates a tale whereby Winston Churchill, in his darkest hour at a particular nadir during the Second World War, went for dinner with some friends before he was due to rush off for an important meeting with the war cabinet. After the meal, there was some entertainment scheduled in the form of a magician and comic called Harry Green. The conjurer placed two cards face up on the table, one red and one black. He then handed the rest of the deck to the Prime Minister and asked him to deal the rest of the pack face down onto the two upturned cards. If he believed the next card to be red, he should place it on the red pile. If he believed it to be black, he should place it on the black pile.

Churchill did as instructed, hoping for nothing more than a few minutes of respite from the troubles weighing heavily upon him. When he had finished sorting the pack, he was absolutely amazed to discover that he had sorted the cards into two perfect piles, one red and one black.

Again and again, the Prime Minister repeated the trick, and every time, he achieved the same result. Now believing in the impossible, he rushed to his meeting with the cabinet and laid out his orders afresh. He probably believed he had magic powers at this point, such was the potency of the cards.

Dynamo, real name Steven Frayne, is a young magician riding the crest of a magical wave. He, too, is synonymous with a pack of cards. He seemingly reinvented the genre by taking his skills out onto the street where he would approach members of an unsuspecting public. In real life, people tend to be guarded when a stranger walks up to them unannounced. The magician had to work fast. For this, a card trick would be perfect. In Dynamo's hands, they usually were, and the result was outright amazement.

The difference between Tommy and almost every other magician, with the possible exception of Paul Daniels, is that nine times out of ten, Tommy Cooper would play it for laughs. This would include even the simplest tricks, such as 'I have here in my hand a pack of fifty-two cards'. He lifts the pack to his ear and drums his thumb along the edge. 'Sorry. Fifty-three!' Then he would hold up a card and ask someone to pick a card and then shout it out, to which Tommy would reply 'correct' before tossing it away. One time, on television, he asked an audience member to think of a card and not to tell him. Then he asked the man if he had thought of a card, and the bloke shouted it out.

Tommy, who may well have led the man into the mistake of shouting it out, either through verbal or physical suggestion, then has fun with the fact that he had told the man not to say anything. He made a joke out of it, playing it up to the rest of the audience, bringing them in on the gag.

According to Gwen, Cooper would even take a pack with him to the lavatory. He did not want to waste a minute and could spend the time practising as he was spending a penny. John Fisher, in his biography, thinks Tommy might well have slept with a pack of cards under his pillow. He wanted them to hand in case he should wake in the night and want to practice.

Then there was the pack containing a mouth organ, which Tommy raised to his lips before belting out a tune and announcing, 'Playing cards!' Who can forget the time he attempted to throw a card into his upturned fez at the *Royal Variety Performance*? Each failed attempt was followed by the shout of 'missed!'

Another trick, which he spent hours trying to perfect, was one that had been conjured up by an American impresario named Johnny Paul. He would get a member of the audience to sign a card from the pack then insert it randomly in between the other cards. Johnny would then throw the complete pack at a nearby wall. All would fall to the floor upon impact, but one would miraculously glue itself to the wall. That, invariably, would be the card with the signature written on it.

Tommy was impressed and practised the trick for hours. He decided to test it out on his daughter, Vicky, one Sunday at home. She duly signed one of the cards, and Tommy then threw them against the living room wall, where the entire pack descended unceremoniously to the floor. Tommy and Vicky, realising the trick had failed miserably, both fell about laughing hysterically.

Unlike the seventeen cases of props and tricks that would sometimes accompany Tommy on tour, a pack of cards fit snugly into the pocket of an overcoat and could be produced while standing at a bar to impress a friend or a member of the general public. It was all just audience to Tommy. After hours spent practising in his dressing room or hotel suite, the pay-off would come with the beguiled expression of the person on the receiving end. With sleight of hand, or dare I say magic, the card effect would be accomplished, and Tommy would be completely thrilled to see the trick work out.

There were many ways to include them in his act.

'These are Russian playing cards. No kings and queens,' he would say.

'Pick a card. Any card,' is known the world over as the prelude to almost every card trick. 'From this "ordinary" pack of cards' was another regular teaser. Of course, in the hands of a serious magician, no pack of playing cards is ever ordinary. They are one of the most important props in their act. Tommy, certainly, had more than his fair share of fun with them.

At the regular meetings of the Magic Circle, or the social gatherings at the various London magic stores, card tricks were a staple. Tommy's own set lists constantly refer to their inclusion. They are peppered throughout his act. Tommy made another reference to the chair of the Magic Circle.

'Jasper Maskelyne gave me this trick,' he said. 'And he was glad to get rid of it!'

If he had visitors at home, or even the odd journalist over to conduct an interview, he would usually be asked to do a bit of magic. He never refused. An audience was the very thing he wanted.

The request would be met with a big grin from Tommy and the response, 'Right, where's my pack of cards?' Then, having found them, he would reel off a small performance. 'Pick a card. Any card'. The guest would select a card and then hand it to Tommy.

'Which one have you picked?' he would say.

'Eight of hearts' (or some such thing) would come the answer.

'No. This one's called Fred,' and Tommy would turn the card over to reveal the name 'Fred' on the back, before collapsing with a huge guffaw.

Playing cards are seemingly the most simple of objects. They are a common household item, but in a magician's hands they really come to life. As Tommy once said, 'All the greatest magicians are dead. Houdini is dead. Devant is dead. Horace Goldin is dead. And I don't feel too good myself!'

What they all had in common was their love of a pack of cards.

38

A House Full of Memories

There are two major auction houses in London—Christie's and Sotheby's. The former was chosen to host an auction entitled 'Hats off to Tommy Cooper' in December 1990. The sale was accompanied by a catalogue outlining the various lots. Inside, as well as a sneak preview of what would be on offer, came a selection of gags to give a taste of what was to come and, also, no doubt, to put prospective buyers in a good mood. The gags, the catalogue said, cover a range of subjects from childhood to school, dentists, doctors, sex, sport, dogs, drunks, and wife jokes.

'Yesterday, I went round to see the doctor. There was nothing wrong with me. I just felt like sticking my tongue out at somebody'.

'My wife went to the hairdressers and had her hair set into the shape of a hand. I said, "What's that?" She said, "A permanent wave."'

'My favourite sport is the fight game. My father was a boxer, with just a dash of terrier on my mother's side'.

'My first day at school—I was so excited I cut myself shaving'.

'It was love at first sight. And what a sight it was. She had a beard!'

'Last week I made a killing in the stock market. I shot my broker!'

'I was in the Army. I got the military cross. I got the Navy pretty mad as well'.

The various lots included a collection of stage hats, original handwritten gags, cue cards, and lyrics. The various hats were divided into eight groups, with estimates of their value ranging from £150 to £500. There was a fez with an exceptionally high brim, worn by Cooper for a *Royal Variety Performance*. This came with an estimate of between £800 and £1,000. Then there was Tommy's own favourite fez; this came with an estimated value of £1,000 to £1,500.

The catalogue goes on to say that the collection provides a fascinating insight into Tommy Cooper's humour and methodology. The cue cards, for example, apart from their entertainment value, are important for their preservation of the text of Cooper's shows and provide evidence that Cooper's apparently haphazard act was actually planned to the finest detail, and that a specific structure lay behind his genius for timing.

One assortment, Lot 29, was a collection of tricks, props, and novelties including the Dippy Duck card selection trick, a collapsible suitcase, a bath hat, a rubber dove, a painted target, and an over-sized playing card—the three-and-a-half of spades. These were accompanied by a letter of authenticity from Gwen confirming that these were the tricks and props taken by Tommy for his very last performance in April 1984.

Lot 30 was described as a burgundy wool fez lined with scarlet cloth and decorated with a black silk tassel, with Gwen confirming that this was the fez that Tommy wore most often. The high-brimmed fez, especially made for Tommy, was said to come from *c.* 1960. It was meant to add extra inches to Tommy's already gargantuan frame, for added comedy value, as he was due to appear with the diminutive Arthur Askey.

Lot 36 was a large collection of assorted hats, including ladies' hats, knitted hats, straw hats, and a number of wigs including a judge's and a barrister's wig. All were confirmed by Gwen as having been worn by Tommy Cooper during theatre or television performances. There was a policeman's helmet, a British Army cap, a pith helmet, and a naval cap bearing the legend SS *Cooper*. There was even a dunce's cap. Other hats were collapsible or contained detonators or white rabbit glove-puppets. Their comic potential was plain for all to see.

This was not the first collection of Tommy's to come to auction, but even six years after his death, one can imagine Gwen was still in possession of a large amount of memorabilia from a man who toured with up to seventeen suitcases full of material. Gwen claimed they took up two bedrooms and a garage at the Chiswick home she shared with Tommy for twenty years. The house had six bedrooms and the props took up a third of the available space. 'God knows why I kept them all,' she said. She still retained a wardrobe full of fezzes, and almost every surface of the family home was covered with photos of the comedy giant. These included pictures of him with the Queen, or posing alongside one of his idols, American comedian Bob Hope. All of Tommy's awards were kept polished as if they had been won the day before, with the recipient due home any minute and about to inspect them.

The house had previously been a hive of activity. There were the two kids, who lived at home well into their twenties, plus the housekeeper who had been with them for thirty-five years, not to mention the two Alsatians and a dovecote full of fantails. Add to this Gwen's own larger than life character and you pretty much have a full house. As if all that were not enough, throw Tommy Cooper, the nation's favourite comedian into the mix. They should have filmed it; life in the Cooper house would have been a reality show that I would have liked to have seen. Many years before the Osbournes kept us all enthralled, *Life with Cooper* would have been a sure-fire hit.

By 1990, life had not been kind to Gwen. She had lost Tommy so publicly, and then four years later, Thomas Jr died of cirrhosis of the liver. It was a tragic end for a young man of just thirty-two years of age. Dove was devastated. She said that it was just as well that Tommy was not around to see it. He had worshipped his boy, and he could not have coped with the news. He would have fallen to pieces, she said.

It is true that father and son were very close. One nightclub owner said Tommy was always asking for him whenever they were on tour. 'Where's Thomas?' he would say. 'Go and get him for me. Tell him I want him'. He did not actually want him for anything, other than that he wanted him nearby. An excellent father, in Gwen's own words, Tommy idolised his son, and the feeling was mutual.

That Dove idolised Tommy is not in doubt. Slowly, over the course of several years after his demise, she began to de-clutter the home and released some bits from his act.

Dove would sometimes turn up at a club to watch Tommy work. Mary Kay, no doubt forewarned by young Thomas, who must have been aware of his mother's schedule, made herself scarce on such occasions. When Dove was in the room, everyone knew about it. She had to be a big personality to match Tommy Cooper, and she was certainly that. She would tell the person in charge of the venue that they had better be looking after her Tommy or else. She sang his praises. 'He's clean,' she would say. 'There's not many acts that are these days'. She was very proud of the fact that his material never ran blue. When Tommy died, she felt like she had been cleaved in two. She had worried about him that day. He had left the house for the theatre at 11.30 a.m. He kissed Gwen five times at the top of the stairs, then slowly, painfully, made his way downstairs.

'He looked dreadful,' she said. 'White as a sheet'. She had called out to him, 'Do you want a hot or a cold meal when you come in?' He did not reply. He either never heard her or was already preoccupied with the live performance that lay ahead of him, and which was causing him unusual concern. Dove wished that she had shouted something more intimate—something like 'I love you'.

Tommy would struggle up the street. The varicose veins and the ulcers on his legs were causing him a great deal of pain. During the day, Thomas Jr found a gap during rehearsals and phoned home. He told his mum that Tommy looked unwell. His next phone call came after the show. It was to tell Gwen that her husband had died.

'I couldn't believe it,' she said. 'I couldn't get it into my head. I sat in an armchair in the living room in a complete daze'. The next few weeks were a blur. She remembers the funeral and sprinkling Tommy's ashes in the garden, and that there were lots of people in the house, but she is pushed to remember who they were or anything that might have been said. She missed the little things: the cuddles, the kisses, the fact that he would tell her he loved her, and the times when he would appear at her bedside after he'd had a few drinks, just to look at her, the love of his life.

She had forty years of memories to fall back on, from that first kiss atop a tour bus in Egypt, which she described as lovely. She fell in love with him there and then and remained very much in love with him until the day he died—rather, until the day that she died. She could have done without the call that came from a newspaper two years later, saying they were about to serialise Mary Kay's book and did she have a comment for their publication. One imagines that she did.

She certainly had a tongue on her, no doubt honed in the many quarrels she had with Tommy over the years as the pair of them downed too much wine and told each other a few home truths. She dismissed 'That bloody woman' as an obsessive, who may or may not have had a one-night stand with her husband but nothing more.

She says if she had known about the situation while Tommy was still alive, she was not sure how she would have reacted. Reflecting on it long after his death, she said simply that he was only human after all. 'I know it was me he really loved,' she told a reporter for the *Daily Mail* in 1994, with tears welling up in her eyes. She missed looking after him, and cooking for him. If he had a club gig, he would sleep through the morning. He probably had not arrived home until 3 or 4 a.m. She would call him when it was time to get up. Like a lazy schoolboy, he would require several prompts before he would eventually surface. When he did so, his breakfast or dinner would be waiting on the table for him. The kids would be there, as was Sheila the housekeeper, as were the dogs and the other animals that they kept.

In the middle of all this activity would be Tommy Cooper, and at the heart of the house would be Gwen. Yet any analysis of the relationship between Dove and Tommy must take into account Mary Kay. While Gwen is surely correct in thinking that it was her that Tommy truly loved, Mary's dealings with Tommy, either on a professional or personal basis, gave her an insight into the man that Dove cannot provide.

Mary fancied herself as an artist of sorts. While away on tour, and probably to fill the hours that Tommy spent practising his routine, Mary took to capturing intimate scenes on canvas with her paint brushes and oils. There is one of Tommy aboard a train, travelling to the next destination on his itinerary. Another shows the two of them in a hotel room, containing two single beds, with Mary relaxing on one and Tommy sitting at the end of another. A third painting is of Tommy in the hotel bathroom, standing in his vest and shorts, brushing his teeth. In an interview, she talked about the enormous amount of medicines he would store on his dressing table, there for his many ailments.

She describes him as a bit of a hypochondriac, though admits he was often in pain. She also revealed how superstitious he was. He would always place his fez upside down on a table, never the right way up, for fear that it would trap the spirits inside.

The funny thing about Tommy and his fez is that, as much as it was his trademark, he never referred to it once during his act. It was just there, like it was a part of him. Another superstition of his was that he would never practice in front of a mirror, something which many performers, and especially magicians, did a lot in order to master the sleight of hand techniques necessary for a successful outcome. Tommy refused to do so.

Mary Kay told how Tommy broke down in tears when he reached fifty years of age. The milestone resonated with him and offered a reminder of his mortality. 'I don't want to grow old,' he said. Words that would sadly come true. Other than that, apart from the first five minutes after a show, which were a time for calm and reflection, he would always be optimistic, upbeat, and on form. She described him as 'Wonderfully buoyant. Nothing got him down'.

Bob Monkhouse says that Tommy was never curious about the world. He never seemed to have a book with him. He had no interest in anything outside of show-business and his family.

Tommy later appeared in a series called *Heroes of Comedy* alongside such luminaries as Les Dawson, Frankie Howerd, Mike Yarwood, Max Bygraves, and Ken Dodd. He comfortably took his place in such company. Even now, Tommy remains one of the most popular of entertainers. He was the comedian's comedian. Fellow professionals say that there is simply no one to compare him to. Jimmy Tarbuck said he cannot recall a single Cooper performance where he failed to upstage the other acts and steal the show.

For Dove, he was simply the man that she loved. Despite her heartbreak, made even more unbearable by the loss of their son four years later, she kept herself going through a resolute belief in the afterlife. She eagerly awaited the family reunion that would result. She said that they would all get together and have a good laugh. 'Oh, it will be so nice,' she said.

In 2002, Gwen passed away and departed for the big stage in the sky.

39

A History of Magic

What is so magic about magic? Maybe it is about capturing that sense of wonder that we had when we were children, before we became cynical adults, and before we thought we knew it all. Most of us had a hobby when we were young. Some of us wanted to be train drivers or astronauts or professional footballers when we grew up. Then, most of us grew out of our earlier obsessions. Tommy found magic at an early age. It was a passion that coursed through him for the rest of his days.

It has been said that you do not get into magic, magic gets into you. David Blaine compares performing a magic trick to a game of chess where you try to outwit your opponent. Moves are planned in advance, and the more moves you can think ahead, the better able you are to ultimately win; not only should you think of your own moves in advance, you should also try and anticipate those of the person that you are competing against.

Whether Tommy Cooper ever thought about it in such terms is surely in doubt. He favoured practice over analysis, and he had a lifelong fascination and childlike enthusiasm for his craft. If he could, Tommy would have liked to have been a pure magician. Yet with his flair for comedy, and the overwhelming audience response to his humour, he was never going to be allowed to do what he enjoyed doing best. Backstage, his tricks all worked. Many a fellow performer was beguiled by his mastery. On stage, he had to play it for laughs. The audience expected nothing more and would have accepted nothing less.

Does this mean that Cooper had to leave his magic ability in the dressing room? It does not. He found countless ways to employ his skills as he tread the boards before an adoring public. He wore the attire of a magician, his props table resembled that of a magician, and everyone watching thought that they were watching an amateur magician delivering sublime comedy. We forgave him for bringing his hobby on to the stage, because it was clear that he genuinely loved magic.

One area where Tommy could practice a magician's art on stage was in the use of suggestion, otherwise known as misdirection. It is described as a skill that magicians use to make their audience look where they want them to, when they want them to. On stage, Tommy Cooper, with his impeccable comic timing, would also employ this device, either to help him to occasionally make a trick go 'right', or to elicit some response or participation from the audience that would further his act or set up a gag. It would be wrong to suggest that Cooper ever needed to employ subterfuge to create the audience response he would always receive, yet such an accomplished and well-practiced magician must have used certain 'tricks' to help achieve his aims.

The history of magic goes back some 5,000 years. The earliest recorded magic stories relate to the Pharaoh Cheops, the man thought responsible for building the world's first pyramids. There was a magician in his court called Dedo, who was summoned to render someone deceased and then bring them back from the dead. Now the underworld was a precious thing to those early Egyptians, and Dedo refused to put anyone in that sacred place, even if he was planning to bring them straight back again. Instead, he chose to practice on a goose. He proceeded to rip the bird's head from its torso, placed both parts on the ground several feet apart and then, to the astonishment of the pharaoh and his subjects, brought the bird back to life, where it squawked loudly and ran among the crowd to the amazement of everyone present. From there on in, magic and its practitioners were heralded for their unworldly gifts, their tricks shrouded in mystery, their aura and status assured.

An early definition of the art of misdirection came from Nevil Maskelyne, founder of the Magic Circle. He said that it consists admittedly in misleading the spectator's senses in order to screen from detection certain details for which secrecy was required. Another magician, Harlan Tarbell, said, 'Nearly the whole of sleight of hand depends on this art of misdirection'.

Indeed, a fellow practitioner, Dariel Fitzkee, stated that 'The true skill of the magician is in the skill he exhibits in influencing the spectator's mind'. Misdirection, it is claimed, is the central secret of all magic.

That said, there is some concern among the magic fraternity about the negative connotations of such a term; 'direction' would be just as accurate a description, and one unencumbered by the idea that the magician may be somehow misleading and therefore cheating the audience.

For Tommy Cooper, of course, who took sheer delight from confounding as well as elating an audience, there can be no such accusations that he was somehow cheating his fans. In fact, so few of his tricks ever turned out right that it would be nonsense to claim anything other than he was under-playing what he could actually do.

One way that most magicians attempt to achieve the result of misdirection is through the use of 'patter'—saying one thing while doing another. For Tommy, who had audiences in the palm of his hand, their attention distracted by the tears of laughter filling their eyes, the patter consisted of an endless stream of gags. It is tempting to think that he could have made it as a magic act after all. A comical one, of course, for we would never have let him deprive us of that, but maybe he could have been the accomplished magician he was no doubt equipped to be. His patter would have been second to none as we would have been too busy laughing.

When discussing magic, words such as 'illusion' and 'manipulation' are all brought to bear. The very idea of magic was linked to the occult and with the notion of witchcraft. It was only when we stopped burning people at the stake did the fun element of magic begin. In the eighteenth century, conjurers and illusionists, better known to us today as magicians, saw the reputation of the craft improve and finally deemed the occupation safe enough for them to appear at fairgrounds and circus attractions.

In the last century, men such as Houdini achieved widespread fame, and the practice of magic was elevated to the level of art-form. Houdini first performed under the banner of the 'King of Cards'. Again, these simple props proved invaluable for their versatility and ubiquity.

Dai Vernon, card magician, went under the impressive moniker of 'The Man Who Fooled Houdini'. It seems that even the greatest could still be confounded and undone. So, if it is possible even for the King of Cards to be fooled, what hope do the rest of us have?

While Tommy Cooper was capable of doing more magic than he ever showed his audience, his intention was never to cheat, and never to misdirect, except in the most positive sense. His aim was to charm, and to engender that child-like glee into the hearts and minds of an adoring public. That he never took advantage of his audience makes him more endearing still.

Wherever he travelled, Tommy would seek out the magic shops, always looking for the latest gadget. Wherever he toured and worked, he would do the same. He went to conventions, gatherings, Magic Circle conferences, anything to support the cause and to soak up as much knowledge as he could about his favourite pastime. He studied the craft and delighted in its mysterious and magical ways.

Cooper dedicated his life to sharing his love for magic with audiences across the land. To those watching, he may have been more comedian than magician but, to Tommy, the magic always came first.

40

Tommy's Heroes

Tommy walked on stage and addressed the audience. 'This is a genuine camel hair coat. It is. It is! What, you don't believe me?' He turned around and there were two large humps stuck on the back.

From the most inauspicious of props, Tommy could raise a laugh. 'See this glove?' He held up a glove, before another dropped down beside it; the pair were sewn together at the finger tips. 'Second-hand!' No one else would have dared as it was all in the delivery, the timing, and his unique bumbling presence. He was constantly laughing. It was as if he were sat in the crowd, watching and enjoying the show along with the rest of them. He laughed as hard as they did, at his own jokes.

Ronnie Barker has said that there have been precious few performers in the history of comedy who had the gift that Tommy had. He suggests W. C. Fields as someone who maybe had it. He posits Oliver Hardy as another, and that is it. Tommy would have been honoured to be mentioned in the company of such legends. W. C. Fields was famous the world over for the curmudgeonly character he portrayed on stage and screen. Oliver Hardy was one of Tommy's all-time favourite heroes. Fields took his first stage bows as a juggler, and only turned to comedy when he failed to make the grade with his favoured routine. Hardy trained on the American vaudeville circuits before finding fame and universal acclaim when he teamed up with Stan Laurel to create some of the funniest films ever made.

Cooper was such a fan of the duo that he took a projector on tour with him so he could delight in the exploits of the pair from the comfort of his hotel room. From the twenties to the forties, Laurel and Hardy made some of the most popular comedy films of all time. Such was their success that they were required to churn out movie after movie, feeding the Hollywood machine in the golden age of cinema. When, after almost twenty years of continuous endeavour, the pair decided to take a well-earned break, they headed to the UK. Stan Laurel intended to visit family that he had in Scotland. Oliver Hardy decided to tag along and spend a fortnight playing golf, which was an all-consuming passion for the larger than life star.

Amazingly, the comic pair had no idea of the hysteria that was to greet them when their ship pulled into Southampton. Soon, sensing the publicity coup, their film production company, MGM, arranged a tour for them, which took in London, Birmingham, Manchester, Newcastle, Edinburgh, and Glasgow. In the latter, more than two dozen people were hospitalised as a result of being crushed in the crowd. Both Stan and Ollie were amazed at the reception. They had spent so much time in the studio that they had no idea just how big they had become. When they were in London, greeting fans in Leicester Square, there among the crowd was a certain Thomas Frederick Cooper. It was, he later said, the only time in his life that he had ever queued up for an autograph.

On a couple of occasions, while Tommy was performing on television, he would have an Oliver Hardy look-a-like cross the stage behind him, stopping just long enough to wave at the audience and catch Tommy's attention before wandering off. That famous Hardy walk—an agile and graceful meander, almost a saunter—came about as a result of being cast in several early films. His large size had caused him to be bullied in school, and he was worried about how he would appear on the screen. It would be unseemly to have a big man lurching about all over the place, so he decided to change tack. 'I always try to walk slightly,' Hardy explained. 'I've always loved to dance, and I suppose that's why I've learned how to walk easily'.

Funnily enough, if Tommy Cooper's bemused and bewildered expression brings anyone else to mind, it has to be Stan Laurel. There is more than a passing resemblance between them. There is that air of innocence, of befuddlement with the world around them—a look of desperation never too far from the surface, and one that was synonymous with them both. Stan was also blessed with magical powers, at least on screen. His ability to spark a flame by flicking his thumb and using it to light his pipe is one of the more surreal episodes in the history of filmmaking; it is apropos of nothing yet manages to be everything.

If the two film giants had ever had the opportunity to see Tommy's act, I am sure they would have appreciated his unique clown-like style. Stan Laurel had toured the music halls of Britain before making the move to the States, and Oliver Hardy had run away from home aged just eight to join a Vaudeville troupe. With Tommy's theatrical experience, all three would have had a lot in common. The difference is that the duo was steeped in film—it was the medium that loved them best—while Tommy responded best to a live audience.

Also, according to Eric Sykes, Tommy could not act. In a tribute video made after Tommy's passing, Eric is standing in front of an enlarged photo of his old pal, and after stating his thoughts on Tommy's lack of acting ability, he turns and repeats it into Tommy's ear. 'Did you hear that? I said you can't act'. It is a tender moment. He then relates a story from the making of his film, *The Plank*. They were sitting in a canteen with the rest of the cast and crew, the former all fine actors, according to Eric. There they sat, stuffing their faces because 'They don't get paid much but what they can do is eat,' talking in plummy voices because 'They're so highly trained they can talk and eat at the same time!' Then, in the midst of all this worthy chatter, and in the setting of a public restaurant, Tommy got up out of his chair, moved to the centre of the room, and lay down on his back. He stayed there a moment and then stood up and returned to his seat as if nothing had happened.

'What did you do that for?' Eric asked.

'I just wanted to do something visual,' Tommy replied.

Eric went on to say that one look from Tommy was worth ten years at RADA, the famous British acting school.

When it came to Sykes's appearance on *This Is Your Life*, the biographical television show hosted by Eamonn Andrews, Tommy stole the show by coming on with a plank of wood and then doing essentially five minutes of stand-up, interacting with Eric as well as invited guests such as Hattie Jacques, Frankie Howerd, Max Bygraves, and Spike Milligan, who can be seen wiping tears of laughter from his eyes at Tommy's recollection of working with Eric.

It is hard to work out if it was scripted or not. There were a couple of visual props in play, but most of it is off-the-cuff banter between Tommy, the host, and the celebrities in attendance, as well as the show's star guest. Tommy does a couple of his stock-in-trade gags. 'I can't help laughing. I know what's coming next'. He had long built up a stable of such gags, and they helped to pad out his sketches, stories, and routines. He would never hurtle through the telling of a tale as there was always a rich seam to mime, and Tommy had gems in abundance that he could sow along the way. This included, 'Good evening. Have I got time for one more?' as well as many variations of this, or the way that he would break off in the middle of a funny story to engage with the audience, halt the flow, saving the punchline for later as he engaged in witty banter, such as this story he told about a man going into a bar.

'A fella goes into a bar and he orders a pint. The barman serves him and the bloke drinks the pint like that and puts the empty pint down on the counter. He turns to the people on his right and says, "You're a bunch of idiots," and then he turns to the people on his left and he says, "And you're a bunch of fools." And then he walks out. The next night, the same bloke comes back into the pub and orders a pint. The barman serves him and the bloke drinks the pint and puts the empty glass down on the counter. Then he turns to the people on his right and says, "You're a bunch of idiots," and then he turns to the people on his left and he says, "And you're a bunch of fools." And then he walks out. Well, there's this bloke sitting there, and he says to the barman, "If he comes in tomorrow night ..."' Then Tommy breaks off and speaks to the audience. 'I mean, he might not.

I don't know. He might do or he might not'. Getting slightly frustrated now 'I don't even know the bloke. I don't know, do I? But he might'.

Tommy goes back to the story. 'So, the next night, the bloke comes in again, and he orders a drink. The barman serves him, and he drinks the pint and puts the glass back down on the counter. Then he turns to the people on his right and says, "You're a bunch of idiots" and then he turns to the people on his left and he says, "And you're a bunch of fools." Now the bloke from the night before has had enough and he says, "Right you, I'm not a fool!" and the other fella says "Well, get over there then with the idiots!"'

Only Tommy Cooper could get away with such material. It is in the telling, the ability to string it out and let us spend even more time with him, where the key to the chemistry and the relationship he formed with an audience are to be found. Eric Sykes calls stand-up comedy the most dangerous profession in show-business. He went on to wonder if we would ever see Tommy's like again.

Tommy Cooper had his own heroes from the world of entertainment. For sure, he also became a hero himself to the performers who followed in his wake.

41

Drinking to Excess

'Two guys were standing at a bar, drinking, when all of a sudden one of them fell face down on the floor. His friend turned to the bartender and said, "That's one good thing about him. He always knows when to stop"' If only Tommy knew too.

Max Bygraves tells a story about Tommy and Gwen having a fight one Sunday morning at their bungalow in Eastbourne. They had one of their usual arguments and Dove stormed off in a huff, jumping in a cab and heading for a hotel in nearby Brighton that the couple used to frequent. Tommy took a few minutes to calm down and then jumped into a cab himself and gave chase. During the cab ride, Tommy began to get undressed. He removed his jacket and shirt and stripped down to his underwear. Then, he walked into the hotel, through the reception, and into the bar, where he found Dove sitting down, nursing a drink. Tommy approached his wife and said 'Dove, where's my clean shirt?' She and the whole room fell about laughing. Tommy then got dressed and the pair carried on with their afternoon.

At their Chiswick home, Gwen would joke with guests about how they did not have a matching set of chairs in the dining room. They had all been broken in various conflagrations, to be replaced in *ad hoc* fashion whenever a replacement had to be found. The cause of these many arguments was the drinking binges they would embark upon.

Vicky Cooper says her father only ever took his temper out on the furniture. She said he once got so angry that he picked up a chair and smashed the legs off it. Then, a few hours later, he looked at it and said, 'Oh God. That was my favourite one as well'.

Tommy's alcohol habit, picked up on the road, did not stop when he got home. Instead, it continued apace. There is the time when Tommy poured gin on his cornflakes as he deemed it to be healthier than full-fat milk. From his club days, one owner revealed a little of Tommy's drinking habits. As he was the star attraction and a very welcome guest, as every show had sold out, Tommy had the run of the bar. He would go and pour himself a drink, and then ask, 'What are you having?' of anyone nearby. He would not have been so magnanimous if he had to pay for it, but it was all completely gratis.

The reply would come, 'Vodka and coke'. Tommy would pour the drink and have one of the same for himself. Then he would ask someone else. The reply might be 'Whiskey and lemonade'. Tommy would pour the drink and have one of the same for himself. Then the owner would appear and Tommy would ask him 'What are you having?' Just half of Guinness would come the reply, and Tommy would pour them both a glass of the black stuff. Mixing your drinks does not come into it. It seemed that Tommy would down anything.

These were the years that finally took their toll on Tommy. Eventually, after his heart attack in 1977, the cause of which was chronic alcoholism, his doctor advised him to slow down. It took some time for the message to get through although, eventually, he did cut back on both his drinking and his smoking. Bob Monkhouse was working with Tommy one time, and in the hours before the show Tommy cracked open a can of lager and lit up a slim panatela cigar.

'I thought you had stopped drinking and smoking,' said Monkhouse, surprised.

'You can't call this drinking, and you can't call this smoking,' Tommy replied.

It seems that Cooper was doing his best to follow doctor's orders, but it cannot have given him much pleasure to have had to miss out on the things he enjoyed.

Clive Mantle played the role of Tommy in the play *Jus' Like That! A Night Out with Tommy Cooper* following in the footsteps of Jerome Flynn in a touring production. He says that he believes Tommy drank because of the pressure of being such a big star. 'Imagine having to be Tommy Cooper all the time. The only thing that could help him deal with the expectations of millions was alcohol'.

Bob Monkhouse described Tommy as a child with an infant's rage, adding that a lot of waiters could testify to the fact. It is true that he did have a temper, and obviously this would be exacerbated when drunk. Mary Kay claims that Tommy knocked her to the floor in a restaurant, after she had laughed at him for protesting that his pork crackling was soggy. Tommy's daughter Vicky has acknowledged that her father could be volatile. 'He had a lousy temper but he came down quick,' she said.

Dennis Kirkland said he could not take Tommy seriously if he ever rose to anger. Once, Dennis had brought a suit for Tommy to wear in a sketch, and it just was not right. The more Tommy ranted at him, the more the television producer laughed, until eventually he had tears rolling down his face. In the end, Tommy said, 'I'm going. You're fucking nuts!'

Kirkland then met Tommy one lunchtime in the bar at the television studios in Teddington. Tommy said he was allowed one glass of wine and then proceeded to work his way through three whole bottles. When Dennis asked what had happened to the supposed restriction, Tommy said, 'Well, I've only used one glass'.

Backstage, Tommy would lock his booze away, lest any of the stagehands help themselves to it. He would do the same with the phone in case anyone made a call that Tommy would be charged for. John Fisher, Tommy's biographer, and himself a gold member of the Inner Magic Circle, puts this caution down to the fact that Tommy was known as the meanest (i.e. the most tight-fisted) man in show-business. Tommy's daughter Vicky acknowledges that the performer would grow increasingly nervous as the curtain call approached. He once said to her, 'People don't know real fear until they've stood in the wings every night'.

John Fisher claims Cooper drank simply because he was successful. He enjoyed it, he could afford it (though he did not like to pay for it), and therefore he simply went ahead and did it to excess. Tommy once remonstrated with a television producer who showed concern that Cooper would be in a fit state to perform: 'I'm the star of this show. I'll drink if I want'. There is that childlike temper again that Bob Monkhouse referred to.

He would often arrive home drunk after a performance. He once jumped in a cab, held up the bottle of brandy he was holding, and asked the driver if he thought he had enough to get him to Chiswick. Once he got back to the house, there would be Dove, who would often advise the cabbie to, 'Bring him in, throw him on the couch, and fuck off!' Mary Kay believed Tommy drank to help him forget his various physical ailments. It was getting increasingly difficult to drag that huge frame around, as age, his drinking, and his illnesses all exacted their toll.

Miff Ferrie recorded in his diary that Tommy drank all the time, buying bottles of spirits like anyone else would buy beer. Gwen related to Miff how Tommy would sit at the dressing table in their bedroom, drinking whiskey all night. She said he got violent when drunk. When his drinking was at its worst, he could certainly be abusive. In a series of nuisance phone calls to Miff, often occurring at all times of the night, the manager and his wife began turning on the answering machine to record the increasingly bizarre rants that Tommy would direct at both Miff and his wife, Beatrice. One time, Tommy said to her, 'Are you still ill, Beatrice? You've been ill for thirty years!'

It seems that Tommy abused himself with alcohol for a decade or more. The 1970s were the worst, leading eventually to his heart attack in 1977. At least the diagnosis was accurate, and it should have served as a wake-up call. Instead, Tommy seems to have shrugged it off. A routine check-up the following year, demanded by Miff who was desperately trying to look after his artist, saw the doctor surmise that Tommy had liver problems caused by drinking too much. On top of his other health issues, it really was time to cut back. Yet, it seems that this did not happen, and though he eventually slowed down a little, he never did manage to stop.

Tommy was a guest at many Variety Club luncheons, or guest of honour, I should say. On many such occasions, he would be accompanied by Dove. At many of these functions, certain members of the audience would don their own fez, joining in with the fun. There was one notable dinner where every one of the 400 people in the crowd, in unison, put a fez on their head just as Tommy rose to speak. Quick as a flash, Tommy put on a fisherman's cap. The whole place fell about laughing. For all his fame and fortune, and despite his occasional outbursts, Tommy remained down to earth.

He was not one for interviews. He was a performer. He refused to appear as the subject on *This Is Your Life*; instead, he was content to turn up only in support and praise of friends. Probably the only major television interview he gave was on the hugely popular Michael Parkinson show in the 1970s. Tommy appeared to the accompaniment of the house band playing 'The Sheik of Araby'.

Parky was a skilled interviewer, but he manages to extract absolutely nothing out of Cooper. Instead, he is seduced into allowing Tommy to simply perform a succession of jokes and tricks. Maybe Tommy never wanted to look behind the curtain. Maybe he did not have the character for self-evaluation. Perhaps he just did not care. How many jokes could he tell in the time it would take to analyse himself, and which was more important? To Tommy, it would always be to make people laugh. That said, the Parkinson interview almost ended in tragedy as Tommy failed to activate the safety switch on a guillotine trick in which Parky played the condemned man. Only the prompt intervention of a studio technician prevented serious injury or worse. It could have been the end of Tommy's glittering career. Maybe Cooper had taken his eye off the ball by enjoying a pre-interview drink. Though his popularity was still intact, the cracks were starting to show. That said, he was still capable of making a lasting impression. He was still one of the funniest people alive.

There is a story that Miff and Tommy were once in Japan and they had to take a cab to their hotel. Tommy and Miff spoke no Japanese, and their driver spoke no English, but Tommy made the cab driver laugh so much that he crashed into a wall!

It would be one of many trips that Tommy made abroad. Though he never 'conquered' America, he was a frequent visitor, enjoying New York and Las Vegas and, of course, his many appearances on *The Ed Sullivan Show*. He played all over Europe, and also ventured to the Middle East, playing concerts at Abu Dhabi and Doha. With drinking restricted in these places, Tommy was not best-pleased to find that he would be limited to Coca Cola. Cooper demanded that some brandy be found to accompany it. The message was passed around and some brandy was procured. Tommy refused to go on stage without it.

He was always at ease with a drink in his hand, no matter where he was. Dove was a willing drinking partner, though even she could not keep up. Tommy had recorded a couple of television series in the middle of the decade, the audience response being captured and used as the laughter track for many other shows, but it was on the cabaret circuit where he most plied his trade, and it was here where Tommy's problems were most noticeable.

Still, murmurs of discontent filtered back to Miff from club owners across the land. He was forced to return fees or take lesser payments. Tommy wanted to cut back on his workload. At first, he was to take one week off for every two that he worked. He then asked Ferrie if this could be the other way around. They eventually settled for two on and two off. It still would not be enough to restore Cooper to health, not when the underlying causes had yet to be addressed.

He had insomnia. Mary Kay, whenever he was on tour, would encourage him to take a nap before a show. Her rationale was that if he could not sleep at night, perhaps he could during the day.

It was another way to keep him out of the bar, too. Whatever was tried though, it was not enough. As the '70s turned into the '80s, the damage had already been done.

42

The Final Performance

Miff Ferrie was an astute manager, and Tommy's earnings throughout the 1970s were well over £100,000 annually. It allowed them to pick and choose from the many offers that continued to pour in. For all their fallings out, the two men had chartered a course that saw Tommy Cooper as a valuable yet available commodity. It had endured for almost four decades, enough time to allow for some reflection.

'We have to look after him,' the agent explained in one interview. 'He's a very valuable property'. Asked how Tommy felt about being the most impersonated man in the country, Miff said 'He loves it. He will start to worry when they stop impersonating him'. He had the best of both worlds. He could go on tour and earn several thousand pounds a week; meanwhile, he was ubiquitous and popular as other people were telling his jokes for him, in character, on television screens across the land. Occasionally, he would pop up on television in person to remind everyone how good the real thing could be.

As his health began to falter, Tommy understandably slowed down. His earnings were reduced accordingly, but he was already a wealthy man. Jackie Mason does a terrific gag where he said, 'I have enough money to last me for the rest of my life ... as long as I don't buy anything!' Tommy had more than he could ever spend, and too little time left to enjoy it.

He made concessions to his lifestyle, checked himself into a Hampshire health farm for a short spell, and took as many holidays as his schedule would allow. His Army days had given him a taste for hot climates and any break he got, he would head for the sun; Tenerife, Spain, and Gibraltar were favourites. America too held a fascination for him. Wherever he went, he would continue to seek out the magic shops—that lifelong love for the craft never left him.

Dove recalled a lost six hours in New York where Tommy vanished from their hotel to go and visit a magic shop that he had heard about, and then could not find his way back to their accommodation. It summed him up perfectly, as he was forever lost, forever late, and seemed to bumble his way through everything. He was pretty much the same in life as he was in his act. Maybe that was one of the reasons that people loved him. There was no artifice. He really was just one of them.

While he tried to modify his behaviour to accord with his doctor's wishes, he had simply placed himself in the path of temptation by continuing to work the cabaret circuit. These were boozy, smoke-filled, testosterone-laden environments. Tommy felt completely at home there and was having too much fun.

He was not a well man by the start of the eighties. Audiences could see it. The man himself could see it, but still he kept going, still the best-loved entertainer in the country. Even when he was not at his best, he still was the best, and the demand for him was still there.

Tommy's movements had always been a delight. They were a large part of his act. No one moved like Tommy Cooper. His frame, looks, and sheer physicality marked him out as an anomaly, and he played them to great effect—hands constantly moving, his feet constantly moving. These were now to be attempted by someone unsteady on their feet. His voice was now more of a mumble. Words were occasionally slurred. Mary Kay said that, when mingling with the crowd while Tommy was on stage at a nightclub, she would hear people mutter that Cooper was not as good as he used to be. Yet he was still fully booked. He was still Tommy Cooper. He could still pick and choose. After almost four decades in the business, he could have retired, but a performer is a performer. The show, and Tommy, just had to go on.

He lived to make people laugh. It was simple as that. He lived to entertain an audience, and nothing gave him more pleasure than to see and hear a group of people enjoying his act.

Vicky Cooper says, 'The way he has been painted as self-obsessed is untrue. He was a kind person, someone I went to with my troubles, but I would say his failings were his deep insecurity and his neediness'.

It is easy to see the neediness in his workload, the constant need for appreciation. His insecurity may have derived from his own father's lackadaisical approach to life. It may have come from the age of austerity in which he grew up. For sure, his attachment to money, his devotion to duty, speak of a man who was never able to rest on his laurels. He appears never able or willing to really relax.

Then, with club-land going into a steep decline as the 1970s became the '80s, Tommy continued to work, drink, and smoke. He was burning the candle at both ends continuously. Daughter Vicky wanted him to slow down. She tried to warn him. 'I said to my Dad, "Don't think you're just going to conveniently drop dead. You'll end up in a wheelchair, and you won't like that, will you?" As it happened, dropping dead was exactly what he did, and it was actually a very fitting way for it all to end. He was on stage, doing the thing he loved most in the world: making people laugh'.

As the intervals became longer between each television outing, Tommy proved as popular as ever whenever he chose to appear. As such, he was the headline act for his performance on *Live from Her Majesty's*. Miff took the booking, little knowing that it was going to be Tommy Cooper's last.

At 11.30 a.m., Tommy left the family home in Chiswick and made his way into London's West End, the cultural quarter. Thomas Jr was with him. Dove had called out to him from the top of the stairs, asking what he wanted to eat when he got back. She received no reply. Tommy was already thinking ahead to the evening's performance. Using an alarm clock that they kept in the kitchen, the couple had timed Tommy's act to perfection, just as they had done so many times before. As an accomplished pianist, Gwen knew a lot about timing. They practised Tommy's act until he had filled every second of the seven-minute slot that his performance required. They had bickered slightly over how much time to allow for the audience laughter that was sure to come his way. Eventually, the routine was finished and polished, and Tommy and his son set off for the venue.

When they arrived, they were met by Mary Kay. She was, by now, a permanent fixture for his every performance. The theatre had a resident doctor on hand, and he looked Tommy over before giving him the all clear. Young Thomas later phoned his mum and told her that Tommy did not look particularly well, but no alarm bells were ringing just yet.

Rehearsals went well. Jimmy Tarbuck was there as the compère. Les Dennis and Dustin Gee, two rising young comics, were also on the bill. Tommy was pleased to be on the stage and reassured that everything was going to plan. He needed that reassurance as he had been anxious that the show was going out live. He had appeared only fleetingly on the nation's screen in the previous couple of years. If not exactly a comeback, it would serve as a timely reminder that he was still king of the comics, the daddy of them all. Mary Kay suggested that Tommy have a nap for half an hour. He looked peaky and tired. When she went to check on him, she took him some apple crumble, which he did not eat.

Jimmy Tarbuck recalls Tommy opening a can of non-alcoholic lager. It seemed that Tommy was taking no chances before his performance, and also heeding the doctor's advice at long last. Then, the show began and soon it was Tommy's turn to entertain the nation. He did not disappoint. He began with a word to the band. 'I want you to play tonight like you've never played before. Together!' Then he proceeded through the act with consummate ease until he came to the Magic Cloak trick. That was when he slumped to the floor. The audience laughed, but backstage and in the wings, no one found it funny. They knew something was wrong. They knew this was serious. They cut to an ad break and brought the curtain down. The house doctor tried to revive Tommy but, sadly, it was to no avail. The ambulance arrived, and Tommy was rushed to hospital. He did not recover, and his death was announced that evening on the 10 o'clock news.

The show-business world went into mourning. His funeral was like a who's who of British entertainment. He was said to have emanated the most expansive comic aura of any comedian of his generation. You could expand on that and call him the most popular performer of the twentieth century.

His friends spoke about his legendary tightness with money, and they did not gloss over the fact that he had sometimes let them and himself down by displaying an occasional mean spirit. Yet no one could hold anything against him, for he had simply given them so much joy over so many years. All was forgiven, because no one could quite believe the sheer power and magic of this true comedy great. That he had graced their lives was something they all gave thanks for. To a nation of fans, he was simply the best there ever was.

Thirty-plus years after his death, it is like Tommy Cooper has never been away. He continues to top polls for the nation's favourite comedian, and he continues to excite the attention of writers and producers who are keen to keep his memory alive. As well as several books about Tommy, he has recently been the subject of a controversial drama series on television, as well as several shows at the Edinburgh festival, including my own play, *The Tommy Cooper Show*, which continues to tour at venues up and down the country.

Vicky Cooper says that her father's biggest worry was whether he was actually ever funny enough. As he departed the stage for the final time, it was to the sound of laughter. That is how I am sure he will be remembered—as possibly the funniest man who ever lived.

43

The Legacy

The Tommy Cooper Society has more than 2,000 members, the most famous being Sir Anthony Hopkins. Its chairman is Chris Brunt, and as well as coming together to celebrate the work of their eponymous hero, they also do a lot of charitable fundraising in his name, most notably for the British Heart Foundation, and understandably so. They recently bought a defibrillator machine for a local school. Perhaps, if one had been present at the theatre that fateful night, Cooper's own life might have been saved.

The organisation also raised £45,000 for a nine-foot sculpture of Cooper that was erected in Caerphilly, Tommy's town of birth, where it stands proudly today, a local and famous landmark to a much-loved son of the town.

Tommy would have approved. Though famously mean with his own money, he did a lot for charity. He was a regular fundraiser and performed at hundreds of events to raise money for worthy causes. Thomas Jr recalls his father on many occasions handing a fiver to a tramp on the street.

That said, when Cooper died, Gwen was surprised to hear about the existence of a safe deposit box held in Tommy's name at a branch of the Nat West bank in Eastbourne. On opening it, they discovered over £30,000 in cash. This probably represented all the drinks he had failed to buy when it came to his round.

The secretary of The Tommy Cooper Society, Tudor Jones, described the comedian's appeal thus: 'Tommy was never topical. He lived in his own world. His act was clean. You could watch him with your grandmother or with your grandchildren'.

It is true that Tommy was a safe pair of hands. Ever respectful and polite, he drilled into his own children the importance of good manners. Vicky Cooper says, 'Woe betide us if we forgot to say please or thank you'.

Vicky says that she was watching television with her father once, and they were watching Morecambe and Wise. Tommy kept saying, 'God, they're so funny. How can I follow them?' He did not have to. Tommy blazed his own trail. He did not need to follow anyone. Fellow comedians acknowledged that he was the king of comedy.

The man who began as the manic magician, the crazy comic, eventually settled into himself and became, simply, the comedian's comedian.

Tim Vine is an excellent comic, and his is the act that resembles Tommy's most in terms of style. The jokes come quick and fast. Many are one-liners. All are incredibly silly. 'A boy was riding his bike past me the other day and said, "Look. No hands." I thought "Shame" because he had no hands'. Vine has enough class to get away with it, but he does not come close in terms of sheer stage presence. Tommy filled up the largest room.

The society that exists in his name, and theatrical plays such as *The Tommy Cooper Show*, will keep reminding audiences of the sheer joy that the man brought into the lives and homes of millions of people. Here is another selection of jokes from the Tommy Cooper files:

'It was so cold, I opened my wardrobe door and my best suit was wearing my overcoat!'

'If you want to get into show-business, you have to have an agent. In fact, I've got two. They're double agents!'

'We were so poor my mother used to buy me one shoe at a time'.

'I took her to the pictures and we held hands all through the film. It would have been better if our seats were together!'

'Last night I dreamt I was a cannon. When I woke up, I shot right out of bed'.

'I can't write in the daytime. I went to night school'.

'There's only one way to diet ... Watch your food. Don't eat it. Just watch it!'

'I said to my doctor the other day, one of my legs is shorter than the other. What shall I do? He said "Limp!"'

'Last week, my grandfather celebrated his 103rd birthday. Unfortunately, he couldn't be there. He died when he was thirty-nine!'

'I always call a spade a spade, until the other night when I stepped on one in the dark!'

'Our next act needs no introduction, because he hasn't shown up!'

'He may talk like an idiot and look like an idiot, but don't let it fool you. He is an idiot!'

'Did you hear about the millionaire who said to his chauffeur, "Drive off the cliff, James. I'm committing suicide!"'

'I learned Japanese with records that play while you're asleep. Now I speak perfect Japanese, but only when I'm asleep!'

'I was at a party the other night. My wife said, "Stop saying one more for the road. We live here!"'

'There's an easy way to find out the value of money. Try and borrow some!'

'I missed my nap today. I slept right through it'.

'They always say start at the bottom if you want to learn something, but suppose you want to learn to swim!'

'My wife watches so many medical shows, I only talk to her during visiting hours!'

'I discovered a great way to avoid getting parking tickets. Remove your windscreen wipers'.

'I was a genius at school. I had so many original ideas, especially when it came to spelling'.

'Electricity is a wonderful thing. Do you realise, if it wasn't for electricity, we'd all be watching television by candle light!'

'Now I'm going to play like I've never played before, because I've never played before!'

'I used to be a one-man band. I played the drums with my feet, the tambourine with my elbows, and the vibraphone with my knees. What did I do with my hands? Held them to my ears!'

'I've got a voice like Caruso. Robinson Caruso!'

Tommy said once, 'If I had to live my life over again, I wouldn't have the strength!' As they say, many a true word is spoken in jest. Tommy Cooper, the hulking, preposterous performer, gave us everything that he had for almost four decades as a professional entertainer.

He is remembered as a giant of entertainment, a unique performer, whose legacy refuses to dwindle, even with the passing of the years since his sad and public exit from the stage.

As the great Max Miller used to say, there will never be another.

He was simply the best—the one and only Tommy Cooper.

44

The Magic Lives On

In 2003, I sat down and wrote my first play. It was called *One Bad Thing* and was about the murder of John Lennon. I had been script editor for a play that had won the *Liverpool Echo* Best Writing Award in 1999, and that gave me the confidence to go ahead and put my first piece on stage.

The Lennon play, with myself as writer, director, and producer, was performed at the Unity Theatre in Liverpool in April 2003 over three nights. We got a standing ovation and a sell-out crowd. Then, in 2010, a friend of mine was entertaining a German film crew, drawn to Liverpool to record a segment about the Beatles. My mate introduced me as a playwright. They asked me what I was currently working on. The answer was nothing. Despite having earned a Masters degree in writing and having written a couple of books in the interim, I had nothing coming up. I felt like a has-been. It was time to do the Lennon play again. So, in 2010, at the Actor's Studio in Liverpool, that is what we did.

During rehearsals, Daniel Taylor, who played John Lennon, was messing around doing Tommy Cooper impressions, except these were not mere impressions. This was an embodiment of the highest order of the great comedian, complete with the requisite physicality, not to mention the inherent funny bones. As I watched, I thought to myself, 'I have to share this with an audience'. I began to research Tommy Cooper, reading John Fisher's excellent biography, and watching countless hours of the comedian on television. I wrote to the Tommy Cooper Society and informed them of my plans to put on a play, seeking the relevant permissions, and heard nothing back.

My plans were temporarily thwarted. It did not matter as Danny, one of the leads in the musical *Blood Brothers*, continued with that show up until the end of the year. The production normally closes in early December, which would have allowed me to do a Christmas show; however, they extended their run for a further two weeks, and so my little show remained but a dream.

The following year, I tried again. I continued to watch Tommy on television, all the while adding to the script. I wrote again to The Tommy Cooper Society to tell them of my plans, and again I heard nothing back. Danny was back touring with Willy Russell's acclaimed musical, while I still had my eye on the Christmas break to put on our show. Then Danny got the chance to play Smee, the lead pirate next to Henry Winkler (the Fonz himself) who was going to play Captain Hook at the Liverpool Empire in that year's pantomime. That was some tough competition, and my own production again had to take a back seat.

My wife and I went along to see Danny and the Fonz in the panto. Also in the cast was Les Dennis, who had covered for Cooper when he had died live on stage. At one point during the show, a few kids were called to the stage. Dennis asked one young boy where his mother was. 'Over here', shouted a man in the audience. As quick as a flash, Les Dennis quipped back 'She's got a deep voice, hasn't she?' A highlight of the show, yet there was still no sign of a show from me.

In 2012, when the *Blood Brothers* run ended in early December, Danny went off to play the part of Father Christmas at a grotto in Milton Keynes. He did not even get paid, and still I could not tie him down. Without him, I did not have a show, as the whole reason for doing it was to show everyone how good he was. I liked Tommy Cooper, and the more I watched his stuff, the bigger fan I became, but really, I just wanted to write a play for my mate. For the best part of three years, I kept writing and adding to the script, but still there was to be no production, and though I kept trying, I still did not have the relevant permission.

Then, in February 2013, I wrote once more to The Tommy Cooper Society; this time they replied. What they said was that they were just a sophisticated fan club, and they did not hold the rights to the material. However, they knew the man that did, and they gave me his details. I got in touch.

Later that year, we did the Lennon play again. I asked Danny, during the course of the run, if he would consider playing Tommy Cooper. 'Have you got a script?' he asked. The answer was yes. Knowing it would appear as a Christmas show, I gave it one last polish, adding a few festive jokes, turning the 'four live ducks' into 'four live Christmas turkeys' and that sort of thing. Two weeks later, I gave the script to Danny.

I then received a panicked phone call. Having agreed to do the show, Danny was wondering what he had gotten himself into.

'It takes years to learn magic,' he said.

'Don't worry,' I told him, 'it's magic that isn't magic'.

I had deliberately chosen jokes and routines that looked like magic but required none of the skill involved to do it. So, to an audience member, whichever card they took was the right one. The glass and the bottles change places, but no one but Tommy can see it; the hardest part of the trick is to make the objects change back again, thus magic that was not magic.

In December 2013, *The Tommy Cooper Christmas Show* debuted at the Lantern Theatre, Liverpool. It is now touring as *The Tommy Cooper Show*. I had asked the Cooper estate for permission to put on the show and told them it would be a tribute to Tommy's life and work. I was thrilled when they agreed to grant the rights. I then contacted the Tommy Cooper Society to thank them for their help and support and invited their chairman up to see the show. It was a wonderful celebration of a much-loved comedian. Audiences knew the jokes (and their punch-lines) off by heart. They were still greeted like long-lost friends. It was a triumph. Sometimes, people would shout out the punch-lines as soon as Danny set them up.

'I backed a horse at twenty to one'.

'Came in at twenty past four,' someone would shout.

One time, Danny did Tommy's line about 'I can't help laughing. I know what's coming next'.

Quick as a flash, an audience member shouted out, 'So do we!' It did not matter as there was love and comedy in the room. It was like having Tommy himself in the room, and the praise continued to pour in. These are some of the comments the play has received.

Chris Brunt, chairman of the Tommy Cooper society, described it as 'Extremely funny. A tour de force'.

Dave Jennings of the British Theatre Guide wrote, 'It is difficult to conceive a better recreation of such a unique and memorable character as Tommy Cooper'.

The show continues to tour across the UK and is a fitting tribute to the best comedian we have ever had. In 2021, it will be the centenary of Tommy Cooper's birth. Despite his death more than thirty years ago, and the century that has passed since his humble beginnings, I bet Tommy Cooper will still top the comedy charts for many a decade to come—he is the best that there has ever been, and he did it 'Just like that!'